KWÉYÒL / CREOLE

KWÉYÒL / CREOLE

RECIPES, STORIES, and TINGS
from a ST. LUCIAN CHEF'S JOURNEY

NINA COMPTON

with OSAYI ENDOLYN

PHOTOGRAPHS BY BRITTANY CONERLY
and L. KASIMU HARRIS
ILLUSTRATIONS BY FIONA COMPTON

CLARKSON POTTER/PUBLISHERS
NEW YORK

Published in the United States by
Clarkson Potter/Publishers, an
imprint of the Crown Publishing
Group, a division of Penguin
Random House LLC, New York.
clarksonpotter.com

CLARKSON POTTER is a trademark
and POTTER with colophon is a
registered trademark of Penguin
Random House LLC.

Library of Congress Cataloging-in-
Publication Data
Names: Compton, Nina, author. |
Endolyn, Osayi, author. |
Conerly, Brittany, photographer. |
Harris, L. Kasimu, photographer.
Title: Kwéyòl/Creole : recipes,
stories, and tings from a St.
Lucian chef's journey / Nina
Compton with Osayi Endolyn;
photographs by Brittany
Conerly.
Other titles: Creole
Description: New York : Clarkson
Potter/Publishers, [2025] |
Includes index. | Identifiers:
LCCN 2024008915 (print) | LCCN
2024008916 (ebook) | ISBN
9780593578971 (hardcover) |
ISBN 9780593578988 (ebook)
Subjects: LCSH: Cooking, Creole. |
LCGFT: Cookbooks.
Classification: LCC TX715 .C75265
2025 (print) | LCC TX715 (ebook)
| DDC 641.59763—dc23/
eng/20240328
LC record available at https://lccn.
loc.gov/2024008915
LC ebook record available at
https://lccn.loc.gov/2024008916

ISBN 978-0-593-57897-1
Ebook ISBN 978-0-593-57898-8

Printed in China

Editor: Jennifer Sit | Editorial
assistant: Elaine Hennig
Designers: Yasmeen Bandoo
and Stephanie Huntwork
Art director: Stephanie Huntwork
Illustrator: Fiona Compton
Production editor: Terry Deal
Production manager: Jane Chinn
Compositor: Merri Ann Morrell
Food stylist: Tami Hardeman
Food stylist assistant: Matthew
Mosshart
Prop stylist: Audrey Davis
Prop stylist assistant: Janai Cano
Copy editor: Kristi Hein
Proofreaders: Rachel Holzman and
Monika Dziamka
Indexer: Elizabeth T. Parson
Publicist: Kristin Casemore
Marketer: Monica Stanton

10 9 8 7 6 5 4 3 2 1

First Edition

TO MY FAMILY
Janice, John, Sean, Jeannine,
Maya, Fiona, and Larry

Contents

Moulin à Vent
ST. LUCIA
GROWING UP KWÉYÒL
33

Montego Bay
JAMAICA
BIG-ISLAND ENERGY
111

MIAMI
Florida
AN AFRO LATIN DIASPORA
165

NEW ORLEANS
Louisiana
COMING HOME TO CREOLE
215

FOREWORD

Nina Compton's food tells a story. Long before I knew that story, I knew there was a narrative involved in her work, from my own armchair analysis of a dish I hadn't yet tasted. It is described on the menu with the same simplicity as the other offerings:

Curried Goat/Sweet Potato Gnocchi/Cashews.

To what mad mind do we owe this conglomeration?

Curried goat is not from Italy. Gnocchi is not from South America. Cashews are not from the Caribbean. And I might add that Nina, who featured this dish at her New Orleans restaurant, Compère Lapin, is not from the Crescent City.

Brett Anderson, then the food critic for the *Times-Picayune*, prepared diners with this particularly ebullient paragraph from a rave review:

Curried goat is her "piece de resistance," a stew that manages to embody globalism's virtues, studded with cashews, fleshed out by sweet potato gnocchi and bursting with flavors that draw connections from Sri Lanka to Durban to Trinidad. It's one of those dishes that, 10 years hence, you'll likely find on a tourist map.

In *Kwéyòl / Creole*, Nina and Osayi Endolyn tell the story of this chef, this dish, and the many flavors and experiences that have taken her from Moulin à Vent, St. Lucia (her hometown), to New Orleans (mine). The book is organized not by course but by location. Readers travel with the chef, stopping in Jamaica's Montego Bay and Ocho Rios, and a particularly Italian address in Miami. At each stop, she mixes her takes on traditional food of the region with inspirations exemplifying her original creations.

The title, *Kwéyòl / Creole,* requires you to pronounce the genre of this food in the same way as the people who live and eat these cultures. Where else have you seen "green figs" and "ground provisions" listed so prominently in a book whose language you thought you understood? This book is an immersive experience. It is a determined effort to bring you as close to the people and places of these Creole worlds as paper and ink will allow. The chef could wish for no better accomplice in this innovative endeavor than Osayi, who has earned a reputation on Instagram and elsewhere for pointing out the many ways in which traditional food writing has assumed that all readers look and eat like "us."

Speaking of eating like "us," I have developed an informal test of published recipes that claim to be Creole, Caribbean, or African. If they require only a few tablespoons of onion for a vat-sized pot of stew, I know that no grandmother in St. Lucia, Port-au-Prince, or Dakar would approve of so bland a transgression. This book passes my onion test in spades. These recipes are seasoned with care and love and onions and peppers and a desire to demonstrate that *Kwéyòl* is a word and a world with which sophisticated gourmands owe it to themselves to become familiar.

Nina and Osayi make a compelling case for us to expand our palates to accommodate worlds of deliciousness that we may have heretofore neglected.

—Lolis Eric Elie

INTRODUCTION
Kwéyòl and Creole

Sa ka fête.

Back home on St. Lucia, any plate of food tells you a story. The characters in that story tell the history of my island. Ground provisions—root vegetables—are the soul of the soil. A typical plate of St. Lucian home cooking features protein like goat or chicken, a salad of lettuces and tomatoes, and always macaroni pie. But the ground provisions, that's how I know I'm home. Vegetables like cassava were originally used by the Kalinago, our Indigenous people, centuries before Europeans landed in the region. Yams were introduced to the Caribbean through the transatlantic slave trade, with ingredients from historical Senegambia, the Bight of Biafra, and the Gold Coast accompanying the forced movement of people to far-off lands. Breadfruit, a beloved and versatile staple, came to St. Lucia on ships led by enslavers like the infamous Captain Bligh, who transported plantings from Polynesia as a cheap means of sustaining involuntary labor forces. India is a major influence in our layered cuisine, too, brought about by the indentured laborers who arrived after slavery was outlawed in the nineteenth century. They emigrated from the subcontinent, bringing a range of spices and dishes like curry, roti, and dal that remain core aspects of St. Lucian food culture today. The Kalinago used hot peppers not just in their food but as protection. They made a poisonous smoke that caused European colonizers in the early 1600s to die from inhalation or flee into the thick of ready warriors defending their land. Hot peppers today make up our peppa sauce, an indispensable condiment, and throughout the Caribbean, peppers are treated respectfully as protective plant medicine.

St. Lucia is a small country in the Eastern Caribbean, tucked in the center of a crest of islands, just south of Martinique and north of St. Vincent and the Grenadines. What we eat is largely reliant on the season. If it's not the right time of year for guava or mangoes, you're not gonna get guava or mangoes. Ground provisions comprise the backbone of most of our meals, foods that sustain and nourish: yam, sweet potato, cassava, breadfruit, plantain, and green fig—what we call green banana. Green fig and saltfish is our national dish. The banana comes from the South Pacific, and salted cod originated in Europe. Enslaved Africans used salted cod to supplement meager diets on island plantations.

These ingredients are the basis of the Creole cooking that I grew up savoring. In St. Lucia when we say "Creole," we don't mean French-influenced. That has too often been accepted as the definition in my adopted city of New Orleans, which owes much to West Africa for its cuisine as well. Our Creole, or Kwéyòl, celebrates a diverse African heritage, beautifully reflected in the dishes and customs that shape much of what I eat and how I cook today.

The recipes in this book will introduce you to, or remind you of, traditional and innovative Caribbean cooking. I'm acknowledging the rich history of where I come from, while forging something that feels a little new, a little mine. And now, with this book, a little yours, too. I'm inspired by the flavors I seek out when I go back to St. Lucia. Fresh-caught lobster grilled seaside. The smokiness of pit-roasted breadfruit. Sweet mango dipped in the ocean for a burst of natural salt. The countless possibilities of beloved plantain. Conch fritters. Roti. Callaloo with coconut cream. Guava vinaigrette drizzled over banana. Homemade curry with fresh turmeric and ginger. Pickled mango and avocado salad. Whole roasted fish dressed in green seasoning, a ubiquitous St. Lucian condiment (every island has its own adaptation) made of pureed cilantro and other herbs, spring onions, and garlic.

These dishes incorporate the pivotal stops on my culinary journey, and the book is organized this way—from Moulin à Vent, to Mo Bay, to Miami, and finally New Orleans. As an immigrant in the United States, I am always referencing where I come from, with pride and respect for the traditions that shaped me. And, as a longtime resident of my adopted country, I have been eager to learn, improvise, and enhance the American palate by doing what us transplants do best: We bring home with us wherever we go.

In these pages, the weather is warm and tropical, and the vibe is easygoing, just like the places I've lived. The dishes are full of flavor. The mood is chill. We are smiling, sipping rum or coconut water, jamming to music, and whatever is on the stovetop don't need no fuss. Everything is as it should be, especially when it's not— because what can you do about it anyway? I love that feeling when I bite into a ripe mango and the juice drips down my arm. It's the sense of knowing I'm in the right moment, in the right place. Wherever I'm at, I'm home.

NEW ORLEANS
The Place of Many Tongues

MIAMI
Sweet Water

JAMAICA
Land of Wood and Water

ST. LUCIA
Land of the Iguana

The Journey of This Book

The recipes in this book are organized by place, following my cooking journey and how each locale and the food and stories there inspired my palate and broadened my view as a chef:

I was born in ST. LUCIA and I grew up in Moulin à Vent in the north of the island. My island is my culinary foundation and still a guiding light. Our heritage celebrates elements of Indigenous, African, Asian, and European cultures, with other regional Caribbean cultures offering their unique points of view, too. My core pantry is fundamentally a global one. Most of our spices are locally grown: allspice, cinnamon, curry and bay leaves, turmeric, ginger, seasoning peppers. Our land is our primary resource for plentiful fruits and vegetables. Many people have a small home garden with a practice of growing their own herbs, ground provisions, and fruits. Guavas and mangoes grow on wild trees that no one "owns," and anyone walking by can pick one or two (we take what we need and leave the rest for others). We come from a culture where we share our bounty, or we sometimes barter: Someone does repair work on your house, they get a goat as payment. Everything in our household revolved around food. Our kitchen was always alive with energy, a connecting point of conversation, laughter, and good things to eat. St. Lucia laid the groundwork for me wanting to cook professionally.

Next, we go to JAMAICA, where I continued my cooking career. Mo Bay is where, as a small-island girl, I got my first taste of being in a big city. Jamaicans are renowned for their confidence and cultural pride; it's a North Star destination in the Caribbean. I encountered a range of people (and food cultures) from other islands, including Trinidad and Tobago, Haiti, Cuba, and the Dominican Republic. I learned how a professional kitchen operates, moving between different positions on the line.

I was exposed to customs alongside the food, such as Carnival, beach sessions, and liming. Here my personal national identity evolved, as I appreciated the opportunities of my upbringing and what it meant to be a St. Lucian living in another part of the region.

The following stop is MIAMI, Florida, where I landed after eighteen months of formal study at culinary school in upstate New York. At that point, I'd maxed out on what I could learn without additional training. After school, I had a brief stint cooking in New York City, but I wanted warmer weather. In Miami, I saw my Caribbean food culture through an Afro Latin lens for the first time, seeing the tropical ingredients I grew up with being used in ways that were new to me. In St. Lucia, we fry ripe plantain, but being in Miami introduced me to the twice-fried tostones you see in Cuban and Puerto Rican kitchens. Even my idea of what "Caribbean" meant was expanding, with broader impressions of Haitian, Cuban, Puerto Rican, and Dominican cultures. Here I stepped into leadership roles, as executive chef of the members-only Versace Mansion, where we did coastal cuisine with Mediterranean influences, and later Scarpetta, a fine dining Italian restaurant. I learned about food traditions that I wasn't exposed to back home, and I saw ingredients from my home country celebrated in American fine dining in ways I hadn't previously observed. In Miami, I grew confident enough in my cooking that I thought I had a decent shot at becoming *Top Chef*, and I traveled to New Orleans to film the show's eleventh season.

We end the book in **NEW ORLEANS**, where I came for what I thought would be a moment and ended up building a life instead. I quickly learned why New Orleans is often referred to as the northernmost Caribbean city. Like St. Lucia, Jamaica, and Miami, New Orleans was pivotally shaped by the skilled West and Central Africans who expertly blended the many cultures surrounding them into something distinctive, joyful, and nourishing. New Orleans is steeped in tradition and known for being a bit lukewarm on folks trying to change things up. But this city has inspired me as much as it's created space for me. As of this writing, I have my first restaurant, Compère Lapin, a Caribbean restaurant with French and Italian influences; followed by BABs-Nola, with rustic, neighborhood fare; and most recently Nina's Creole Cottage, a fast-casual Caribbean offering. I found similarities to my St. Lucian background in the core recipes of New Orleans, and I learned that folks found aspects of their Creole and Cajun heritage in my food, too. Being in New Orleans has brought me home in new ways, an extension of the Kwéyòl I grew up with, becoming the Creole I'm part of now.

You'll note both my deference to seasonality and the intimate relationship to the land that grounds my understanding of food. In St. Lucia, we don't select fish from a supermarket counter; we drive or walk to the fisherman and choose from whatever he caught that morning. When mangoes are in season, mangoes go in everything. You may not be living on a tiny island while you turn these pages—frankly, neither am I! But I hope to demonstrate how influential and irreplaceable *place* is as an ingredient in the story of a recipe and the dish that comes from it. This book aims to transport as much as it aims to anchor.

Becoming Chef

I was born to Janice and John Compton, the fourth of five children. My mum was born in St. Lucia to my English grandmother, Phyllis Clarke, and my St. Lucian grandfather, Sir Frederick Clarke (more on their story in the recipe for Banana and Brown Butter Tea Sandwiches on page 67). My grandmum used to tell me how she adapted to St. Lucia in the 1940s, then still under British colonial rule (and at other periods, the French; they each ruled my country seven times over the centuries). In a country with limited modern amenities at the time, making tea was suddenly a lengthy affair, once she accounted for building a fire for the coal pot, bringing water to boil, then steeping and finally serving her cuppa. When I was little, I acted as her sous chef for the easygoing lunches we enjoyed as a family. (Lunch was a big, two-hour meal; dinner was for smaller plates and leftovers.) I helped cut the onions and peeled garlic. I looked forward to just being in the kitchen, but especially cooking with my grandmother. By the time I was sixteen, I knew I wanted to become a chef.

I had just come home for holiday from boarding school in Kent, England, when I broke the news to my parents about my future endeavors. I'd been following a family tradition of leaving St. Lucia to study in the United Kingdom. In the 1930s, my maternal grandfather, Frederick, left St. Lucia to study medicine at Edinburgh University. He met Phyllis, who was an English nurse training in midwifery, and in 1944, they got married, making a life in St. Lucia together. My father, Sir John Compton, would eventually become the first prime minister of an independent St. Lucia in 1979. But he began as a boy from St. Vincent and the Grenadines who went to secondary school on St. Lucia, and then onward to the University College of Wales and the London School of Economics. My elder siblings studied abroad as well. When my turn came, I considered going into agriculture on the island. At the time, St. Lucia was not yet a booming tourist destination—an economic model rooted in colonialism with many challenges still—and the bulk of financial opportunity for workers came from the growth and export of our bananas.

But as a teen living abroad, I'd experimented with cooking for friends and loved it. I'd spent most of my childhood in the kitchen with my grandmother—that was where the social action was at family gatherings. My father, whose lineage included a legacy of shipwrights, whalers, boatmen, and fishermen, taught me and my siblings about one-pot meals and the joy of eating fish heads (if you don't know, we'll get into it shortly!). On holiday visits back to St. Lucia, I'd cook meals for my family. I'd fallen in love with the joy on their faces when I prepared hors d'oeuvres or a full meal. When I told my mother, now Lady Janice Compton, that I wanted to be a chef, it took convincing. By this time, I was known to be a rule-breaker, and I was growing up on a small island as the daughter of the leader of our government. When I got up to things, by the time I got home, Mum would know. Sometimes people would even call out to me, "Hey Compy, go home!" Caribbean folks are always in your business! When it came to cooking professionally, Mum worried about the fast-paced working conditions and wisely predicted a litany of future burns, cuts, and nicks. "Is this something you really want to do?" she asked. I was game, and she finally agreed.

My restaurant education landed me more than one thousand miles away from home, in a hotel resort kitchen in Montego Bay, Jamaica. For me, coming out of tiny St. Lucia, Mo Bay's size and energy felt thrilling and overwhelming. Mo Bay is where I learned what to do with all that ackee we had growing in our St. Lucia yard but never ate. My mum was always giving the fruit away to our Jamaican neighbors, as St. Lucians don't customarily eat ackee. In Jamaica, I made ackee every which way I could and froze the leftovers. I called Mum and said, "You've got to keep some ackee for yourself!" and promised to show her how to make it.

After a couple of years in Jamaica, I craved more education. I went to culinary school in upstate New York, and I worked in French fine dining in Manhattan. But it was actually in Miami, where one of my sisters was living, that I learned about Caribbean foodways with a Latin lens. This education happened, in part, by osmosis. In the restaurants, bars, shops, and neighborhoods that define Miami, I was surrounded by a mix of African, Francophone, Anglophone, and Spanish-language culture in music, style, and food. The other aspect of my education was my time as a cook in several fine dining restaurants. I was seeing ingredients from my own culture being treated with the same intention and attention to aesthetics as the European-focused recipes I'd been studying. I realized that becoming a chef was about being able to express myself, not only about achieving a specific skill. I wanted to cook my people's food in ways that celebrated its ingenuity and layered origins. I wanted to serve these foods using techniques from all aspects of my training, my Caribbean heritage, and French and Italian influences.

The producers of *Top Chef* called me up one day—it seemed like it was out of the blue. At that point, I was fifteen years into my cooking career. I loved living in Miami. I'd nailed down executive-level roles at celebrated spots; I had my staff; I had my cute little beach life, enjoying morning croquetas by the Atlantic Ocean before work. Life was good! When the show producers explained that they wanted me to be a part of the forthcoming season, I thought it was a prank. But after more discussion, I started to consider it. What if I could get on this show? Maybe I could even win. Maybe I could get more Caribbean food seen and appreciated by the millions of viewers who tune in every week. Agreeing to compete on the show would mean leaving the work culture I'd worked hard to cultivate. The producers put us through multiple rounds of interviews. The last week, about two months after their initial invitation, they finally revealed the location to me. We would film in New Orleans.

I didn't know anything about New Orleans while growing up in St. Lucia. But when I arrived as a TV show contestant in 2015, it felt more like being in the islands than I could have imagined. For folks with their eye on history, New Orleans is often referred to as culturally Caribbean. The city was a major port for the sale of enslaved Africans and the busiest port in the U.S. domestic trade. I've been a student of its rich culinary history, authored predominantly by the Africans who were brought here to cultivate and serve, who blended their Indigenous practices with ingredients from mostly Acadian, Spanish, and French cultures. New Orleans, like St. Lucia, is fashioned from a unique hodgepodge of people, in both places primarily Black people. New Orleans has Mardi Gras; St. Lucia has Carnival. We have Friday fish fry during Lent in NOLA just like back on my island. Both places have long-standing beliefs about the recipes you best let be. And both places—along with the stops in between—have helped shape my way of cooking.

Filming *Top Chef* took only six weeks, but it planted seeds I couldn't have gotten anywhere else as quickly. In a show framed around competition, insane ingredient or timing challenges, and literally being judged, what you must do well is cook from your gut. Meaning, from your heart. The show helped me understand that I don't have to cook anyone else's food but mine (even if the judges didn't have a frame of reference for my food culture). That ethos served me well. I made it to the finale with only four chefs left out of the eighteen who began. We had a two-month break in production before filming the finale, and everyone went home. When I got back to Miami, I realized that I was no longer a fit for cooking in someone else's kitchen. I needed to open my own place, and I thought Miami would be it (remember, my cute little beach life was poppin'!).

I ended *Top Chef* as the runner-up. For my final challenge, I cooked roasted goat with orecchiette pasta, and a chocolate zeppole with passion fruit crème anglaise. I was proud and happy with my dishes. Contestants are sworn to secrecy so we don't spoil the viewing experience for the audience, and by the time the series aired, I was getting much love from my Caribbean bredren. My mum would tell me, week to week, that people in St. Lucia were making T-shirts with my face on them, and they were having viewing parties. For the finale, St. Lucia's capital, Castries, shut down the main square and projected it on a big screen. I felt bad because I knew they were going to be disappointed that I didn't win. But I did my best!

They tell chefs that offers start rolling in after you make it to the final *Top Chef* episode, because millions of people have gotten to know you and are presumably excited about your food. The show aired. For a couple months my phone did not ring. I focused on finding a spot to open in Miami. But the spaces I looked at didn't feel right. Viewing after viewing, nothing was a match. Then suddenly I was getting calls from around the U.S., but none of those opportunities felt right either. A hotel in New Orleans called; they wanted me to consider opening there. The space was under construction, but I felt the vibe. "This is the one," I said. And I was off to the Crescent City.

I opened my first restaurant, Compère Lapin, in 2015. My vision of cooking Caribbean food my way had come to life. At Compère, we serve accra, or saltfish fritters. I have always believed in my recipe for curried goat with sweet potato gnocchi. It's got heat to it—the goat is tender, the sweet potato dough billows just right. But I didn't know how it would go over with diners; you never know how folks will receive a dish. When we opened, the entrée was so popular that we exhausted the inventory from my goat supplier. Our vegetable dishes reflect what I can get in South Louisiana, and they reflect the best of the season, like mirliton and carrot slaw. Folks in the know order my interpretation of cow heel soup, with its rich broth scented with ginger, lemongrass, and peppers. Back home, the soup is a beloved classic sold at the local Saturday market. It's robust in flavor and resourceful in ingredients. Every bite counts.

My second restaurant, BABs-Nola, is tucked into a former rice mill in the Bywater neighborhood. There we continue our mission of merging influences. The fish we have on a given day—say, snapper—may be pan-roasted with cauliflower and a pecan salsa verde. The coconut rice and peas (in Caribbean cultures, "peas" are pigeon peas) pair well with curried rabbit. And cabbage salad, a staple for me growing up, is refreshing with a toss of herbs and spiced nuts.

We opened a third restaurant in casino row, Nina's Creole Cottage, where dishes like hot fire chicken set it off for folks taking a break from rolling dice. This restaurant synthesizes my understanding of New Orleans recipes, like blackened catfish or shrimp and grits. The food we make in my restaurants or at special events around the globe are reflected in these pages. Starting with traditional household dishes to roadside stall recipes passed down for generations, to dishes that cooks far from home share with their colleagues, friends, and family. They all make up my journey of becoming a chef.

How to Use This Book

This is a story-driven cookbook. You can skip around in it as a reference, for sure. But writer Osayi Endolyn and I worked closely to ensure that these recipes reflect a range of my life and teachings, and that the stories about those recipes make a meaningful narrative. The story is part of the food, and the food exists in my life because of the story.

In my culture and the ones I've learned from along my path, we don't teach cooking through books. That doesn't mean we don't prize literature, but that the root of this knowledge is in our minds, hearts, and hands. Pages come after all of that. Our heritage is part of oral traditions, and our techniques are taught through sharing. In the restaurant industry, we adopt much of this practice. Cookbooks are amazing because they can bring other cultures into your home kitchen, but as anyone who's tried to replicate their grandmother's cooking knows, a lot more than step-by-step instructions go into the pot. I hope my stories remind you of dishes that are special to you, or inspire you to create your own.

Where this book may introduce you to ingredients or dishes that are new to you, I hope you'll find restaurants and markets in your community to explore different nuances and preferences. I hope that the next time you come to the Caribbean or to cities like Miami or New Orleans, you'll seek out foods off the tourist track. It's unfortunate that high real estate costs and gentrification keep pushing out the very cultures whose food and music give city centers their heart. You may have to go farther out to find the good stuff, but it's worth it. Coming from a country whose economy once depended on exporting a single crop and now relies on tourism, we like to have visitors, but keep in mind, people don't owe you. You get to share in local practices when you are kind and respectful.

There are, of course, many examples of cultural blending and expression that extend beyond what I can document in this book. I hope you'll find that I took care to share the traditions I was taught with respect and at the same time I'm also expressing my point of view. People around the world adjust their dishes based on what they have and who they're cooking for, and those decisions aren't always simple. If you ever want a Ph.D. in why that is, just open a restaurant! (Good luck!)

Like I mention in the stories that accompany these recipes, in my culture we learn from standing side-by-side, watching, listening, mimicking. The technique is not "magic," which is not really a compliment but gets thrown around a lot when women and Black folks are doing the cooking. Within the techniques, science, and wisdom, there is indeed magic present. It's the energy of generation after generation of hand-to-hand education. It's respect for nature. It's knowing from scent, or touch, or taste, because someone taught you how to honor scent, touch, and taste. It's allowing time to be its own ingredient.

Ingredients

Many of the ingredients in this book come from cultures based in the tropics, or are deeply connected to them. Markets that sell foods from similar geographic areas will be a good go-to. Visit your local African, Caribbean, Latin, or Asian markets. If shopping at a big retailer, you might be surprised what ingredients they have, if you weren't already looking for them. Chain stores in different parts of a city might offer different items that reflect the clientele in the neighborhood. Shop around.

Whenever possible, shop with your local farmers. They need us, and let me tell you, we need them. There's nothing like meeting the person who has grown your food and supporting their labor year-round. Get to know your fishmonger and butcher, too. They're choosy about what they bring into their shops, and you'll learn about different seafood or meats.

Finally, people who've traversed lands, dialects, and customs learn to call things by different names. Along my journey, I learned that dasheen in St. Lucia is taro in Miami, that cassava back home is yuca in Spanish-speaking areas, and what we call christophine is mirliton in New Orleans. In each location-based chapter, I reference the name of the ingredient as it's called in that place. I feel it's important to honor these cultures and that includes respecting local convention.

BANANA LEAF

We use these often in Caribbean cooking for steaming and boiling, but the use of the banana leaf is common around the world; it was used functionally and decoratively by the Kalinago people. It's both a sustainable resource that imparts flavor and the perfect vessel for everything from fish (Steamed Snapper with Pepper Ginger Sauce, page 48) to traditional African diaspora corn pudding (Jamaican Blue Draws, page 158).

BREADFRUIT

We love our breadfruit trees in the Caribbean; the fruit is often compared to the versatility of a North American potato in that it can be steamed, boiled, roasted, grilled, or fried. We eat it primarily in its mature state when the flesh is firmer. Breadfruit is ubiquitous throughout the Caribbean because it was imported from Southeast Asia by European colonists to feed enslaved Africans, as the plant grows hardily and without much intervention. Many cultures have embraced breadfruit. Its presence in diaspora recipes tells the culinary story of our ancestors' survival, and therefore, our own existence.

BROWNING

Made from darkly charred sugar caramelized with hot water, browning brings depth and deepening of color. I'd say Jamaicans use browning the most, but you'll see it in other parts of the Caribbean. It's used mostly for aesthetics. I recommend buying it, as getting sugar caramelized deeply enough without burning it can be time consuming and tricky; it's easy to find in Caribbean markets or online.

CASSAREEP

Famous for its use in traditional Guyanese dishes like pepperpot and stew chicken, cassareep acts as a glaze. It's made from the juice of cassava root, boiled at length, then cooked down with spices like cinnamon, cloves, and brown sugar. It comes out to a super thick, rich liquid.

COCONUT, COCONUT MILK, AND COCONUT OIL

The coconut perfectly represents Caribbean cooking because it shows how we have multiple uses for the same ingredient at different points in its maturity and can extract several uses at once. Young coconuts offer coconut "water" and jelly; older coconuts offer rich flesh and a "milk"—a natural fat that adds creaminess (I would not recommend "light" coconut milk; it seems to miss the point). For coconut oil, I prefer unrefined or virgin. We use coconut in all kinds of savory and sweet preparations.

GREEN FIG (GREEN BANANA)

In St. Lucia we have our green figs, which might be known where you are as green bananas. This is just what we call them! We eat green figs with saltfish, a fresh, savory combination that has become our national dish. Bananas are delicious and found growing all over the island, but they were also a vital aspect of St. Lucia's political economy, particularly in the twentieth century as we sought national independence.

GROUND PROVISIONS

Local markets and home gardens in St. Lucia are always bountiful with ground provisions: cassava (yuca), dasheen (taro), yam, and sweet potato. We dice them to cook in stews, grill them straight up over coals, or roast them as sides. They rarely get fancy attention, but ground provisions are where you find the nutrition and deep flavor.

MEAT AND POULTRY

Growing up in St. Lucia, we ate primarily vegetables and seafood, with goat and chicken as our typical proteins. We didn't have much beef, and when we did, it was end cuts. (Man, I still cannot believe the cost of oxtail these days. It used to be *cents* on the pound; now it's a delicacy.) We're a small island, and the agricultural space is not conducive to mass meat production. But meat does appear in these pages, and like with other fresh ingredients, where you buy counts. Try to go to a butcher who has a relationship with local or regional farmers. The flavor alone is worth it.

PLANTAIN

In the right hands, a plantain in any state of ripeness is always ready to be cooked. In St. Lucia we enjoy plantain at its ripest—when the skins are black and the flesh is soft to touch—peeled, sliced, and fried. But traveling through the Caribbean diaspora, I learned of uses that take underripe (green-skinned) to kind of ripe (yellowish-skinned, with black markings) plantains and boil or fry them. When I was introduced to tostones (page 182), it was a super bueno day.

SALT

I use Diamond Crystal brand kosher salt for cooking, and *I recommend you use that brand as you cook these recipes.* Kosher salt is unrefined; in general it's a nicer flavor. Diamond Crystal is known for lighter flakes that mix quickly into your dish, so when you taste to adjust for seasoning, you can taste the difference faster. Salts are made in different ways, resulting in different crystals and sodium content, so substitutes for a different brand will change the outcome from what I've planned for you. Please navigate carefully. When the recipe calls for flaky sea salt, I prefer Maldon. It's what chefs call a "finishing" salt, which we add just prior to serving. The flakes are airy and crunchy and really set off a dish. A pinch goes a long way.

SALTFISH

Saltfish is a catchall for any white, meaty fish preserved through salt curing. In preparation, the cook soaks or boils the saltfish to release the excess salt. The fish is usually cod, and saltfish is also known as bacalao, baccalà, or bacalhau. Saltfish is ubiquitous around the world and particularly popular in Caribbean cooking because European colonists inherently tied it to the trade of enslaved Africans who were fed saltfish as part of their sustenance—truly a survival food—aboard ships en route to being sold. The fact that saltfish found its way to many long-standing recipes in the diaspora reflects trade routes throughout the centuries. It further underscores the authorship of Africans who did the cooking in these regions.

SCOTCH BONNET

These peppers have a floral taste with spice that slowly builds; it's not too upfront. They allow a happy medium of adding spice to a dish without overpowering heat. If you can't find Scotch bonnets, habaneros are good replacements. We say, "Meme bête, meme pwel," or "Same beast, same hair." They aren't as floral, but you can control the heat level.

SEAFOOD

Growing up on an island, and now living on the Gulf of Mexico, I am a lover of all seafood. We'll shuck oysters, fry conch, and grill whole fish in these pages, along with cooking fillets. Where I'm from, fishermen wouldn't dream of trying to sell you a fish without showing it to you intact. You judge the clarity in its eyes, the glisten and freshness of the skin. I'm a chef-owner of restaurants where people expect to not have to deal with bones, so if you're squeamish, I get it. But in the Caribbean, we deal with our food at its source, and I invite you to reflect on what that means for you at your table.

SEASONING PEPPERS

Seasoning peppers are literally called seasoning peppers. You might see them listed as Caribbean seasoning peppers. They can look like a habanero or Scotch bonnet, and they do have the floral spiciness that you'd expect. But they're different from their spicier relatives because seasoning peppers have a subtle heat, and they carry a sweetness. It's a universal pepper that can be used as base seasoning, or sofrito, in poultry, seafood, and rice.

SPICES

In Caribbean cooking, we use plentiful seasonings; throughout the diaspora we say, "Black folks flavor our food." This happens in layers of seasoning throughout the cooking process. An overnight marinade, for example, is seasoning. The use of a long-cooked stock is a layer of a seasoning. Well-seasoned food, well-spiced food, is not the same as something *being* "spicy" as in the use of chili pepper to add piquant, numbing, or burning sensations. Our spice staples include bay leaves, cayenne pepper, cinnamon, nutmeg, vanilla, ginger, and turmeric. With the exception of vanilla, all of these grow fresh on the island of St. Lucia, but in other locales you'll do well to simply buy thoughtfully sourced, high-quality spices. In St. Lucia we pick our bay leaf straight off the spice tree, but when you see it in a recipe here, fresh or dried is fine.

Equipment

You'll need a few essentials and, depending on your cooking repertoire, perhaps a few items that may become your new fave kitchen tools. Less common supplies are noted in recipes.

Assorted bowls for mixes and marinades

A good chef's knife (typically 8-inch) and paring knife, both always sharp!

Blender

Cooking utensils: whisk, tongs, spoons, slotted spoon, heat-safe spatula

Food processor

Mandoline, for uniform thin slicing

Microplane (it's finer than a box grater)

Mortar and pestle

Roasting pan

Saucepans, for shallow frying

Sheet pans and baking dishes

Skillet or saucepan, for sautéing

Stand mixer

Stockpot or Dutch oven, for stews, braises, and deep frying

Moulin à Vent

ST. LUCIA

GROWING UP KWÉYÒL

Kouman ou yé?

I'm from a quiet, hilly region of St. Lucia called Moulin à Vent, which means "windmill" in French. We had an old windmill next to our house, which was used to process sugarcane many years ago. Nearby is Gros Islet, a small fishing town. You see the fishermen go out in the morning and come back in the evenings. Whenever we'd go to the beach, I'd see this guy on a small boat, which he adorned with flags from all over the world. The boat was practically drowning in flags. He sold fresh fruit to folks relaxing on their boats. He'd blow his conch shell to announce oranges, grapefruit, or mangoes. Usually he'd come to the shoreline, and we'd get a bag of fruit, which he'd cut for us right there. My childhood is defined by that salty, sweet flavor—the ripe fruit mixed with the briny mist of ocean water. I've always liked to be surrounded by the water.

On the weekends, my four siblings and I would head down to the countryside with my dad to Mahaut, where he farmed. That was my dad's escape from his career in law and politics. He loved working the land. He went to the farm weekly, harvesting whatever he could. When we visited with him, we'd hang out by the river, which was just down the hill. The water was chilly, but we didn't care. We'd climb the rocks and catch crayfish. We'd try to catch fish with our hands, but they were too fast.

Back home, it seems like everything was tied to food. My backyard had every fruit tree I could think of; it's crazy that it seems special now, that you could pick fruit that grows for free. We had guava, lime, lemon, and passion fruit. We'd come home from school, take off our uniforms, and play for hours in the garden. We had three guava trees in a perfect line in front of our house. We'd play gymnastics, pretending the guava trees were uneven bars, because the branches were long.

Mrs. King, a lady who lived near my school, would make patties (Caribbean-style Cornish pasties). There we were, all these kids—a typical Caribbean scene of boys and girls in school uniforms, socks up to our knees, racing to get a snack during the midday break. Mrs. King made patties with roast chicken, potatoes, peas, or corn, then folded over and baked. It was just a thing you had to get, that and her iced lollies—little bags of frozen, sweetened condensed milk with food coloring. We all knew her by these treats.

Family travel consisted of short road trips to the south of the island to visit the rainforests. The roads are winding and curvy, and we drove slowly. On the ride there, I'd bounce around the back of my father's pickup truck, high-fiving banana tree leaves with my sister. We'd try to grab the banana leaves or hit them during the ride. We were troublesome! Once, I fell out of the truck and my sister had to alert my father that I was no longer in the back of the pickup. Upon arrival, we'd have a riverside lunch with fresh fruit, sandwiches, maybe stewed chopped pork with rice and beans. This part of the country has dense vegetation. There aren't a lot of streetlights. You can see all the stars. More traditional cooking happens here. More green figs, more pig tails. If you want to feel St. Lucia at its core, head south. I think the same is true in the United States.

Growing up John Compton's daughter, everyone knows you're John Compton's daughter. He was a lawyer, politician, then farmer, and he led St. Lucia to independence in 1979 as the country's first prime minister. He did a lot of things that helped St. Lucia develop into the country it is now. Caribbean people are playful, and when I was a kid, they'd shout my name—"Compton!"—and keep walking. In a way, it's acknowledgment of my parents, of our family. You get used to that after a while.

When I was a teenager, I was rebellious. I would do things like hitchhike rides. My mother would get phone calls from people she didn't know: "Mrs. Compton, we see your daughter hitching rides in the back of pickup trucks; her father would be embarrassed!" She'd ask them who it was, given that I had sisters. They'd be like, "The tomboy one!" By the time I got home, Mum knew what I'd been up to.

My dad was always down-to-earth. He was from Canouan in St. Vincent and the Grenadines, a tiny island known for sailing and building boats. I remember a story he told us from when he was a kid. One day after school, he had gone to the beach. He put his shoes on a rock and went swimming, but when he came back, his shoes were gone. He was so scared to go home. He searched for hours, yet he finally came home empty-handed. He had to go to school barefoot. That was a hard lesson learned.

Outside of my awareness that my father was a public figure, my dad didn't bring politics home. My mum loves to discuss global affairs and is deeply interested in the political fabric of the world. They'd have those adult conversations, but we weren't part of that when we were young. He was about moving forward and developing the country, with a focus on education and improving peoples' livelihoods.

My dad retired in his seventies. Nine years lapsed between his first retirement and his reentry into politics in his eighties. My mum called me when I was living in Miami: "Your dad is going back into politics." I was like, "But, he's retired!" At that time, the country had changed a lot. Daddy Compton was his name, and people looked up to him.

My early notions of becoming a chef felt connected to my celebratory sense of food. Being in the kitchen was always where the fun was as I grew up. At boarding school in England, I noticed I was bringing my household's entertaining style to my classmates; it was part of my identity. It felt natural to think about being a chef, to connect with people by cooking for them.

The recipes in this chapter showcase classic fare from St. Lucia, like Conch in Sauce Souskaye (page 42), Beef Pepperpot (page 87), and Green Fig and Saltfish (page 40). I share recipes from my family members, like my sister Fiona's Cassava Cookies (page 76), which put a twist on our traditional ground provision; my grandmother's Banana and Brown Butter Tea Sandwiches (page 67), reflecting her English background; Daddy's Milk Punch (page 55), for the rum fans; and Mum's Soursop Mousse (page 71).

GREEN FIG AND SALTFISH

SERVES 4

This combo is the official national dish of St. Lucia. The indigenous (banana) and imported (salted cod) became part of the diets of those living under colonial and enslaved rule for generations. The meanings that foods carry over time are constantly in flux. When writer Osayi Endolyn visited St. Lucia for the first time in 2022, she met with my friend Damian Adjodha, who manages horticulture and farming for Jade Mountain, a luxurious resort in Soufrière. Damian and I grew up together, and he's been proactive in cultivating the local produce that is increasingly appearing on resort menus, showcasing our local cuisine to visitors. It's inspiring to see him contribute to shaping an empowered narrative for Caribbean cuisine. In Damian and Osayi's conversations, he told her that saltfish is indeed part of our tradition—it was imported as inexpensive sustenance for enslaved Africans.

"They came with the cod, they left with the sugar and/or the rum," he said. "But to say it's our 'national dish' is to say that we are still part of that colonial cycle. I think we need to free ourselves from that. Our *real* survival food was: You go catch a fish, you roast it, and you blend or mash up the herbs that you have, squeeze a lime on it and eat your souskaye." We'll get into sauce souskaye in a moment (see page 42, Conch in Sauce Souskaye). I like Damian's willingness to revisit the story we tell about ourselves through our food.

Green fig and saltfish is delicious and filling meal that we often enjoy for breakfast. It's another indicator of our history, as people performing relentless physical labor would benefit from a calorie-rich meal at the start of the day. It's been a mainstay for the generations that followed this difficult history, at once bright, acidic, fresh, and savory. Note the advance preparation of soaking the saltfish overnight.

1 pound saltfish fillet

¼ cup coconut oil (or canola oil)

1 large yellow onion, minced

1 green bell pepper, coarsely chopped

3 garlic cloves, minced

4 seasoning peppers, thinly sliced

2 teaspoons thyme leaves

½ cup thinly sliced scallions

½ cup chopped fresh tomato (optional)

1½ teaspoons kosher salt

1½ teaspoons freshly ground black pepper

8 green figs (these are green *bananas*—not plantains!)

1 tablespoon chopped flat-leaf parsley

GARNISH

Florida avocado (or available avocado), sliced

Cucumber, grated

SERVING SUGGESTION

Bakes (page 83)

In a medium bowl, submerge the saltfish in water and leave to soak overnight in the refrigerator. Change the water at least once during the soaking time. Drain.

Let's cook the excess salt out of the fish: Place the cod in a medium pot and cover with cold water by 2 inches. Bring the pot to a boil, then reduce to a simmer and cook for 20 minutes. Drain the fillets, return it to the pot, and repeat the boiling and draining process once more. Transfer the fillets to a medium bowl. If needed, clean the saltfish by removing all skin, scales, and pin bones. Use a fork to flake it into large chunks, then set aside.

In a medium saucepan, heat the coconut oil over medium heat. Add the onions, green bell peppers, and garlic and sauté, stirring, until the vegetables are softened and fragrant, about 2 minutes. Add the seasoning peppers and stir, then cook until just incorporated, another 3 minutes. Add the flaked saltfish and thyme. Stir to mix thoroughly. Add the scallions and tomatoes (if using) and mix well. Season the mixture with 1 teaspoon of the kosher salt and the black pepper, then mix again. Set aside.

In a medium pot, bring about 2 quarts of water to a boil. Cut the ends off the green figs (green bananas). Make one lengthwise slice just through the skin. Place the green figs in the pot and boil until fork tender, about 15 minutes. Drain the water and allow the green figs to cool just enough to handle.

Remove the peels, using a small paring knife if needed. Dice the green figs into 2-inch cubes. Mix the green figs and the saltfish together. Taste and adjust the seasoning with the remaining ½ teaspoon of salt. Add the chopped parsley.

Garnish: Top with sliced avocado and grated cucumber. Enjoy hot. We serve this dish family style in the pot.

CONCH IN SAUCE SOUSKAYE

SERVES 4

Many St. Lucians would argue that sauce souskaye, prepared with your chosen seafood, is our true, definitive national dish (as opposed to Green Fig and Saltfish, page 40). As my childhood friend, farmer and horticulturist Damian Adjodha, noted about his work on the island, when it comes to feeding yourself, there is nothing more sovereign than catching your own fish, native to our surrounding waters, and preparing it with a foraged medley of herbs and citrus.

You'll find iterations of souskaye throughout the Caribbean (particularly in Martinique) and in dishes in this book. Island foods in this part of the world are often linked by similar moments in history along with climate and customs, not to mention generations of interregional migration and diaspora-mixing. This is another way of saying there are many ways to souskaye, okay! The essentials are oil, peppers, and herbs; my must-haves are coconut oil and parsley.

My take on this recipe is inspired by the souskaye at Fond Doux, an eco-boutique hotel located a thousand feet above sea level in the mountains of Soufrière. It used to be a cocoa plantation. The owners, Lyton and Eroline Lamontagne, gathered and restored nineteenth-century Creole cottages from around the island. With a focus on preservation, the cottages are being repurposed as guesthouses for visitors on the property, all tucked away in lush vegetation. It feels like you're in the jungle.

When we want to say that something is really, *really*, good, we say it's knockin, like it knocks you down it's so good. The souskaye at Fond Doux is knockin! I expect nothing less from your take.

Conch (sounds like "konk") is a firm and mild shellfish that you'll find in tropically driven fish markets or often wherever Caribbean folks are en masse. I'd compare it to a less briny clam or abalone; it has a touch of sweetness. If you haven't seen it around, ask your fishmonger if they can get it for you. Calamari or shrimp make good substitutes.

1 pound conch meat (or 1 pound calamari or 1½ pounds U10-size shrimp, peeled and deveined)

½ cup coconut oil

1 red bell pepper, minced

½ cup roughly chopped scallions

1 tablespoon red chili flakes

3 garlic cloves, grated

2 teaspoons minced celery

2 teaspoons thyme leaves

2 teaspoons marjoram leaves

1 teaspoon peeled and grated ginger

1 teaspoon kosher salt

1 tablespoon white wine vinegar

3 limes, zested and juiced

2 teaspoons chopped flat-leaf parsley

1 teaspoon Baron West Indian Hot Sauce

SERVING

Dasheen Chips (page 43)

Prepare the conch: In a large stockpot, add the conch meat. Cover with water by about 6 inches. Bring to a boil, then reduce to medium heat and simmer for about 3 hours. To check for doneness, use a paring knife to make an incision through the thickest part of the conch. The conch is ready when the meat is tender and there is little resistance. Use a slotted spoon to transfer it to a bowl and allow it to cool. Once the conch has cooled, cut into 1-inch pieces and set aside. (If using calamari or shrimp, bring a large stockpot of water to boil, then poach for 2 minutes. Use a slotted spoon to remove the calamari or shrimp and set aside.)

For the souskaye: Place a medium sauté pan over low heat. Warm the coconut oil, and then add the red bell pepper, scallion, red chili flakes, garlic, celery, thyme, marjoram, and ginger. Sauté and stir just long enough to combine the ingredients, about 1 minute. Season with the salt, add the white wine vinegar, and stir to combine. Remove from the heat. Add the conch (or calamari or shrimp), then add the lime zest and juice, parsley, and hot sauce. Return the mixture to low heat and gently warm through for 1 minute.

To serve: Enjoy right away with the dasheen chips.

DASHEEN CHIPS

SERVES 4 TO 6

We enjoy these chips all around the island. Dasheen, also known as taro root, can be fried, boiled, steamed, or roasted. It's an easy plant to maintain— it's fairly small, and the tubers grow underground, so it doesn't take up a lot of room in your garden. But it reaps a bounty! It's used in our everyday cooking on St. Lucia because we have so much of it. We add dasheen in our bouyon, or we roast it and serve it as a side with fresh seafood and salads. These dasheen chips are a fun snack on their own, but they can also hang with dips, salads, or my suggestion here, a ceviche.

1 large dasheen (about
    1 pound), peeled
Canola oil, for frying
2 tablespoons flaky sea salt

EQUIPMENT
Mandoline

SERVING SUGGESTION
Shrimp Ceviche (page 187)

Use a mandoline to thinly slice the peeled dasheen; you're going for super thin, like $\frac{1}{16}$ of an inch. Add the dasheen slices to a colander and rinse until the water runs clear. This removes some of the starch so the chips won't stick together when frying.

In a large pot or Dutch oven, add canola oil to a depth of 3 inches (about 6 cups) and heat to 350°F; check using an instant-read thermometer. Line a plate or sheet pan with paper towels.

Drop in the slices, one at a time, about 6 to 8 slices maximum. Fry the dasheen in batches, gently stirring the whole time so they don't clump in the pot, until the chips are a faint purple (they won't turn golden brown), 3 to 5 minutes. Use a slotted spoon to remove the chips and let them drain on the paper towel. Repeat with the remaining slices. Season with the salt and allow them to cool before serving.

COCONUT RICE AND PEAS
WITH CHICKEN

SERVES 6

My take on traditional rice and peas is inspired by a Trinidadian pelau. Trinidad and Tobago is geographically close to St. Lucia, and many Trinis come to St. Lucia to work. We'll see roadside roti shops where this dish is served. The Trinis burn the sugar and add onions, bell peppers, ginger, and Scotch bonnets, then add rice and coconut milk to finish and let that steam all the way through. In Trinidad, they usually add chicken cuts, which I've done here. For a vegetarian dish, simply omit the chicken. Note the advance preparation of soaking the peas overnight.

PICKLED ONIONS

2 cups red wine vinegar

½ cup sugar

1 teaspoon kosher salt

1 large red onion, thinly sliced

RICE AND PEAS

1 cup pigeon peas (or black-eyed peas)

6 chicken legs

½ cup Mojo Vinaigrette (page 273)

4 tablespoons kosher salt

1½ cups jasmine rice

4 tablespoons extra-virgin olive oil

¼ cup light brown sugar

¼ cup minced yellow onion

1 red bell pepper, minced

2 tablespoons minced celery

1 tablespoon minced fresh ginger

1 teaspoon minced Scotch bonnet pepper

1 fresh bay leaf

½ cup tomato paste

2 cups coconut milk

GARNISH

Pickled onions

Sprigs of cilantro

Pickle the onions: In a small pot, add the red wine vinegar, sugar, and salt. Stir just to combine. Bring to a boil, uncovered, and boil until the sugar is dissolved, about 2 minutes. Place the sliced onions in a small heat-safe bowl. Pour the hot liquid over the onions. Let the mixture cool to room temperature, uncovered, and set aside. These will keep, refrigerated, for up to 2 weeks.

Make the rice and peas: In a medium bowl, cover the peas with at least 4 inches of water. Soak overnight at room temperature. Drain the peas.

Place the chicken legs in a medium bowl, add the vinaigrette, and turn to coat. Transfer to the refrigerator and marinate, covered, for 1 hour. Remove from the refrigerator and season on all sides with 2 tablespoons of the kosher salt.

Using a fine-mesh strainer or rice bowl, rinse the jasmine rice until the water runs clear, about three times. Drain well and set aside.

In a large Dutch oven, add 2 tablespoons of the olive oil and heat on medium. Add the chicken legs to the hot oil, working in batches if necessary, and sear until golden brown on all surfaces, about 2 minutes for each side. Transfer the chicken from the pot to a plate and set aside.

Raise the heat to medium-high. Add the brown sugar and remaining 2 tablespoons of olive oil. Caramelize, stirring occasionally, until it develops a molasses color, about 6 minutes.

Add the yellow onions and cook, undisturbed, until golden brown, about 1 minute. Follow with the bell pepper, celery, ginger, Scotch bonnet, and bay leaf. Cook, stirring regularly, until softened, about 3 minutes.

Season with the remaining 2 tablespoons of salt. Add the tomato paste and the drained peas and stir to incorporate. Add enough water to cover the peas by 3 inches. Bring to a boil, then reduce the heat to low and simmer uncovered for about 1 hour. Keep 1 inch of water over the peas throughout the cooking time. Check the peas for doneness by gently squeezing one between your fingers. It should be tender and give no resistance. If the pea still feels firm, give them 20 minutes more and check again.

Meanwhile, heat the oven to 350°F.

Add the rice to the cooked peas and return the seared chicken to the pot, arranging it on top of the rice. Remove the pot from the heat and drizzle the coconut milk evenly over the top. Check that there is about 1 inch of liquid over the rice. If there isn't, add a bit more room-temperature water. Bake, uncovered, until the rice is tender, about 20 minutes. Remove bay leaf and discard.

To garnish: Top with pickled red onion and cilantro and serve immediately.

STEAMED SNAPPER
WITH PEPPER GINGER SAUCE

SERVES 4

Banana trees are everywhere on the island, and we use the leaves as a vessel to keep fish moist and juicy while cooking. The ooohs and aaahs roll off people's tongues when you present this fish in the middle of the table, heightened by the theater of pulling away the banana wrap. The colors of the peppery ginger sauce glisten as it leaks into every crevice, offering you the most beautiful, spicy bite. You can find banana leaves in the freezer section at most Caribbean, Afro Latin, or Asian markets.

¼ cup canola oil

1 small Spanish onion, chopped

1 cup Fresno chilies, chopped

¼ cup grated fresh ginger

3 tablespoons minced garlic

1 tablespoon thyme leaves

½ cup white vinegar

¼ cup tomato paste

¼ cup plus 2 tablespoons cold water

4 (4-ounce) fillets of snapper, skin removed

2 teaspoons kosher salt

½ cup extra-virgin olive oil

4 banana leaves

GARNISH
1 lime, halved

SERVING
Coconut Rice and Peas (page 47)

Heat the oven to 375°F.

In a medium sauté pan, add the canola oil and heat on medium-high. Sauté the onions, chilies, ginger, and garlic, stirring to combine, until they begin to develop a golden brown color, 6 to 8 minutes. Add the thyme, then add the vinegar. Raise the heat to high and cook to reduce the liquid volume by half, 2 to 3 minutes.

Add the tomato paste and the ¼ cup of cold water. Reduce the heat to low and simmer until the vegetables soften and the mixture thickens, about 5 minutes.

Transfer the mixture to a blender and puree until smooth (cracking the lid to allow steam to escape).

Using a paring knife and pressing just past the surface of the fish, make three 1-inch scores along each snapper fillet. Scoring in this way helps the seasoning get into the fish and it will cook faster.

Liberally season both sides of the fillets with the salt and then the olive oil.

If needed, trim each banana leaf into an 8-inch square. Put a fillet on each leaf, spoon the blended pepper sauce over the fish, and fold the leaves over to envelop the fish. Ensure that all sides are sealed by tucking the edges underneath (or use toothpicks to help keep them snug). Place the wrapped fillets in one large ovenproof dish, leaving an inch of separation between the banana leaf envelopes. Add the 2 tablespoons of cold water to the dish, to encourage the fish to steam. Place the dish in the oven and cook for 15 minutes.

While the fish is cooking, prepare the garnish: Heat a small, dry skillet on high heat for 5 minutes. Place a piece of foil on the skillet surface, just large enough to fit the lime halves. Follow with the lime halves, flesh side down. Char for 8 minutes, until the sugars caramelize and the lime is blackened. Set aside.

Check the fish by unwrapping one. It should be firm and easy to flake with a fork. Unwrap the remaining fish and garnish with the charred lime.

To serve: Enjoy hot with coconut rice.

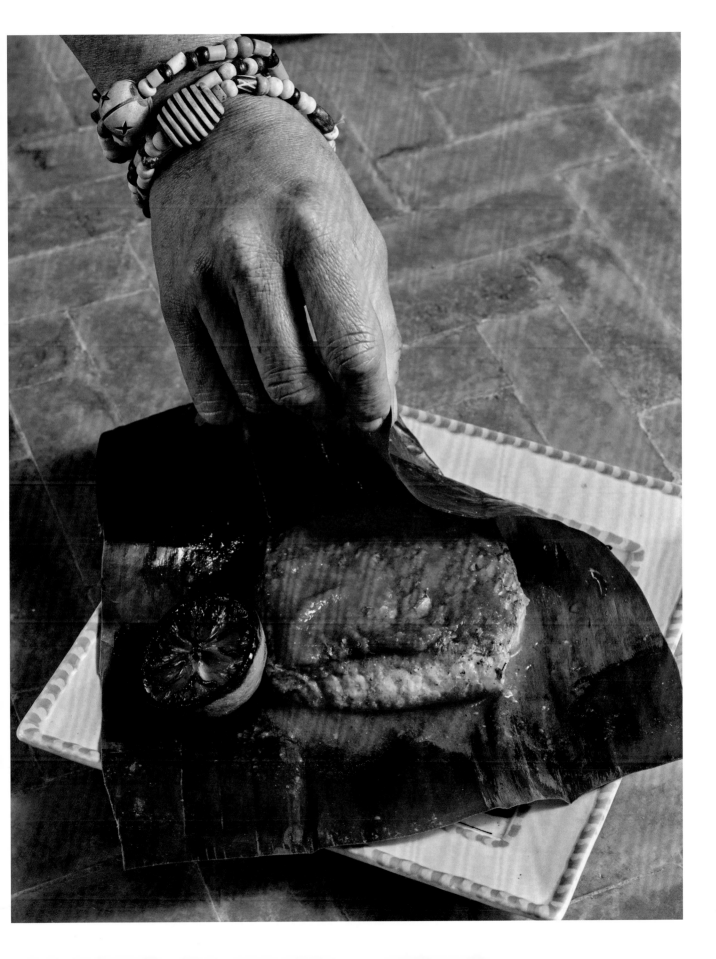

STUFFED CRAB BACKS

SERVES 4

If you step into a St. Lucian restaurant, crab backs are on the menu. Locals hunt for land crabs (also known as brown crabs) in the marshy areas at night or at sundown. Using a wooden stick, they poke around the mangroves. Back in the day they used a flabeau (Kwéyòl for "flaming torch") so as to not use a bright light that would frighten the crabs away. The stick goes into the holes around the mangrove, and the crabs attach themselves to the stick. Sometimes when people hunt a lot they use mesh wire baskets to catch the crabs.

Crab backs are a labor-intensive dish—from catching the crabs, to cleaning them, to carefully removing all the meat. You find them all over the island, but because it takes so much effort to enjoy them, they tend to appear only in fancier restaurants.

We cook the crabmeat inside the shell, but if you can't get your hands on live crabs, you can use a casserole dish or ovenproof ramekin.

Ice water

4 (5-ounce) live blue crabs, or 1 pound jumbo lump crabmeat

3 tablespoons unsalted butter

1 cup diced yellow onion

1 cup chopped fresh tomatoes

¼ cup chopped scallions

¼ cup minced green bell peppers

1 teaspoon cayenne pepper

1 tablespoon chopped garlic

1 tablespoon Worcestershire sauce

2 tablespoons Green Seasoning (page 274)

Kosher salt and freshly ground black pepper

¼ cup panko breadcrumbs, plus more for topping

If you're using lump crabmeat, jump ahead to the stovetop step. If you're using live crabs: Fill a medium pot of water and bring it to a boil. Fill a large bowl with ice water and set aside. Drop the crabs into the boiling water and cook until they turn bright pinkish orange, about 10 minutes. Use tongs to remove the crabs and place them in the ice water. Allow them to cool for 5 minutes.

Once the crabs are cool to touch, you're going to remove the backs. Flip each crab onto its belly and pull the back apart from the body, from just above the eyes. Gently remove the meat and reserve the shell. Use kitchen shears to separate the legs from the body, then cut down the entire length of the crab to fully expose the meat. For the knuckles, separate into smaller sections and use the back of a sturdy knife to crack the hardest part of the shell. Using your fingers, pry the shell open and remove the meat. Pick through the meat again to make sure there are no bits of shell.

Heat the oven to 375°F.

Now you've got your shelled crab or your lump crabmeat, so let's cook the crab: In a medium sauté pan, melt the butter over medium-high heat. Add the onions, tomatoes, scallions, bell pepper, cayenne pepper, and garlic. Sauté, stirring to combine, until the vegetables are softened, 3 to 5 minutes. Add the crabmeat and Worcestershire sauce and cook, heating the crab through and blending the meat well into the vegetables and seasonings, 1 to 2 minutes. Add the green seasoning and stir to evenly distribute.

Once the crabmeat is thoroughly heated, season to taste with salt and black pepper. Remove the sauté pan from the heat and sprinkle in the breadcrumbs. Mix well, then divide evenly among the crab shells (or ramekins if you're using lump crabmeat). Transfer the stuffed shells or ramekins to a sheet pan.

Top the crabs with additional breadcrumbs and brown in the oven just long enough for the breadcrumbs to toast, about 8 minutes. Serve immediately.

DASHEEN DUMPLINGS

SERVES 2

We eat these dumplings on the regular, adding them to stews and sauces. We like them dense and chewy. They are not meant to be light and airy as a pillow. They're meant to have heft to them!

If you can't get dasheen, malanga works well in this recipe. Both have a mild, sweet flesh and almost nutty flavor. You can enjoy these dumplings with a little melted butter and salt on their own, or add to stews.

1 cup peeled and grated dasheen or malanga

1 cup all-purpose flour, plus more for dusting

3 large egg yolks

½ cup plus 1 tablespoon kosher salt

6 to 10 tablespoons water, as needed

In a large bowl, add the dasheen, flour, egg yolks, and the 1 tablespoon of salt. Use your hands to knead the ingredients into a firm but elastic dough. Since the dasheen already has a bit of moisture, you're working in the flour before adding water.

Once you have the dough combined, start adding water, 1 tablespoon at a time. Continue to knead until it feels smooth and elastic, and once the dough achieves this state, stop adding water. Wrap the dough in plastic wrap and allow it to rest at room temperature for 30 minutes.

Fill a small stockpot with 3 quarts of water and bring it to a boil. Add ½ cup of salt. Carefully taste the water. It should have the salinity of a broth. Reduce the heat to medium-low and allow the salted water to simmer.

Dust a flat surface with flour and lightly dust a sheet pan. Remove the plastic wrap from the dough ball and use a dough cutter to cut it into 4 equal pieces. Roll each piece into a ball. Use your flat palm to gently work each ball into a 3-inch-wide, ¼-inch-thick disk. Place each disk on the floured sheet pan.

Drop 2 of the disks into the simmering water. Allow them to float for about 1 minute before using a slotted spoon to transfer to a plate. They'll look pretty much the same, but the texture will become a bit firmer after a minute passes. Repeat with the remaining pieces. (You can also simmer the dasheen dumplings in Curried Goat [page 96], or any sauce of your choosing.) Serve immediately.

CASSAVA DUMPLINGS

MAKES 4

You can treat a cassava dumpling like a dumpling made of wheat flour or pasta. We start with cassava flour, then make it into a dough that can be poached. These are chewier and a bit denser than flour-based dumplings. In Trinidad, the dumpling is shaped to resemble the shape of a cow's tongue. Add it to dishes like Beef Pepperpot (page 87) or if you don't want to do traditional spinner dumplings (made of wheat flour), drop these in your Bouyon (page 88).

½ pound cassava, peeled and diced

6 tablespoons kosher salt

2 large egg yolks

1 cup cassava flour (or 1 cup all-purpose flour)

In a medium stockpot, combine the cassava and enough cold water to cover by about 1 inch. It's important to start with cold water so you can bring up the temperature of the cassava slowly, which allows for more even cooking.

Add 2 tablespoons of the salt and bring the water to a simmer on medium heat. Cook until the cassava is fork tender, about 20 minutes. Drain the water, retaining the cassava in the pot.

Use a potato masher or potato ricer to mash the cassava. Make sure there are no lumps.

Allow the mashed cassava to cool slightly. You want it to be warm to the touch. If the cassava gets too cold it will seize up and become difficult to manipulate.

Season with 2 tablespoons of the salt and add the egg yolks, using a spoon to mix.

Sprinkle the cassava flour onto a dry surface. Transfer the mixture on top and knead gently in the flour until it forms a smooth ball. Leaving the dough on your work surface, cover with a damp towel or plastic wrap. Let it rest for 15 minutes.

While the dough is resting, add about 4 cups of water to a medium pot and bring it to a boil.

Uncover your resting dough and divide it into 4 even pieces. Use the palms of your hands to gently roll each piece into a long rope, about ¾-inch thick (keep the waiting dough covered with a towel). Pull the sides of the dough away from each other to be about 2 inches wide and 4 inches long.

The pot of water should be boiling (or close) by now. Add the remaining 2 tablespoons of salt.

Drop each dumpling into the boiling water. Reduce the heat to medium and allow them to simmer until they float, about 1 minute. Use a slotted spoon or tongs to remove the dumplings.

Serve immediately as a side dish or added to stew.

DADDY'S MILK PUNCH

SERVES 6

My father, John, made this punch every Christmas. It was his contribution to the festivities. Every year you knew Christmas was coming because you'd hear the blender. After mixing the punch, he'd pour it back into the original rum bottle, which was always Chairman's Reserve Spiced or Bounty. In true festive fashion, he'd make extra for visitors stopping by. The rest would be given to friends and relatives when we made our rounds wishing everyone well for the season.

1 vanilla pod (see Note)
1 (750 ml) bottle
   Chairman's Reserve
   Spiced Rum
   (or dark rum)
4 (12-ounce) cans
   evaporated milk
1 (14-ounce) can
   condensed milk
3 large eggs
1 tablespoon Angostura
   bitters

GARNISH
6 star anise pods
1 cinnamon stick

NOTE: After scraping the seeds from the vanilla pod, you can retain the pod and place it in a medium airtight container with about 4 cups of granulated sugar. The pod will infuse the sugar, making the most use of the pod, which is typically pricey in the States. You can keep it at room temperature for up to 30 days, using the sugar however you like. I told you, in the Caribbean we don't waste a ting!

Using a paring knife, slice the vanilla pod lengthwise and scrape out the seeds. In a blender, mix the rum, evaporated milk, condensed milk, eggs, bitters, and vanilla seeds. Blend until smooth. If your blender can't accommodate the full bottle of rum, blend everything else first, transfer the mixture to a pitcher, then stir in the rum.

Fill serving glasses with ice and pour in the punch.

To garnish: Add a whole star anise to each glass and grate cinnamon on top. Serve immediately.

CHRISTOPHINE GRATIN

SERVES 4

Whether known as christophine (in St. Lucia), chayote (in Spanish-speaking areas), or mirliton (as we call it down in the Bayou), this gourd vegetable is beloved throughout the Caribbean and the Southern U.S. In St. Lucia, we slice it up, sauté it, and then layer the pieces in a casserole.

This gratin is distinctive in my mind because my mother, Janice, added grated turmeric root to her light béchamel sauce. The natural yellow coloring, layered in with cheese and sauce and then baked, was always a hit for me growing up. These days, I'd love to see turmeric used more broadly in American dining. In St. Lucia, we include turmeric in teas (such as in a blend of lemongrass, ginger, bay leaf, cinnamon, and turmeric—"bush tea" is what we call it), and many people in St. Lucia grow turmeric in their gardens.

The sauté step is meant to cook out the water in the christophine so that when you bake it, the slices will become translucent and firm up like a potato. Don't skip it.

4 christophine

¼ cup extra-virgin olive oil

2 small Spanish onions, diced

4 tablespoons kosher salt

2 tablespoons finely grated fresh turmeric root

1 garlic clove, thinly sliced

4 tablespoons (½ stick) unsalted butter

6 tablespoons all-purpose flour

1 teaspoon cayenne pepper

3 cups hot whole milk

4 sprigs of thyme

2 cups grated mild Cheddar cheese

½ cup panko breadcrumbs

Heat the oven to 375°F.

Cut the christophine into quarters and remove the pit in the center. Cut into ¼-inch slices.

In a medium sauté pan, add the olive oil and heat on medium-high for 2 minutes. Add the christophine, onions, 2 tablespoons of the salt, 1 tablespoon of the turmeric, and the garlic. Sweat on medium-high heat, stirring occasionally, until the ingredients become translucent, 6 to 8 minutes. Transfer the vegetables to a bowl and set aside.

Make the roux: Reduce the heat to low. Add the butter, the remaining 2 tablespoons of salt, and the remaining 1 tablespoon of turmeric. Cook for 3 minutes to incorporate the turmeric into the butter. Add the flour and cayenne and use a spatula to fold the flour into the butter. Cook, stirring occasionally, until the roux develops into a thick paste, 8 to 10 minutes. This step is important to cook the raw sharpness out of the flour. Taste it; it should have a roasted flavor.

Make the béchamel: Add the hot milk and thyme to the roux, then simmer just long enough for the roux to thicken the milk, stirring constantly, 5 to 6 minutes (the hot milk helps to avoid clumping in the roux). You're going for a consistency similar to gravy—thick, but easy to manipulate. Remove and discard the thyme.

Remove the pan from the heat and add 1 cup of the cheese, stirring until it melts. Transfer the christophine mixture from the bowl to an 8 × 8-inch baking dish (or similar size). Pour the béchamel over the mixture, then evenly cover with the remaining 1 cup of cheese. Sprinkle the panko breadcrumbs on top.

Bake until the gratin is golden brown and the edges start to bubble, about 20 minutes. Remove from the oven and allow to cool for about 5 minutes. Slice and serve immediately.

BREADFRUIT BALLS

MAKES ABOUT 12

Breadfruit is kind of an honorary ground provision throughout the Caribbean. While it grows on trees, we treat it like a root vegetable in our food. It's nutrient-dense and incredibly versatile. We consider it our potato. If you can't find breadfruit, substitute dasheen, cassava, or Russet potatoes.

These breadfruit balls are like a croquette. You mash up the breadfruit and add a sofrito (onions, scallions, celery, seasoning peppers). Flour, eggs, and breadcrumbs give it body. If you're feeling it, you can add 1 cup of crabmeat or saltfish to the batter. My granny, Phyllis, would make breadfruit balls as an appetizer when she made her fried flying fish dish (page 68), though in my family we like to serve it as a side with roasted chicken or fish stew. The breadfruit balls are also great with Conch in Sauce Souskaye (page 42).

1 medium breadfruit (about 2 pounds)

2 tablespoons plus ½ teaspoon kosher salt, plus more to taste

Canola oil, for frying

½ medium yellow onion, finely diced

¼ cup minced scallions

1 Scotch bonnet pepper, minced

¼ cup flat-leaf parsley, minced

¼ teaspoon freshly ground black pepper

Pinch of freshly grated nutmeg

¼ cup whole milk

1 large egg

1½ cups fine breadcrumbs, plus more as needed

On a flat work surface, use a sharp knife to remove the breadfruit stem. Rest it flat side down and cut into 1-inch wedges. Using a sharp paring knife, peel off the skin. Remove the spongy center so your wedges are entirely breadfruit meat. Rinse the wedges with cool water.

In a large pot, add the breadfruit wedges and cover with cold water about 2 inches over the breadfruit. Add the 2 tablespoons of salt. Cook on medium-high heat until the breadfruit is fork tender, 30 to 40 minutes.

In a medium skillet, add canola oil to a depth of 2 inches (about 3 cups) and heat on medium to 350°F; check with an instant-read thermometer. Line a plate with paper towels.

In a large pan, sauté the onion, scallions, and Scotch bonnet on low heat, until the vegetables soften, about 3 minutes. Mix in the parsley and season with the remaining ½ teaspoon salt and the pepper and nutmeg, then set aside.

Using a colander or slotted spoon, drain the breadfruit. While it's hot, transfer to a large bowl and mash with a potato masher or fork until there are no lumps. Add the onion mixture to the bowl and stir together until well combined.

In a small bowl, whisk the milk and egg together until the egg is evenly distributed.

Add the liquid to the breadfruit and mix with your hands. If there are still large chunks of breadfruit, you can crush them with your fingers. The mixture should look and feel cohesive, not soupy.

Put the breadcrumbs in a shallow bowl. For your breadfruit balls, aim for approximately 1½ tablespoons each. Use your hands to form balls. Toss the balls in the breadcrumbs until they're lightly coated. Set aside on a plate or sheet pan.

Once the oil is at temperature, use a slotted spoon to place 1 or 2 balls in the oil at a time, 5 or 6 maximum. Avoid overcrowding, to prevent the oil temperature from dropping and the balls from absorbing too much oil, which can result in a greasy texture. Cook until the balls are completely golden brown on all sides. You'll need to flip the balls and pay attention to doneness, but estimate 5 to 6 minutes total for each batch.

Using a slotted spoon, remove the balls from the oil and drain on the paper towels. Season with additional salt to your taste. Repeat with the remaining balls and serve hot.

BREADFRUIT PIE

SERVES 6

It's hard to overestimate St. Lucians' love for starch and cheese combos (it's me, raising my hand). We have our Macaroni Pie (page 63), but the breadfruit version hits different. St. Lucians treat breadfruit like a potato, so we think of this dish as Americans might think of a potato gratin. We cook seasonally, so when breadfruit is in season (typically August to November) it might replace macaroni pie as a side dish. The breadfruit is boiled, peeled, then sliced into thin wedges. Add a little béchamel situation amped up with a Scotch bonnet, and you're minutes away from a slice of comfort.

2 large breadfruit (about 4 pounds)

2 tablespoons kosher salt, plus more to taste

2 cups (4 sticks) unsalted butter, plus more for the pan

½ cup finely diced yellow onion

¼ Scotch bonnet pepper, finely diced

2 cups all-purpose flour

3½ cups whole milk, plus more as needed

2 cups grated sharp Cheddar cheese

2 tablespoons minced flat-leaf parsley

¼ teaspoon freshly ground black pepper

Pinch of freshly grated nutmeg

On a flat work surface, use a sharp knife to remove the breadfruit stem. Rest it flat side down and cut into 1-inch wedges. Using a sharp paring knife, peel off the skin. Remove the spongy center so your wedges are entirely breadfruit meat. Rinse the wedges with cool water.

In a large pot, add the wedges and salt, then cover with water, about 2 inches over the breadfruit. Bring to a boil, then reduce the heat to low. Place a heat-safe bowl with water in it inside the pot, on top of the breadfruit wedges. This weighs them down, allowing them to cook evenly. Simmer with the weighted bowl on top until the breadfruit is fork tender, 30 to 40 minutes. As the breadfruit boils, you'll notice it develops a darker hue. To be sure it's fully cooked, pierce with a sharp knife and make sure there's no resistance. Remove it from the water using a slotted spoon or drain in a colander and set aside to cool.

Heat the oven to 350°F. Grease a 9 × 12-inch baking dish with butter.

In a medium saucepan, heat the butter, onions, and Scotch bonnet pepper on low heat. As the butter melts, whisk in the flour and cook, continually whisking, until you have a smooth paste, 4 to 5 minutes. It's important that you constantly whisk it, so the flour does not clump or burn. Add a pinch of salt.

Now add the milk. Raise the heat to medium and whisk constantly. Add 1 cup of the cheese and cook, continuing to whisk, until the cheese begins to bubble around the edges and the sauce becomes thick but smooth, 2 to 3 minutes. Add a bit more milk or water if it's too thick. Add the parsley, black pepper, and nutmeg. Stir well to combine, then set aside.

Return to the cooled breadfruit. Cut each wedge lengthwise into ¼-inch-thick slices. Arrange a layer of the sliced breadfruit in the prepared dish. Follow with about 1 cup of the sauce, poured in an even layer, then continue to alternate between wedges and sauce. Pour the remaining cheese sauce over the top of the dish and finish with the remaining 1 cup of cheese.

Bake until the cheese is bubbling around the edges, about 30 minutes. Place the dish on a high rack in the oven, then turn on your broiler for about 2 minutes—watch carefully! Everyone's broiler is different. You just want to crisp up the crust, so it's a beautiful golden brown color.

Remove from the heat and allow it to rest on the stovetop for about 5 minutes. Slice and enjoy hot.

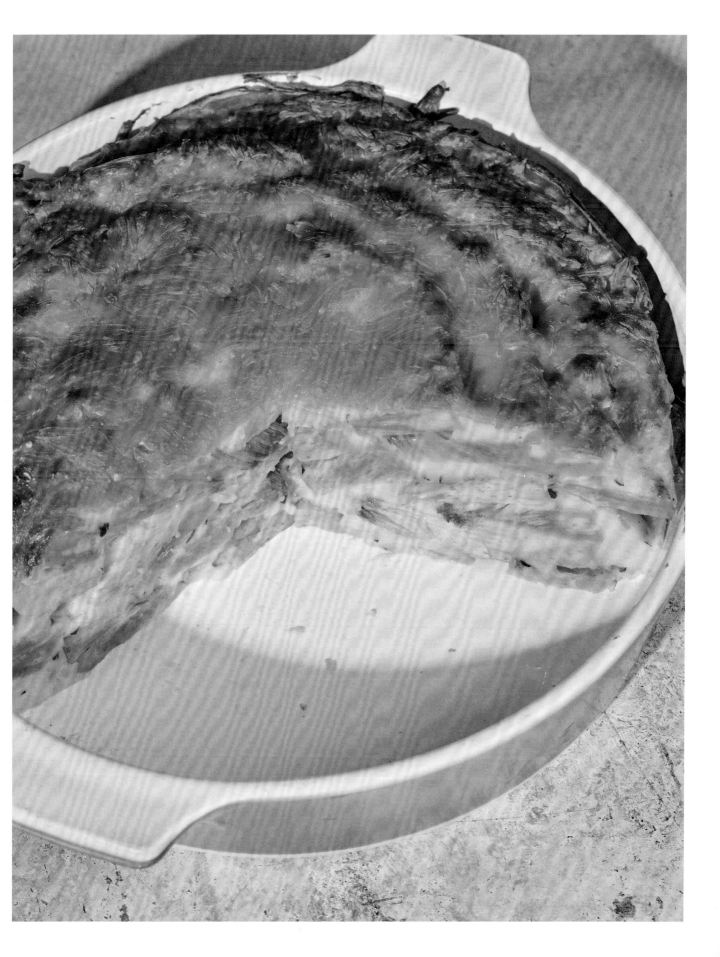

MACARONI PIE

SERVES 6

Pretty much any restaurant in St. Lucia—the roadside stops, the fast-casual places—serves macaroni pie as a side dish. We love our carbs! We probably eat more carbs than proteins. The macaroni pie is cooked to be firm; it's not runny or saucy like a lot of American mac and cheese. When you slice into macaroni pie, it keeps its shape. One thing my mum does that is typical for Caribbean people: we save the wrapper from the butter in the refrigerator so it can be used to grease pans, like you'll do in the first step below. We don't waste *anything*!

I like to add poblano and jalapeño peppers to my macaroni pie, which differs from the typical approach in St. Lucia. It adds spice without being overpowering. Back home, you'll find macaroni pie served at lunch or dinner alongside baked chicken, rice and peas, and a small green salad—great options here as well.

Butter or nonstick cooking spray

4 quarts water

1 cup plus 3 tablespoons kosher salt, plus more as needed

2 cups elbow macaroni

¼ cup extra-virgin olive oil

2 jalapeños, seeded and minced

2 poblano peppers, seeded and minced

2 tablespoons all-purpose flour

3 cups hot whole milk

1 teaspoon cayenne pepper

1 teaspoon sweet paprika

¼ teaspoon freshly ground black pepper

3 cups grated Cheddar cheese

1 cup grated fontina cheese

Heat the oven to 350°F. Grease a 9 × 12-inch baking dish with butter or nonstick cooking spray.

In a medium pot, bring the water to a boil. Add 1 cup of salt to the water (this seasons the pasta; don't skimp on it!) and the macaroni. Cook until the pasta is cooked through and chewy to the bite, about 8 minutes. Use a colander to drain the pasta and set aside.

In a medium saucepan on low heat, add the olive oil and sauté the jalapeño and poblano peppers, stirring to coat in the oil, until aromatic, about 3 minutes. Add the flour, stir to blend well, and cook for 1 minute. Add the remaining 3 tablespoons of salt and the hot milk, cayenne, paprika, and black pepper (the hot milk helps to avoid clumping). Stir until combined. Allow the mixture to come to a simmer. Whisk in 2 cups of the Cheddar cheese and the fontina, then remove from the heat. Continue whisking until the cheese is fully melted.

Stir in the drained macaroni. Check your seasoning and add a pinch of salt if needed.

Pour the pasta mixture into the prepared baking dish. Top with the remaining 1 cup of grated Cheddar. Bake until firm and the top is golden brown, 35 to 40 minutes. Allow the macaroni pie to rest for 10 to 15 minutes before slicing to serve.

BLACK CAKE

SERVES 6

December in St. Lucia is all about Christmas festivities—visitors, decorating the house with family, good food, strong drinks, and fun times. When the end of November hits, everyone is talking about the ham they're going to buy for Christmas dinner and so on. You can't get much business done in St. Lucia in December. As a kid, I looked forward to a slice of this black cake and a taste of my dad's milk punch (page 55) every year.

We understand that black cake derived in the Caribbean from British Christmas plum pudding, also known as Empire Christmas Pudding (they really were telling on themselves!). Both are extremely rich and make use of fruits soaked in liquor (brandy for the pudding, rum for the cake because it developed in the British-colonized Caribbean). We celebrate the British Boxing Day in St. Lucia, and it's common to begin soaking the dried fruit in rum on Boxing Day in preparation for the following year's black cake. Some folks use fruit soaked for two years; it's serious!

My mum follows the tradition of soaking her fruit a year in advance, and when she reached for that jar, we always knew what time it was. And yes, even us kids would get a small pour of the rum milk punch served with this cake. As in many cultures, our parents watered it down for us, but we got to feel part of the special occasions. Highly recommend this pairing for you, no matter the time of year.

1 cup dried fruit medley (such as dates, raisins, and cherries)

1 cup plus 3 tablespoons Chairman's Reserve Spiced Rum, plus more for serving

1 cup sugar

1 cup (2 sticks) unsalted butter, softened, plus more for greasing

1½ cups all-purpose flour

1 tablespoon baking powder

1 teaspoon kosher salt

1 teaspoon ground nutmeg

1 teaspoon ground allspice

1 teaspoon ground cinnamon

5 large eggs

1¼ cups molasses

½ cup browning (store-bought)

2 teaspoons fresh lime juice

1 teaspoon vanilla extract

For the fruit: In a small bowl, add the dried fruit. You want an even distribution of whatever types you choose. Add ¼ cup of the rum and soak the fruit for 20 to 30 minutes (the rum doesn't need to cover the fruit; we're just using it to rehydrate). Add the soaked fruit and rum to a small pot and transfer to a stovetop. Heat on low, uncovered, until the fruit softens and plumps up, for 10 minutes.

Heat the oven to 350°F.

Transfer the cooked fruit to a blender. Add the remaining ¾ cup of rum and puree until smooth. Set aside.

In the bowl of a stand mixer fitted with the paddle attachment, add the sugar and butter. Cream together on medium speed until it looks pale yellow, light, and fluffy, 8 to 10 minutes. In a medium bowl, sift together the flour, baking powder, salt, nutmeg, allspice, and cinnamon. Set aside.

Set the stand mixer on low speed and add the eggs one at a time, allowing each one to incorporate thoroughly. You don't want to add all the eggs at once because it can cause the mixture to break. Add the pureed fruit, molasses, browning, lime juice, and vanilla extract and mix on low to incorporate, stopping the mixer to scrape down the sides of the dough as necessary, 3 to 5 minutes.

Continuing on low speed, slowly add the dry ingredient mixture and mix until the batter comes together and looks smooth and thick, about 5 minutes. Do not overmix.

Grease a 6-cup Bundt cake pan with butter, making sure to coat the entire surface. Pour in the batter and bake until a cake tester comes out clean, 30 to 45 minutes. Allow the cake to cool in the pan for 10 to 15 minutes. To flip the cake out of the pan, place a plate on top of the pan, then turn it over; the cake should slide out easily. Drizzle about 3 tablespoons of rum over the surface of the cake. Slice and serve.

The cake keeps for up to 1 month, wrapped in plastic wrap, at room temperature. You can rehydrate the cake with a splash of rum before serving as the days go by; just lightly brush it across the top and allow it to absorb.

BANANA AND BROWN BUTTER TEA SANDWICHES

SERVES 2

My grandmum, Phyllis Clarke, was a nurse in Edinburgh, Scotland, during World War II. There she met my St. Lucian grandfather, Frederick Clarke, who was studying to be a doctor. They courted for several years during his studies; this was the late 1940s. He planned to return to St. Lucia upon graduating because there weren't a lot of doctors on the island. They were in love and wanted to start a new life together. They tried three times to get married in England before finally finding a church that would perform the ceremony for an interracial couple. Grandad left before Granny to set things up, as he hadn't been home in years. My grandmum made the journey in 1946, when she was pregnant with my mother, Janice. She took a troop ship from England to Trinidad, with Jamaicans and Trinis who'd fought in the war, then waited another week to get a boat to St. Lucia. It was her first time leaving England.

When she arrived in St. Lucia, she was shocked. The buildings and landscape were different then. It wasn't that developed yet. People would take ferries because most of the town was on the coast. An electric stove was basically unheard of. She was cooking with a coal pot, essentially a Dutch oven made of clay that you build a fire underneath. "When I came to St. Lucia, it was forty-five minutes to make the fire, boil the water, and then I could make my cup of tea." An Englishwoman through and through, my grandmum always had teatime at 4:00 in the afternoon, and you know it had to be English Breakfast tea.

My grandmum used to eat so many bananas. Truly, between her and my dad, my household could have kept every banana farmer on the island in business. Granny would take salted butter and sliced bananas and make a tea sandwich with brown bread—we never called it "whole wheat" bread, just brown. She'd cut them into little crust-free triangles, I think mostly for aesthetics, and also because the crust is a different texture. She would feed the crust to the birds to keep the peace. The birds on the island are friendly but bold, and our window structures are open, so nature is your kitchen. They seemed to have an understanding with Granny: Stay away from her bananas, get a little bread!

This sandwich is a delicate bite, so you gotta lean into the daintiness. Raised pinky fingers are totally optional. Ripe bananas work best, but try to avoid mushy ones, as they can be harder to handle. When you taste that salty butter with the banana, it all makes sense.

¾ cup (1½ sticks) salted butter, softened

2 ripe bananas, halved lengthwise (we use Gros Michel or Cavendish)

6 slices rye or multigrain bread

1 teaspoon flaky sea salt

SERVING SUGGESTION
Hot tea

In a small sauté pan, add ½ cup (1 stick) of the butter and gently brown on medium heat, undisturbed, until the butter is foamy and develops a darker color as the milk solids toast, 3 to 5 minutes. Do not burn the butter! The butter should be a deep golden brown, but it shouldn't become smoky or burn.

Add the bananas and sauté to soften them (they're not going to develop any color), about 30 seconds on one side, then flip and repeat. Remove the bananas from the pan, leaving the brown butter behind.

Use a knife to trim the crust off the bread slices.

Use the remaining ¼ cup (4 tablespoons) butter to smear one side of each bread slice. Divide the bananas evenly between half the buttered bread, season with the salt, and drizzle the brown butter on the bananas. Top each sandwich with another slice of buttered bread. Cut in half.

Enjoy immediately (ideally with tea!).

FRIED FLYING FISH
WITH GARLIC PARSLEY SAUCE

SERVES 4

This recipe was Granny's favorite dish to make. As an Englishwoman, she had never experienced flying fish, and the Caribbean exposed her to the bounty of seafood we have in the region. Flying fish is a mild, flaky fish, a tad larger than a sardine. When we went sailing with my father, they would jump alongside the boat, "flying." Nothing got Granny excited like flying fish. She'd see it at the market and say, "I have to make this for lunch!"—which was the biggest meal for us back home. We'd have a two-hour lunch when everyone comes home to eat with their families. Our home had an herb garden, and parsley, thyme, and marjoram were the most consistent year-round. Granny would make a parsley sauce for the fish, then bread and fry it.

Flying fish is central to St. Lucia and Barbados foodways; it's not as common on other islands. But these days flying fish are nowhere near as abundant as they were when I was a child, due to climate change and the impact of heightened oceanic temperatures. When they're available, the fishermen will display the fish on their carts. Whiting works great if you're not on island time.

MARINATED FISH

1 cup roughly chopped scallion

¼ cup chopped flat-leaf parsley

¼ cup white vinegar

2 tablespoons Worcestershire sauce

2 tablespoons chopped marjoram

1 tablespoon thyme leaves

1 teaspoon minced Scotch bonnet pepper

1 garlic clove

¼ teaspoon freshly ground black pepper

⅛ teaspoon ground cloves

¼ cup extra-virgin olive oil

8 (1½-ounce) fillets flying fish (or whiting)

COOKING THE FISH

Canola oil, for frying

2 cups all-purpose flour

3 tablespoons kosher salt

2 large eggs, beaten

4 cups fine breadcrumbs

GARLIC PARSLEY SAUCE

¼ cup (½ stick) unsalted butter

1 garlic clove, peeled

1 cup extra-virgin olive oil

¾ cup chopped flat-leaf parsley

1 lemon, zested and juiced

SERVING

Lime wedges

Baron West Indian Hot Sauce

Marinate the fish: In a food processor, add the scallion, parsley, vinegar, Worcestershire sauce, marjoram, thyme, Scotch bonnet, garlic, black pepper, and ground cloves. Pulse for a few seconds to incorporate the ingredients, then add the olive oil. Pulse again until it becomes a smooth paste. Rub the paste generously on the fish fillets and refrigerate for 30 minutes (no need to cover).

Cook the fish: In a medium sauté pan, add canola oil to ½-inch depth and heat on medium-high to 325°F; check with an instant-read thermometer. Line a plate with paper towels.

Set up 3 shallow bowls to prepare the fish for frying. In the first bowl, add the flour and season it with 2 tablespoons of the salt. In the second bowl, add the beaten eggs. In the third bowl, add the breadcrumbs. Using tongs, dip the fillets one at a time in the flour, then coat them in the beaten eggs and let the excess drip off. Next, coat them all over in the breadcrumbs. Gently place the coated fish in the hot oil. Repeat with a few more fillets, taking care not to crowd the pan. Fry the fillets until they brown lightly, turning once, about 2 minutes on each side. Use a spatula or tongs to remove the fish from the pan and drain on the paper towels. Repeat with all the fillets. Season them with 1½ teaspoons of the salt.

Make the garlic parsley sauce: Going back to the pan, drain the excess oil into a small heat-safe bowl and set aside. Put the pan over low heat and add the butter. Heat until the butter begins to foam. Add the garlic and sauté until gently browned, about 1 minute. Remove the pan from the heat. Add the olive oil, parsley, and lemon zest and juice. Season with the remaining 1½ teaspoons of salt. Drizzle the fish with the parsley sauce.

To serve: Enjoy with lime wedges and Baron hot sauce.

MUM'S SOURSOP MOUSSE

SERVES 6

When I was growing up, we had a soursop tree in the garden. Picking the ripest soursop was my job, because the tree was outside my bedroom window. Each day, I'd look outside, waiting for the right moment to pick them. It was always worth the wait. When you cut into the spiky fruit and take a bite of the tangy, custardy flesh, you can't help but smile. Soursop mousse is my mum's specialty, and this is her recipe. I'd watch her whip the cream and create a light, fluffy mousse and serve it with seasonal fruit. At Compère Lapin, I pay homage to Mum with a soursop semifreddo that's sometimes on the dessert menu. You can find soursop puree in Latin and Asian markets in the frozen section, or online.

¾ cup sugar

12 large egg yolks

½ cup soursop puree (such as Primor)

1¾ cups heavy cream

1 teaspoon kosher salt

4 fresh guava or 1 large fresh ripe mango, cut into 1-inch cubes

Set up a double boiler on the stovetop. Start with a medium pot of hot water over medium heat. In a large heat-safe bowl, add the sugar, yolks, and soursop puree. Once the water begins to simmer, rest the mixing bowl in the pot (the bowl should be large enough that it does not fully drop into the pot of water). Whisk the mixture constantly until it's pale yellow and develops a thick, creamy consistency and an instant-read thermometer reads 170°F. Remove from the heat and set aside.

In the bowl of a stand mixer fitted with the whisk attachment, add the heavy cream and salt. Whip on medium speed until the cream doubles in volume and develops stiff peaks, 6 to 8 minutes.

Use a spatula to fold the cream into the soursop mixture. Mix gently just to combine, without stirring too much air out of the whipped cream. Transfer to your preferred serving bowl(s). Chill in the refrigerator for 30 minutes to allow the mousse to set.

Serve immediately, topped with fresh guava or mango.

MUM'S RUM-SPICED RICE PUDDING

SERVES 4

My mum hates cooking, but she loves baking. She prides herself on making sweets. She would always make the family a baked rice pudding on the weekends. This was our household tradition; for us kids, excitement would build up as soon as we saw her mixing it. It's quick and easy, and the rice pudding becomes thick and creamy. The rum spice adds a little surprise, but it's not boozy. For us, the best part is the "skin" of the caramelized milk. It's crunchy and just covers the surface of the dish. Because there's a limited amount and it's so sweet and good, my siblings and I would all fight for it. This is Mum's recipe.

¾ cup raisins

1 cup Chairman's Reserve Spiced Rum (or dark rum)

1½ cups water

¾ cup white basmati rice

½ teaspoon kosher salt

1 star anise pod

1 cinnamon stick

2 whole cloves

5 cups half-and-half

½ cup sugar

1½ teaspoons pure vanilla extract

Heat the oven to 325°F.

In a small bowl, combine the raisins and ½ cup of the rum. Set aside.

In a medium heavy-bottomed saucepan, combine the water, rice, salt, star anise, cinnamon, and cloves. Mix to combine and bring to a boil. Stir once, then reduce the heat to medium-low and simmer, covered, until most of the water is absorbed, 8 to 9 minutes.

Stir in 4 cups of the half-and-half and the sugar and bring to a boil. Use tongs or a slotted spoon to remove the anise, cinnamon stick, and cloves. Remove from the heat.

Add the remaining 1 cup of half-and-half and the vanilla extract and stir to combine.

Transfer to a 9 × 9-inch baking dish and drizzle the remaining ½ cup of rum over the top. Bake until the rice is tender, about 30 minutes.

Enjoy warm or cold: Refrigerate the rice pudding until chilled, about 3 hours, or up to overnight.

COCONUT PIE

SERVES 4 TO 6

This recipe is from my mum. Back home she gets the brown, fresh coconuts and uses their firm flesh, removing the coconut meat from its shell. It's labor-intensive, but worth it for that clean, creamy flavor. We use the brown coconuts because they're older than green ones. (Brown coconut is where coconut milk comes from; green is where we get coconut "water.") As the coconuts age, the jelly goes from a soft texture to a firmer flesh, which works better in a pie like this. If you can't get fresh coconut, you can soak dried coconut flakes overnight in the refrigerator.

This pie shell calls for butter that's as cold as you can get it. You can pop it in the freezer for 30 minutes before you begin the filling preparation. The texture of the finished pie is similar to buttermilk pie.

FILLING

1 cup coconut milk

1 cup freshly grated coconut or fresh coconut flakes

¼ cup granulated sugar (or use coconut sugar)

1 teaspoon kosher salt

½ teaspoon freshly grated nutmeg

2 large eggs

PIE SHELL

1¼ cups all-purpose flour, plus more for dusting

½ teaspoon kosher salt

½ teaspoon granulated sugar

½ cup (1 stick) unsalted butter, chilled, then grated

4 to 6 tablespoons ice water, plus more if needed

2 cups any dried bean, for blind baking

SERVING SUGGESTION

Enjoy with your favorite store-bought ice cream (try a coconut ice cream or hibiscus sorbet).

Start the filling: In a medium saucepan, bring the coconut milk to a boil. While it's boiling, add the coconut, sugar, salt, and nutmeg. Allow the mixture to cook until the ingredients come together, about 2 minutes, then remove from the heat and set aside to cool slightly. Transfer the slightly cooled mixture to the refrigerator to cool completely, about 30 minutes. No need to cover.

Make the pie shell: In the bowl of a food processor, mix the flour, salt, and sugar. Add the chilled, grated butter and pulse until the butter becomes pea-sized chunks. Slowly add ice water, a bit at a time, while pulsing, until the mixture becomes incorporated and a soft dough forms.

Wrap the dough in plastic wrap and transfer to the refrigerator. Chill the dough for 15 minutes.

Heat the oven to 375°F.

On a flat work surface, sprinkle a few pinches of flour—just enough to evenly cover it. Using a rolling pin, roll the dough into a disk that's just larger than a 9-inch pie pan, and about ¼ inch thick.

Gently place the pie dough in the pan. Use a fork to prick the bottom a few times. Trim any dough that's hanging over the sides of the pan and discard. Chill for 10 minutes.

While the dough is setting, come back to the filling. In a medium bowl, beat the eggs lightly until frothy. Remove the coconut milk mixture from the refrigerator and use a spatula to fold in the beaten eggs.

Line the chilled pie shell with parchment paper. Spread an even layer of the dried beans on top of the paper and bake for 10 minutes, until the shell is firm. Discard the beans (or reserve for another pie!) and the parchment paper. Evenly pour the filling into the shell. Bake until the filling center sets, 30 to 40 minutes. Let the pie cool completely before slicing and serving.

FIONA'S CASSAVA COOKIES

MAKES 18 COOKIES

My sister, Fiona Compton, is one of my biggest inspirations. A historian and artist, she's known to more than a quarter-million social media followers as the cultural ambassador @KnowYourCaribbean, an account she established to celebrate the unfiltered, nuanced history of the Caribbean and its African and Indigenous roots.

Let me tell you, Fiona does not come to play around! She is firm and unflinching in her commitment to bring the full scope of history to the table: She doesn't minimize the brutal impact of European colonial reign and gives proper due to the African traditions and innovations that shape our languages, dance, music, fashion, and food customs. Through archival images and videos, news clippings, and her in-the-field research, she's become a master at merging history with the present.

Fiona's recipe features cassava, a ground provision we have in St. Lucia and throughout the Caribbean. She has shared how cassava originated in South America and became popular in West Africa through the immigration of free Africans returning to the continent. Like many plants, cassava was a way for African and Indigenous people in the Caribbean to resist colonization. Consumed raw, the juice of cassava is poisonous, and Africans could use it against enslavers as a form of rebellion.

Today in St. Lucia, imported goods are often perceived to be higher quality, largely because of the way colonialism teaches people to disregard their own history in order to uphold minority rulers. Cassava is everywhere, but younger generations haven't been as likely to use it; and what's worse is it's often sold back to St. Lucians at a premium cost (Africa has been subjected to the same abuses). But with a greater sense of cultural pride and more connection to our rich history, this knowledge gap is closing. We're remembering that what's in our own backyard is not just available; it offers its own bounty of health.

Cassava flour is nutty in flavor. These cookies will be delicate and flaky, and of course they're gluten-free.

½ cup (1 stick) unsalted butter, softened
⅓ cup honey
¼ cup coconut sugar
1 teaspoon vanilla extract
1 cup dark chocolate chips, chopped cashews, or shredded coconut (optional)

1 cup cassava flour
½ teaspoon baking soda
½ teaspoon baking powder
¼ teaspoon flaky sea salt

In the bowl of a stand mixer fitted with the paddle attachment, add the butter, honey, coconut sugar, and vanilla extract. Mix on medium speed until smooth and creamy, 6 to 8 minutes. If you're adding the optional chocolate chips, nuts, or shredded coconut, do so now. Mix for another minute on medium speed to incorporate. Set aside.

In a separate medium bowl, add the cassava flour, baking soda, and baking powder. Mix well.

Add the dry mixture to the wet ingredients in the stand mixer bowl. Beat at low speed until smooth, about 5 minutes.

Heat the oven to 350°F. Line a large sheet pan with parchment paper.

Refrigerate the bowl with the dough, uncovered, for 10 to 15 minutes.

Scoop dough balls of about 2 tablespoons each and place them on the prepared sheet pan 2 inches apart. Don't press down on the balls. Sprinkle the salt evenly over the balls. (You can use a second sheet pan for the remaining balls, or repeat the process using the same pan later.)

Bake the cookies until golden brown, about 10 minutes. Allow the cookies to cool completely on the sheet pan—do not attempt to transfer them while they're still hot. (The cookies are very delicate without gluten in the cassava flour.) This will be hard, because they'll smell so good, but resist the urge to eat them right out of the oven. For the best experience, give them time to finish setting as they cool.

Once the cookies are completely cool to the touch, remove them from the sheet pan and serve. The cookies will be soft and chewy at room temperature and become more firm, yet still chewy, after refrigeration. I prefer them after they've been chilled. Store leftovers in an airtight container in the refrigerator for up to 3 days. Enjoy!

WHOLE ROASTED SNAPPER

SERVES 2

Fish is a social affair in St. Lucia, and Sundays at the beach are a big grilling day for families. Friday nights, you'll see whole snapper in full force. Up in Gros Islet, we have a big block party, and all they serve is grilled whole fish. It's a vibe. The grills are set up like the old drums with grates on top. At any given time of day, six people will be grilling fish. "Peppa sauce or garlic sauce?" they ask you. They hand over whatever the fisherman got that day, such as marlin, dorado, or of course, snapper, beautifully grilled. Sometimes they serve grilled corn or green fig salad and coleslaw. You take your foil-wrapped fish and head to the bar next door. Grab a cold Piton. Nobody has shoes on. Music is playing, and the energy is relaxed.

1 (2-pound) whole red snapper, cleaned with head on

1 cup extra-virgin olive oil

¼ cup Baron West Indian Hot Sauce

3 tablespoons kosher salt, plus more to taste

2 lemons, zested and thinly sliced in rounds

1 cup minced flat-leaf parsley

½ cup Garlic Oil (page 271)

1 grapefruit, peeled and supremed (see page 187)

1 small green papaya (½ to 1 pound), peeled and thinly sliced

6 basil leaves, torn

6 mint leaves, torn

SERVING SUGGESTION

Steamed rice, Coconut Rice and Peas (page 47), or Callaloo (page 126)

Heat the oven to 400°F.

Use a paring knife to score the snapper belly with crosshatches. In a small bowl, add ¾ cup of olive oil, the Baron hot sauce, and 2 tablespoons of the salt. Mix to combine well, then rub generously into the fish flesh and spoon over the outsides. Insert the sliced lemon rounds into the belly (make sure you've zested the lemons before slicing them).

Place the fish in a roasting pan, transfer to the oven, and bake until the skin develops a golden brown color and the flesh looks white and flaky, about 35 minutes. Use a cake tester or toothpick to check the fish. The flesh should flake easily with no resistance, and the fish should feel hot to the bone. Transfer the fish to a serving plate.

In a small bowl, add the parsley, garlic oil, and lemon zest. Taste and season with the remaining 1 tablespoon of salt. Gently squeeze the supremed grapefruit to add a little juice to the bowl, then add the fruit itself. Add the papaya. Dress with more salt to taste, then add the remaining ¼ cup of olive oil and the torn basil and mint leaves. Stir to incorporate.

Spoon the dressed papaya salad on top of the fish. Enjoy with steamed rice, Coconut Rice and Peas, or Callaloo.

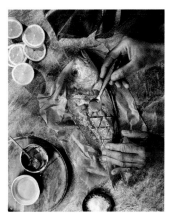

COCOA TEA

SERVES 4

St. Lucians drink black tea and cocoa tea; you don't see much coffee. We drink tea in the morning and in the afternoons, the latter signaling that the day is almost over. But cocoa tea is by far our more popular morning beverage.

Cocoa (also cacao) trees are native to the island and particularly present in the lush rainforests on the south side. The trees produce cocoa pods with bright exterior hues of yellow, red, pink, and brown. The flesh of the cocoa pods houses the pulpy beans, which we often suck on for the creamy flavor (no chewing, lest you come to a new understanding of "bitter"). The beans are dried and fermented in a process that involves air-drying them in the sun, in massive wooden trays the length of a small house, which can be collapsed when rain comes. The beans get mashed into a paste, then rolled into a cocoa stick. Cocoa sticks are a staple in any St. Lucian pantry. You grate the unsweetened cocoa into simmering hot milk. Most folks add a little flour or cornstarch, and aromatics like cinnamon, star anise, cloves, or fresh bay leaf, all of which grow in St. Lucia. Our cocoa tea might remind you of pre-Hispanic champurrado in Mexico, as cacao and chocolate are ingredients that their Indigenous cultures also treasured. You can find traditional St. Lucian cocoa sticks online from retailers based in the Caribbean.

3 tablespoons cornstarch

2 cups water

4 cups whole milk

½ cup Demerara sugar, or to taste

1 vanilla bean, split and seeds scraped, or 1 teaspoon vanilla extract

1 fresh bay leaf (or 1 dried)

1 large cinnamon stick

⅛ teaspoon freshly grated nutmeg

1 cup grated cocoa stick or ¼ cup unsweetened cocoa powder

⅛ teaspoon kosher salt

SERVING SUGGESTION

Sip alongside warm Bakes (page 83)

In a small bowl or cup, dissolve the cornstarch in 1 cup of the water. Stir into a smooth paste and set aside.

In a medium pot, add the remaining 1 cup of water and the milk, sugar, vanilla beans and seeds, bay leaf, cinnamon, and nutmeg. Stir to combine. Bring to a simmer over low heat, and simmer for 10 minutes to fully marry the flavors. Add the cocoa and salt, stir to combine, and simmer for another 5 minutes. Whisk in the cornstarch slurry, then raise the heat and bring to a boil. Cook until the mixture thickens, about 5 minutes. Strain the cocoa tea into mugs and serve immediately.

BAKES

SERVES 4

Bakes are a quick bread, and they're standard fare in a St. Lucian breakfast (a variation on bakes is a "float"—an airy version that includes yeast). Bakes are dense and sweet and are great plain, but more than likely they're a vessel for whatever else is on your plate, be it stewed mackerel, sardines, saltfish, or a Cheddar cheese wedge. I love to pile my bakes with Ackee and Saltfish (see page 122), a combo I learned about when I moved to Jamaica, or avocado slices. (Note that in Jamaica, their breakfast fried bread is called "fried dumpling," but it's essentially the same thing as our bakes.) Another traditional route is to enjoy your bakes with Cocoa Tea (page 80). It's hard to have a bad day when the morning starts off this good.

2 cups all-purpose flour, plus more for dusting

1 tablespoon baking powder

1 teaspoon sugar

½ teaspoon kosher salt

1 teaspoon unsalted butter

1 cup water, plus 1 tablespoon if needed

Canola or coconut oil, for frying

In a medium bowl, mix the flour, baking powder, sugar, and salt. Use your hands to combine the butter into the dry mix until the butter is pea-sized and evenly incorporated.

Make a hole or well in the center of the flour and add ¾ cup of the water while mixing and stirring in a circular motion with your hand. At this stage, the dough should resemble coarse crumbs.

Add the remaining ¼ cup of water and continue mixing gently with your hand until a soft dough forms, about 5 minutes.

Depending on the humidity level where you live, your dough might need adjusting. If the dough is too sticky, dust it with 1 tablespoon of flour and gently mix. If the dough is too dry after you've added all the water, add 1 tablespoon of water and mix. Once your mixing is done, allow the dough to rest for 3 to 5 minutes. Dust with 1 tablespoon of flour and gently knead to form a smoother dough.

In a large saucepan, add oil to a depth of 2 inches (about 3 cups) and heat on medium heat to 350°F; check with an instant-read thermometer. Line a plate with paper towels.

Divide the dough into 8 equal portions (about 2½ ounces each) and roll them into balls. On a clean, flat surface, use a rolling pin to roll each ball into a disk about 3 inches wide and ½ inch thick. (Note: When preparing the fried dumplings for Ackee and Saltfish, page 122, skip this flattening step.) Cover them with plastic wrap or a damp towel as you finish and let the dough rest for 10 minutes.

When the oil is ready, fry the bakes a few at a time, taking care not to crowd the pan, until golden brown, about 45 seconds on each side. Use a spatula or slotted spoon to transfer to the paper towels to drain and repeat with the remaining dough. Serve immediately.

ACCRA FRITTERS

SERVES 2 TO 4

Accra is a definitive St. Lucian street food snack, especially at outdoor markets like in Castries. Every vendor has their specialty. You'll see one guy frying fish, another stewing goat meat. Then there's the woman frying accra, and the aroma hits you. When the balls pop up in the oil, she flips them. When I see those huge pots of bubbling oil with spoonfuls of batter at the top, I know what time it is.

Accra consists of saltfish, a raising agent like baking powder, flour, and scallions. We use a lot of seasoning peppers, often a mix of green, yellow, and red, but they're not that spicy. You'll see accra on special occasions or holidays like Good Friday, but it's also an everyday food that doesn't require fuss. Saltfish was brought to the Caribbean by European colonists who imported the cod fish as cheap rations for enslaved Africans. Like elsewhere in the African diaspora, the beloved dishes we enjoy today emerged from this combination of available resources and pieces of memory. Saltfish is as definitive to my culture's cuisine as the oceanic waters that surround my island home.

This recipe is a loose batter; it takes shape when it hits the hot oil. However it lands in the pot, that's what it is; that's your fritter. In St. Lucia, accra is served straight-up plain, but when I host cocktail parties in New Orleans, I serve them with my take on tartar sauce, slightly sweet with the addition of fresh pineapple. It's a perfect contrast with the saltfish. Cooking accra fritters places me in the market in Castries. I hope it transports you, too. Note the advance preparation of soaking the saltfish overnight.

½ pound boneless saltfish (dry salted cod)

1 cup all-purpose flour

2 teaspoons baking powder

1 teaspoon sweet paprika

1 teaspoon curry powder

1 teaspoon cayenne pepper

2 scallions, minced

¼ cup finely diced red bell pepper

¾ to 1 cup water, as needed

Canola oil, for frying

SERVING

Kosher salt

Lemon wedges

Pickled Pineapple Tartar Sauce (page 273)

In a medium bowl, submerge the saltfish in water and leave to soak overnight in the refrigerator. Change the water at least once during the soaking time. Drain and set aside.

Let's cook the excess salt out of the fish: In a medium pot, add the drained saltfish and enough cold water to cover the fish by 2 inches. Bring the water to a simmer and simmer for 30 minutes. Drain, add enough water to cover by 2 inches, and simmer for another 30 minutes.

Drain the water and allow the saltfish to cool. Using a fork, gently pull the fish apart into small flakes. Double-check for small bones and skin and discard any you find. Set aside.

In a large bowl, add the dry ingredients: the flour, baking powder, paprika, curry powder, and cayenne. Mix well.

Add the flaked saltfish and the scallions and bell pepper. Add water incrementally and use a whisk to mix until the mixture is smooth and the consistency of a thick pancake batter. (The batter can sit in the refrigerator, covered, for up to one night. Just make sure to bring the batter back to room temperature before frying the next day.)

In a large saucepan, add canola oil to a depth of 2 inches (about 3 cups) and heat on medium heat to 350°F; check with an instant-read thermometer. (If you don't have one, you can do a little drop test of the batter to see if it's hot; just spoon a tiny drop—if it sizzles, the oil is ready.) Line a plate or sheet pan with paper towels.

To shape the fritters, use two spoons—one to scoop 1 heaping tablespoon of the batter and the other to scrape the batter into the oil. Continue adding the batter, but don't crowd the pan; don't cook more than 6 at a time (you'll have about 12 fritters in total), as that will drop the temperature of the oil and the accra will absorb too much oil before it gets crispy. Flip each fritter after it becomes golden brown on one side, about 2 minutes. Use a slotted spoon to transfer the fritter to the paper towels to drain. Repeat with the remaining batter.

Serve the fritters: Season with salt and eat right away with a lemon wedge and pickled pineapple tartar sauce.

BEEF PEPPERPOT

SERVES 6

We have a strong Guyanese influence in St. Lucia. Several of my secondary school teachers were from Guyana, and of course with proximity to people comes access to their food. And aren't we lucky. Many of the Guyanese in St. Lucia keep small shops as extensions of their home, where they sell prepared food. St. Lucians don't eat a lot of beef; we eat more seafood, chicken, and goat. Most small nations simply don't have the physical space to account for housing cows for meat production. But Guyana is a much bigger country, and they have more access to large farm animals. This recipe is a Guyanese-style pepperpot that's served on Christmas Day or around Christmastime.

Guyanese pepperpot is basically braised beef using cassareep—caramelized cassava juice infused with spices like cinnamon, cloves, sugar, and cayenne pepper. (Importantly, the juice of the cassava is caramelized and not consumed raw, as in that form it is toxic.) You'll also find the popular Jamaican pepperpot that's mostly done with callaloo, potatoes, cassava, and coconut milk. You can substitute short ribs for oxtail, or stewed beef cuts. Note the advance preparation of marinating, ideally overnight.

4 pounds boneless short ribs, cut into 2-inch pieces

1 cup cassareep

4 tablespoons kosher salt, plus more to taste

1 teaspoon minced garlic

1 teaspoon thyme leaves

2 tablespoons light brown sugar

2 tablespoons canola oil (optional)

2 cups diced Spanish onion

1 Scotch bonnet pepper

1 cinnamon stick

4 quarts Brown Stock (page 279)

3 tablespoons Angostura cocoa bitters

Peel of 1 orange

Freshly ground black pepper

GARNISH

½ cup chopped fresh flat-leaf parsley

2 scallions, diced

SERVING

Steamed rice or crusty bread

Place the short ribs in a large bowl or zip top bag. Add ½ cup of the cassareep, then the salt, garlic, and thyme. Mix until the short ribs are well coated. Set aside in the refrigerator to marinate overnight (you can reduce to 2 hours if needed, but overnight will give more flavor depth).

When ready to cook, shake off any excess seasoning from the meat. In a large Dutch oven or heavy-bottomed pot, add the brown sugar and cook over medium heat, stirring continually, until it caramelizes and begins to turn deep brown, about 3 minutes. Be careful to not let it burn. Add the short ribs to the pot, meat side down, giving the pieces plenty of room. It's okay to work in batches if you need to. Let them sear, unbothered, until browned, for about 2 minutes. Continue until all meat surfaces are browned. If your short ribs are on the leaner side and not rendering fat, add 2 tablespoons of canola oil as you're browning.

Remove all the short ribs and reserve. Add the onions and Scotch bonnet to the pot and cook until the onions are brown, stirring occasionally, 3 to 5 minutes.

Add the cinnamon stick. Thoroughly mix and continue cooking to heat through, 1 to 2 minutes. Return the seared short ribs to the pot in a single layer. Add the brown stock to the pot, making sure all the meat is covered by the liquid. Bring to a boil, then reduce the heat to low and allow it to simmer, with the lid on, for about 40 minutes.

After 40 minutes, add the remaining ½ cup of the cassareep. You want the liquid to be about 2 inches above the meat, so add water if it's low. Stir in the bitters and the orange peel. Continue cooking, uncovered, until the beef is fork tender, 2 to 3 hours. Leave it be as it cooks. The sauce should be thick. Adjust seasoning with salt and black pepper to your liking.

To garnish: Top with parsley and scallions.

To serve: Enjoy with steamed white rice or crusty bread for dipping.

BOUYON

SERVES 6

Bouyon, a traditional stew of pork, beans, and dumplings, is one of my favorites. It's a homey dish whose name is derived from the island's French influences, as bouyon in Kwéyòl translates to "broth" ("bouillon" in French). But our bouyon is a far cry from a clear broth. St. Lucian bouyon becomes a hearty red bean stew, and we add ground provisions like cassava, potatoes, and yams. Iterations of bouyon can also be found in the Lesser Antilles, like Dominica, St. Vincent, and Grenada.

You want to take your time with this one. There's a ritual to soaking the beans, roasting the pork. Pig tails add a beautiful gelatinous element to the dish. In my current home of Louisiana, I get salted pig tails from the butcher. You can look for cured pork, too. Normally we get the tails, snout, or back fat, and in Louisiana we have a lot of pig lips (my staff at Compère Lapin often come in with a snack bag of jerky-like dried pig lips; they're *good*). For the ground provisions, I like tannia, as we call it back home, or malanga—it's a small yam with grayish-white flesh. You can often find them at Asian, Afro Latin, or Caribbean markets. You likely won't need additional salt thanks to the cured pork, but have it on hand just in case.

The spinner dumplings in this recipe, named for how you form them with your hands, are chewy; they look like torpedoes and have a real bite. To shape the dumpling, you put a piece of dough between your palms, rolling the dough by moving your hands in opposing directions. The dumplings flick or spin off your hand and land in the pot of simmering bouyon. As you cook the dumplings with the beans, they pick up the flavor. This is traditional, but sometimes we substitute cassava dumplings (page 54) for the spinners. Note the advance preparation of soaking the beans overnight.

1 cup dried kidney beans

2 pounds salted pig tails (or cured salt pork, or salt pork belly)

2 tablespoons canola oil

1 large yellow onion, diced

1 medium seasoning pepper, chopped (or use habanada, or jalapeño)

2 scallions, chopped, plus more sliced for garnish

6 garlic cloves, crushed

3 sprigs of thyme

6 cups Brown Stock (page 279) (or use beef or chicken stock)

2 medium peeled tannia or malanga root, large diced

1 cup peeled and diced pumpkin

1 large carrot, diced into 1-inch pieces

1 small yellow or white yam, diced

1 cup peeled and diced cassava

2 cups packed fresh callaloo or spinach

Kosher salt to taste

SPINNER DUMPLINGS

1 cup all-purpose flour

½ cup cornmeal

1 teaspoon kosher salt

1 cup water, or as needed

(recipe continues)

Put the beans in a large bowl and add enough water to cover by 4 inches. Soak overnight at room temperature.

Wash the salted pig tails in running water for 10 minutes, to ensure the excess salt is removed. Cut them into 2-inch pieces.

In a medium stockpot, add the cut pig tails. Cover them with enough water to submerge, then bring to a boil. Boil, uncovered, for 20 minutes.

Add fresh water, enough to submerge the pig tails again, and bring to a boil again. Reduce the heat to low, then simmer, uncovered until the pig tails are tender, 30 to 45 minutes. Set aside.

In a separate large pot over medium heat, add the canola oil and heat for 2 minutes. Add the yellow onion, peppers, scallions, garlic, and thyme, and sauté, stirring occasionally, until the vegetables soften, about 5 minutes.

Drain the kidney beans. Add the beans to the pot, followed by the stock. Bring to a simmer, then reduce the heat to low and simmer until the beans are tender, 30 to 40 minutes.

Add the pig tails and the ground provisions: tannia, pumpkin, carrot, yam, and cassava. If you're using callaloo, add it now, then simmer everything on medium-high heat until the roots are tender, about 15 minutes. If you're using spinach, simmer the root vegetables until tender first, then add the spinach and cook just until wilted. Season with salt to your taste.

Meanwhile, make the spinner dumplings: In a medium bowl, add the flour, cornmeal, and salt and combine. Add water, about 1 tablespoon at a time, mixing with your hands until the mixture forms a firm dough. Using your hands, roll the dough into small balls of 1 to 2 tablespoons.

Place one ball of dough between your hands and as you move your hands in opposite directions to form a torpedo shape, flick the dough into the bouyon. Repeat with all the dough, then simmer on medium-high heat until the dumplings are cooked through, another 5 minutes. Don't overcook! These are thick dumplings, so they won't float, but this is sufficient time for them to finish.

To serve, spoon the bouyon into bowls and garnish with sliced scallions. Enjoy immediately.

Caribbean Tales

In the Caribbean, we have many storytelling expressions that connect to African spirituality and religions. Storytelling is our cultural ancestral practice. Throughout the islands and mainland countries, we share overlapping histories that reflect our origins. Our stories are truths that connect to the Other World. They refer to magic and the afterlife. They have moral lessons and outcomes that can be moving, humorous, or tragic, and they extend from a soul-filled canon of iconic characters. Some of these beliefs evolved to incorporate the religions of colonizers, who used their religious texts to justify violent methods of domination and conversion and to demonize the sacred rituals of Indigenous African people.

As one example of this, Vodun, which became Voodoo in the U.S., is a broad religion and philosophy, a tradition of existing with spirit; it defies any one term in English. It is practiced by many groups throughout West Africa, and with the movement of those peoples you now see elements of this sacred history in Cuba, the American South, Brazil, Haiti, and so on. But Voodoo, as it is expressed in tourist traps in places like the New Orleans French Quarter, has become diluted and commercialized, completely separate from its origins. So much has been lost to the violence of colonization, but our ancestors retained the lifeblood of our oral stories, our histories. Many of these story traditions remain present city to city, village to village throughout the region today. We grow up hearing about creatures, ghosts, spirits, shape-shifters, and tricksters, guides in other dimensions that can support or challenge your present journey. These are tales of love and lust, justice and loss, told with style, narrative rhythm, and repetition, and sometimes expressed through music, song, and dance.

COW HEEL SOUP

SERVES 6 TO 8

Cow heel soup is inspired by the St. Lucian lore of La Jablesse or La Diablesse, the beautiful and mysterious siren spirit rumored to prey on men during the night. As the tale goes, she lures them away into the quiet and kills them, making the men a sacrifice to her allegiance with the devil. But how can you distinguish a gorgeous woman from La Jablesse? The spirit is dressed in a large hat and a long, slitted dress that grazes the ground so you don't see her cloven hooves. You won't find La Jablesse in bustling cities; she's more at ease in remote villages, the forest, or seaside. They say she has a strong-scented perfume and that only idiot men fall victim to her ways.

Patrons of Compère Lapin will recognize this dish, as I make a version of it at the restaurant. But I wrote *this* recipe like how we would eat it back home, heartier with bones and all (we omit the bones at the restaurant). This is a humble and profoundly delicious soup, boasting fresh aromatics and brought together in a gelatinous braise from the feet. A dish worthy of praise, if not respect—just like La Jablesse!

3 pounds veal feet, chopped into 1½-inch to 2-inch pieces (ask your butcher!)

3 cups yellow lentils

¼ cup canola oil

2 medium yellow onions, diced

1 stalk lemongrass, finely chopped

½ cup minced fresh ginger

2 tablespoons minced fresh turmeric root

2 Scotch bonnet peppers, minced

4 cups okra pods, cut into ¼-inch rounds

GARNISH

5 scallions, thinly sliced

Chili Oil (page 271)

In a large pot, cover the veal feet with at least 5 to 6 inches of cold water and bring to a simmer over medium-low heat. Use a ladle to skim and discard the foam that floats to the surface. Continue to simmer, uncovered, until tender, about 4 hours. Using a fork, test for doneness; the meat should easily pull away. Remove from the heat and continue to pull the meat from the bones. You're not shredding it; it's okay to leave it in chunks. Save the cooking liquid, and if you prefer, you can discard the bones.

Rinse the lentils in cool water. Drain and repeat until the water runs clear, then set aside.

In a large pan, add the canola oil on low heat. Add the onions, lemongrass, ginger, turmeric, and Scotch bonnet and sweat on low heat, stirring occasionally, until the vegetables become fragrant, 6 to 8 minutes. Add the lentils and reserved broth, then simmer, stirring just to incorporate, until tender, about 20 minutes. If the lentils become too thick during cooking, add a bit of water.

Transfer half of the mixture to a blender and puree (be careful of the hot steam as you're blending, and crack the lid to allow it to escape). This step helps give the soup an even texture. Return the blended soup to the pan, then add the sliced okra. Cook until the okra is tender, another 5 minutes. Add the meat back to the soup. Heat through for 3 minutes. Spoon into bowls and garnish with the scallions. Drizzle with chili oil for an added kick. Enjoy immediately.

CURRIED GOAT

SERVES 8

Curried goat is a staple in many cultures and countries, owing to the movement of people and their go-to ingredients. In St. Lucia, we credit the arrival of foods like turmeric, garam masala, and curry leaves to indentured laborers from India, whose diverse food cultures go back thousands of years. When the British Empire finally ended slavery in its territories, sugar plantation owners experienced a vast labor shortage. They sought alternatives to continue the skilled, primarily agricultural work once performed by Africans and their descendants, who'd brought their millennia of knowledge and generated centuries of international wealth. The British turned to another colonized country, India, and brought more than a half million workers to fulfill labor demands in places like Trinidad and Tobago, Guyana, Jamaica, and of course, my home island.

Slow-stewed proteins appear around the globe, but this mix feels particularly personal to me. Curry makes me happy—the steady layering of flavors, the leisurely cook time, all comprise a dish that gets better as you eat it. The flavor is earthy and herbaceous. We enjoy curried goat from a vendor on the roadside in St. Lucia, usually folded into roti for a hearty handheld meal (see Buss Up Shut Roti for an interpretation of this mash-up, page 141). For me, this dish feels as close as I can get to representing my culinary roots; you always find it in the Caribbean. It's a badge of honor that it resonates with diners at Compère Lapin, where I serve it with Sweet Potato Gnocchi (page 263) as a nod to my local environment in the American South. In my version, I add arugula and cashews to the ragu. The greens bring brightness to every bite, and the nuts give texture that I love. No tradition is static, and every household has their way to curry goat; this is mine.

You're going to spend time on this curry, even as it's straightforward and considered a humble meal where I'm from. A whole lot of history says the effort is well worth it. Note the advance preparation of brining the goat overnight.

BRINED GOAT
4 quarts room-temperature water

2 cups kosher salt

1 (5-pound) bone-in goat leg

SPICE SACHET
2 cups curry leaves

3 cinnamon sticks

3 tablespoons smashed green cardamom pods

2 tablespoons star anise pods

2 tablespoons coriander seeds

1 tablespoon whole cloves

1 Scotch bonnet pepper, torn in half

BRAISE
¼ cup extra-virgin olive oil

3 medium yellow onions, thinly sliced

½ cup roughly chopped fresh ginger

½ cup roughly chopped fresh turmeric (or ¼ cup ground turmeric)

3 garlic cloves, roughly chopped

¼ cup garam masala

4 quarts Brown Stock (page 279)

RAGU
¼ cup extra-virgin olive oil

3 medium yellow onions, thinly sliced

1 cup minced fresh ginger

1 cup minced fresh turmeric

2 tablespoons garam masala

1 Scotch bonnet pepper, seeded and minced

4 (14-ounce) cans coconut milk

1 cup fresh arugula

Kosher salt

GARNISH
1 cup toasted, chopped cashews

1 cup cilantro leaves

SERVING
Sweet Potato Gnocchi (page 263) or steamed rice

Brine the goat: In a large lidded container or large pot big enough to comfortably fit the goat, mix the room-temperature water and salt until the salt is dissolved. Submerge the goat in the brine, cover with the lid, and refrigerate to brine overnight.

Make the goat: Heat the oven to 400°F.

Carefully remove the goat from its brine and place it in a large roasting pan. Roast, uncovered, until golden brown, about 1 hour. Don't bother the goat while it's doing its thing; just let it roast. Once the goat reaches that golden brown point, remove it from the oven and reduce the oven temperature to 300°F.

(recipe continues)

Make the spice sachet: While the goat roasts, cut a 6 × 6-inch piece of cheesecloth. Place the curry leaves, cinnamon sticks, cardamom pods, star anise, coriander, cloves, and Scotch bonnet in the center, bring together the edges to form a bundle, and secure it tightly with string.

Make the braise: In a medium stockpot, add the olive oil and heat on medium for 2 minutes. Add the onions, ginger, turmeric, garlic, garam masala, and the spice sachet and sauté, stirring to incorporate the ingredients and letting them sweat, until the vegetables soften, about 5 minutes. Add the brown stock and bring the mixture to a simmer.

Carefully pour the hot stock over the goat in its roasting pan. Be sure to include all those aromatics; they've still got work to do.

Roast the goat in the stock for about 3½ hours. This time, because you've got a basting liquid, you're going to rotate the leg every 30 minutes to get evenly roasted meat. When the thickest part of the leg is fork tender and pulling away from the bone, remove the pan from the oven and allow the meat to rest in its roasting liquid for 20 minutes. Transfer the goat to a sheet pan to cool slightly. Use your hands to pull off the meat until the goat leg bone is picked clean. Dice the pulled meat into roughly 1-inch cubes. No need to be too precious here; we're just making the goat a bit easier to eat.

Strain the liquid into a large container and set aside. You're going to use the strained stock for the ragu in just a moment. Reserve that superstar sachet as well and discard the remaining aromatics.

Make the ragu: In a medium pot, add the olive oil and heat on low for 2 minutes. Add the onions, ginger, turmeric, garam masala, and Scotch bonnet, and sauté, stirring occasionally, until the vegetables soften, about 5 minutes. Add the coconut milk, the reserved spice sachet, and the strained stock. Bring to a simmer and let the flavors marry for about 45 minutes. The aroma will become more fragrant and the ragu thickens as it simmers; it will become glossy and nearly coat a spoon.

Add the diced goat meat to the ragu and simmer to warm through, 3 to 5 minutes. Add the arugula and gently wilt it into the stew. Taste and adjust with salt as needed.

Top the ragu with cashews and cilantro.

To serve: Enjoy with Sweet Potato Gnocchi or steamed rice.

SPLIT PEA DAL

SERVES 6

This stew is inspired by a lunchtime snack I had in school. My mother always packed a lunch kit of homemade sandwiches when I was in secondary school, but what I really wanted was dal from the Dal Man. That's what we called him. He served curried lentils as a filling in rolled, fried flatbread (not to be mistaken for dal puri, which has the lentils cooked into the center of the flatbread and is griddled on a tawa). He would come over to the school grounds at noon and stand in the corner with a big basket, a towel draped over the top to keep in the heat and moisture. "What do you want today?" he'd ask. "I have dal, saltfish, chicken." I always got the dal. For years I've known this guy, and he's still around. On a recent trip home he was selling beachside on the weekends. He was always and still is the Dal Man.

3 cups yellow lentils

¼ cup extra-virgin olive oil

1 teaspoon jeera (cumin) seeds

½ medium Spanish onion, diced

2 small scallions, thinly sliced

1 medium tomato, roughly chopped

¼ cup tomato paste

2 tablespoons kosher salt

¼ Scotch bonnet pepper

1½ teaspoons grated fresh turmeric

½ teaspoon freshly ground black pepper

1 garlic clove, roughly chopped

SERVING SUGGESTION

Steamed rice or Buss Up Shut Roti (page 141) with a dollop of plain yogurt

Rinse the lentils in cool water. Drain and repeat until the water runs clear, then set aside.

In a medium pot, add the olive oil and heat on medium for 2 minutes. Add the jeera and toast until the seeds become aromatic, about 30 seconds. Add the onion, scallions, tomato, tomato paste, salt, Scotch bonnet pepper, turmeric, black pepper, and garlic. Stir to incorporate. Add the lentils and 2½ quarts of water. Raise the heat to medium-high and cook on a rolling boil, with the lid slightly ajar and stirring occasionally, until the lentils are tender, about 20 minutes. Serve hot.

FISH TEA

SERVES 6

Fish tea, a light broth made from the whole fish carcass to extract a delicate flavor, is found throughout the small fishing villages along the southern coast of St. Lucia. It's also served as a light starter throughout the Caribbean. In typical lore, this is considered an aphrodisiac (to "make your back strong," wink wink). Fishermen on the beach will make a fish tea after they fillet the fish. They'll bring their boats to shore, grab vegetables from nearby vendors, and build a fire on the beachside. Then they make the fish tea. It's not really something they sell, but if they're gathering with friends after a day on the water, they'll share it. Our food culture in St. Lucia is to not waste, so we make the most of all ingredients. Traditionally we keep the fish heads in the pot; it's considered a delicacy. My mum would eat the eyes. In many cultures eating the eyes is considered good luck!

My fish tea uses the whole fish, not just the bones. It exudes a hearty flavor, but it's deceptively light. Serve it with hot sauce. While many American hot sauces have strong vinegar notes, Baron is straight pepper vibes and one of my favorites. At home we just call it "peppa sauce." It's balanced and bright, not scary-hot for the sake of giving you a breathless taste bud attack.

1 (2-pound) whole red snapper, head on, cleaned, and filleted (see Note)

4 tablespoons extra-virgin olive oil

1 lemongrass stalk, thinly sliced

¼ cup minced fresh ginger

1 medium Spanish onion, diced

1 large carrot, diced

½ cup diced celery

Kosher salt and freshly ground black pepper

2 garlic cloves, minced

2 tablespoons minced thyme leaves

1 Scotch bonnet pepper, chopped

2 cups peeled and diced cassava or Yukon gold potatoes (½-inch pieces)

SERVING

1 cup roughly chopped cilantro (about 1 bunch)

1 small red onion, thinly sliced

1 cup thinly sliced scallions (about 1 small bunch)

Baron West Indian Hot Sauce

6 lime wedges

NOTE: If you know how to fillet the fish, good on you! If you don't, best to rely on your fishmonger. Ask them to reserve the bones and keep the fish head (this is irreplaceable flavor).

Dice the snapper fillets into 1-inch "cubes" and keep them refrigerated.

In a medium stockpot, heat 2 tablespoons of the olive oil over medium-high. Add the lemongrass and ginger and sauté, stirring just to distribute evenly in the pot and long enough for them to become aromatic, about 1 minute. Add the fish head and bones. Add enough water to just cover the fish. Raise the heat and bring to a boil. Then reduce the heat to medium-low and simmer for 45 minutes; you're giving time for the fish to impart its flavor to the broth. The flesh on the bones will be cooked through.

Strain the broth using a fine-mesh strainer and transfer the liquid to a medium bowl, then set aside. In the medium stockpot, add the remaining 2 tablespoons olive oil and heat over medium-high. Add the Spanish onions, carrots, and celery, plus a pinch of salt and pepper. Sauté, stirring frequently, until tender, 7 to 9 minutes. Add the garlic and thyme to the pan along with the Scotch bonnet pepper. Sauté, stirring just to mix, until fragrant, about 30 seconds.

Take the diced snapper out of the refrigerator and set it aside. Add the cassava to the pot, along with the reserved broth. Stir well. Bring to a simmer over medium-low heat and cook until the root vegetables are tender, about 15 minutes. Season with another pinch of salt.

Once the root vegetables are tender, add the snapper. Simmer until the fish is cooked through and all the flavors have combined, 15 to 20 minutes. The fish will look firm and flaky.

To serve: Divide the broth among the serving bowls and garnish with the chopped cilantro, red onion, scallions, Baron hot sauce to taste, and a lime wedge. Serve hot.

CREOLE BREAD

In St. Lucia, Creole bread is generally found at the super-small bakeries in town. They use stone ovens, and they're open mostly when they feel like it. Sometimes you drive by and the shop is closed; sometimes a line is wrapped down the road.

One of the most popular is a roadside bakery by the Thomazo family. I look forward to visiting their shop because it's at the base of a scenic, loopy hill. We don't really have a grid with street names. You go up this one road, pass the mango tree, and take a left. You pass this gap and drive two hundred feet, and there they are. The father established the bakery and built his own wood-burning oven. As he's gotten older, he supervises, and the sons prepare the dough and bake it. His daughters run the cash register, while the grandkids run around. People hang out and enjoy the house-made, fruit-infused rum. It's a true vibe.

Creole bread is similar to a rustic baguette, with a touch of sugar. It's rolled at the ends into pointy shapes we call "tot tot," which means "nipple." The crunchy ends are the best part. The middle is soft and chewy. We serve it with butter, fresh from the oven, plain and delicious.

2 cups warm water

5 cups bread flour, plus more as needed

2 tablespoons sugar

2 teaspoons instant active yeast

½ cup coconut oil, plus more for the bowl (optional)

1 teaspoon kosher salt

Unsalted butter, for the bowl (optional)

SERVING

Soft unsalted butter, or try Bacon Butter (page 275) or Honey Butter (page 274)

Flaky sea salt

In a small bowl, combine the warm water, 2 tablespoons of the flour, 1 tablespoon of the sugar, and the yeast. Set aside for 10 minutes to allow the yeast to bloom.

In a medium bowl, add the coconut oil, remaining 1 tablespoon of sugar, and the kosher salt. To dissolve the sugar, heat on a stovetop over medium heat for about 20 seconds. Stir and set aside to cool for 3 to 5 minutes. Then add the oil mixture to the yeast mixture.

In a large bowl or the bowl of a stand mixer fitted with the dough hook, sift the remaining flour. Add the wet mixture to the flour. Use a wooden spoon (or mix on low speed in the stand mixer) to combine the dough. Mix for 10 to 12 minutes to make sure you're working that gluten, until the dough is a smooth mass.

If the dough is sticky, add flour in ¼ cup increments until you have a dough that is smooth but not shiny or wet. Grease a large bowl with butter or oil and transfer the dough to the bowl. Cover it with a damp cloth and let the dough rise until it doubles in size, about 2 hours.

Dust a clean work surface with flour and dump the dough onto it. Make fists and punch down the dough, then knead into a round ball for about 3 minutes. This removes air pockets from the dough and helps make it easier to handle when you roll it.

Grease a sheet pan or line it with parchment paper.

Use a dough cutter to divide the dough into 10 equal portions, then shape each into a ball. Roll each ball into a torpedo-style oval 5 to 6 inches long, like a small baguette. Make sure the ends are pointy; that's the definitive Creole bread look! Place evenly spaced on the prepared sheet pan and cover for 30 minutes to proof at room temperature, until they double in size.

Meanwhile, heat the oven to 400°F.

Bake the loaves until the tops are golden brown, about 30 minutes. Use a spatula to gently raise the bread so you can check that it's golden brown underneath. Tap it—when it sounds hollow, it's ready to go.

To serve: Enjoy immediately with soft butter and sea salt.

CASSAVA SWEET BREAD

SERVES 4

The southern part of St. Lucia has countless hills and curvy roads. Many of the rustic, smaller bakeries are in the South, and if you know where to go, you wind up or down looping roads to get the best baked goods. They're not like typical businesses in the U.S.; you can't just look for a big sign or online presence. You have to know who people are, and you never really know when they're going to be open. You drive by and look, and if you see action, you pull over—it's that good.

Plas Kassav is one such family-owned bakery in Canaries. It seems like from the moment they open, they automatically have a line out the door. Their specialty is cassava bread, and when they run out, they're out. They prepare the batter, wrap it in banana leaves, then roast or steam it in the oven. Their bread is like a dense cake, almost like a bread pudding. Mine is a lighter texture. At Plas Kassav the bread can feature banana, spiced coconut, or cherries, which I've also chosen for my version.

Heat the oven to 350°F. Spray a 9 × 5-inch loaf pan with nonstick cooking spray or line it with a piece of parchment paper (keep the side pieces long to use as handles to remove the bread).

In a medium bowl, whisk the eggs and sugar well until light and fluffy, about 8 to 10 minutes. The eggs should look pale yellow and have a creamy consistency. Pour in the canola oil, water, and cane syrup, then whisk to combine. Set aside.

In a large bowl, add the cassava flour, baking powder, and salt. Whisk together the dry ingredients. Slowly add the wet ingredients, then follow with the dried cherries, stirring with a whisk as you go. Continue to whisk until the mixture is free of lumps.

Pour the cassava batter into the prepared loaf pan and transfer to the oven. Bake for 30 to 40 minutes. Check for doneness using a cake tester or toothpick, which should come out clean.

Allow the bread to cool for 10 minutes, then carefully remove from the loaf pan and place on a cooling rack for 30 minutes before slicing and serving. Enjoying cassava bread fresh is always best, but you can store it in an airtight container at room temperature for up 2 days.

Nonstick cooking spray (optional)

6 large eggs

1 cup sugar

½ cup canola oil

½ cup room-temperature water

1 tablespoon cane syrup

2 cups cassava flour

2 teaspoons baking powder

1 teaspoon kosher salt

1 cup dried cherries

SERVING SUGGESTION

Serve warm with butter, or a compound butter (such as the Chili Butter, page 275, Bacon Butter, page 275, or Honey Butter, page 274), or your favorite jam.

COCONUT BALLS

MAKES 12

In my experience, we don't eat a lot of manufactured sweets in the Caribbean. You do find treats like coconut balls—dried coconut flakes cooked with caramelized sugar, coconut milk, then rolled to form balls just as the sugar starts to cool. You could say that's our bonbon. You'll see these balls wrapped in small plastic baggies by the checkout at the market, and folks make these at home, too. During special occasions or holidays, people will add food coloring to their coconut balls to make them seasonally festive. During Easter, they'll be pastel-hued pink, green, and light blue. Sometimes we'll add unsweetened or lightly sweetened chocolate to the coconut balls, or we make tamarind balls, mixing the fruit with fresh vanilla, cinnamon, and nutmeg, all rolled in sugar. Store leftovers in plastic wrap, but I'm not sure you'll have any!

¾ cup sugar

5 cups shredded unsweetened coconut

½ cup dark rum (like Chairman's Reserve)

¼ cup finely grated fresh ginger

Zest of 1 lime

Line a plate or sheet pan with parchment paper.

In a medium heavy-bottomed saucepan, caramelize the sugar on low heat, swirling the pan to encourage faster and more even melting, until it develops a light golden brown color, 8 to 10 minutes.

Carefully add 4 cups of the shredded coconut and the rum and ginger and use a spatula or large spoon to combine.

Remove from the heat and allow the mixture to cool on the stovetop until it's cool to touch, 3 to 5 minutes.

Transfer the mixture to a large bowl. Dampen your hands with water. Use a 1-ounce scoop to measure the mixture, then form the coconut balls with your hands (or portion them into 1½-inch balls if you don't have a scoop). Place the balls on the parchment paper.

Add the remaining 1 cup of coconut to the same bowl. Place 3 to 4 balls at a time in the bowl, then gently toss to coat in the coconut. Return the coated coconut balls to the plate or sheet pan. Repeat until all balls have a coconut coating.

Zest the lime over the top of the coated balls. Serve immediately or keep in an airtight container at room temperature for up to 1 week.

Montego Bay

JAMAICA

BIG-ISLAND ENERGY

Wah gwaan.

I wanted to get out of St. Lucia, but I didn't quite want to move to the States yet. The U.S. felt too big, too daunting. When you're growing up in the Caribbean, the islands, they kind of bicker with each other. Bigger islands are like, *Ah you small-island people.* Cuba, Jamaica, they're the big islands. I was twenty years old, and I wanted to go to the big islands. I'd been working at Sandals La Toc near Castries for almost two years. I'd rotated through the various outlets at the resort: a bakery, Japanese and French restaurants, and one that highlighted local fare. I was cooking things I'd read about but didn't make at home, like hollandaise. I felt like I had learned everything I could at that point, and I wanted more exposure to Caribbean cuisine from other islands. I asked to go to another property; Antigua was available, but I thought it was small like St. Lucia. They had properties in Jamaica, though, so I was on my way to Sandals Montego Bay.

Montego Bay, or Mo Bay, as locals call it, was so developed; the bustling nature of the commerce and traffic was exciting and energizing to me, so different from my hometown. I was suddenly around people whose culture I knew nothing about. I also couldn't understand a word they were saying! I felt their accents were thick, but they were of course speaking English, same as me. Jamaicans carry themselves differently from people on every other island in the Caribbean; they have a distinctive confidence to them. They're right to be proud. You think of their music, their food, their contributions to sports, and especially their political identity as a nation (globally it was known that Africans in Jamaica launched well-organized revolts during slavery, as many of them were warriors in their home nations before being stolen). Anyone I met, they'd be talking about everything from their national history to their rivers and waterfalls. They are their own advertising campaign. Everyone I met reflected to me how great the island is. Jamaicans' vibe is like: *We are who we are and if you don't like it, we don't give a damn.*

I have found that on many Caribbean islands, with our colonial history and forced dependence on tourism as the main economic driver, there is a sensitivity to being of service that taps into our desire to share and be hospitable. But this can sometimes lead to placating visitors, even those who come to our islands and don't always treat our people or our land well. But the Jamaicans! They don't roll like that. It's not cockiness, really; it's a swagger. You're gonna respect the Jamaicans or you can get out. I loved being around that energy.

Each part of the island is different. The landscape in Negril is flat, with stunning white sand. I walked along the seven-mile beach. There's this spot where people do cookouts, and it's laden with conch shells. You can see a makeshift grill, people grilling conch. In Port Antonio, it's got lush lagoons. In the center of the island, you see big mountains in a rainforest. You feel the changes in each geographic area. There's a stretch from Ocho Rios to Kingston, part of the Fern Gully rainforest, where you feel like you're in the middle of the Amazon.

I remember taking the public bus from Mo Bay to Kingston. They cram as many people together as possible in those buses. Someone told me, "Oh, there's space in the back," and the driver pulled out a little wooden stool so I could sit in the walkway of the bus. And that became my seat. Everyone was saying to me, "Small up yourself!" Meaning, "make room." The bus took off with little me squatted in the aisle, people jam-packed together.

I think I had ackee every day that I lived in Jamaica. It was often sautéed with peppers and onions. Breakfast in the Caribbean is hearty. In St. Lucia, it's green fig and saltfish or saltfish with steamed dumplings. In Jamaica it's ackee and saltfish. I'd often have a lunch of ackee, callaloo, rice and peas, and steamed vegetables. So much of what we eat in the Caribbean is connected to the plant-based diets our ancestors had in West Africa. A lot of these small restaurants, they make everything from scratch. At Sips and Bites, the joke was, "How long did you wait?" They don't batch anything, so you're going to wait a minimum of thirty to forty minutes. People refuse to be rushed in the Caribbean. In the U.S., everything has to be now, it has to be quick. In the Caribbean we're going to take our time, and it is what it is.

The food culture of everyday folks probably taught me more than being on staff in the resort kitchen, and I share those stories and recipes in this chapter. I saw the intersection of food with the lifestyle, which becomes easier to observe when you're away from your home environment. I was shifting from my family's customs to being introduced to how others gathered.

I worked with a woman named Rita; she was like an aunt to me. She took me under her wing, recognizing I was out of my element. I was so relieved; thank God for Rita! She'd break down the Jamaican patois for me and helped fast-track my fitting in. Every weekend she'd say, "We're going to the bashment." I'd only heard of these in reggae songs. Rita must have been about forty-five. When she picks me up, it's her and her daughter, and she's wearing a green one-piece leotard, neon green bob wig, green eyelashes, her nails done. Her daughter had on a white wig with white hot pants. I had no idea you had to be dressed in the freshest gear. I was in jeans, sneakers, and a T-shirt.

We went to a dancehall and I just watched. This was the height of the dancehall culture, and the focus was on the emcees (but we called them DJs) and beautiful women in custom outfits who'd dance opposite the DJ in competition. Separate from the performances, the crowd was moving nonstop. Different rhythms had different dances, and it seemed like everyone knew what to do when. Outside the venue, you'd see smoke plumes from folks roasting jerk chicken or barbecuing meats.

Throughout the city, street vendors recycle old car parts and repurpose them as grills. I saw a lot of folks use a wheel spoke as their grill. They'll put together a stand and their coals, and they cook dishes like stewed chicken with rice and peas. You see them in these makeshift stalls along the street, along the coast, driving from Negril to Montego Bay.

Of course, I encountered many jerk pits. Jerk chicken, charred and juicy, with a piece of white bread. It was the best. I loved the way they had the food packaged, snacks in perfectly folded wrappers, spicy peanuts, fruit in a bag. *It was the best!* I'd see vendors with their food in a perfect pyramid, of fresh-cut oranges or pineapples, or whole pineapples with the tops still on, wrapped in plastic. They'd be perfectly carved in such a way so it was easy to remove the brown studs.

There was this guy called the Pudding Man. He had a dish you could compare to a tamale. It's prepared with cornmeal and then steamed. What I love about Caribbean people, their focus is on making one thing. You perfect your craft in that one offering and you do it well. You'll see Miss Jones do a stewed chicken on Fridays and Saturdays from her house. And when she sells out, she sells out. I learned from all these cooks how important it is that you do one thing really well; don't deplete your time trying to do a bunch of mediocre dishes.

I moved to Ocho Rios after a while. It was smaller than Mo Bay, but still had a lot going on. I loved being surrounded by the rivers. I went to Miss T's restaurant, where she cooked local fare like oxtail with the spinner dumplings. It's so good—she braises it with just spices, no onions. You can taste all the spices, the Scotch bonnet peppers. In the Caribbean, the dumplings we make are chewy. We don't make delicate pillows of air. It has to comfort you, fill you up! Sometimes diners in the U.S. will say to me, "Oh, these dumplings are dense." I say, "Yeah, that's just how we do it." The spinner dumplings simmered in Miss T's oxtail braise. You almost didn't even need the meat, because the dumplings carry so much of the flavor.

I visited Kingston often because I had family there. No one goes to Kingston for the beaches; it's the city. I had this cornmeal peanut porridge from a man who had a wooden structure, maybe 5 × 3 feet. The porridge is all he serves—no fruit, no coffee. Just the porridge. You get this beautiful, creamy, buttery porridge, but what set it off for me was the molasses. The taxi driver even said to me, "You gotta have a shot of molasses with your porridge." They cook it in either evaporated milk or coconut milk, and it's sweetened with condensed milk. Then they add ground peanuts and peanut butter. It's not overly sweet; it's just right. Add the molasses and it's over the top. I also loved Devon House in Kingston; it's been around forever. It's a historical landmark, and they're known for their patties (like hand pies, if you don't know). They do curry goat, beef, chicken, and vegetable patties. The curry goat always sells out.

In Jamaica, I learned about the influences of Rastafarian culture throughout the island and how important their Ital diet is to everyday life. I learned about the process of making jerk—this pit-roasting method was new to me. Coming from St. Lucia, where we prize everything coming out of the ocean, I related to the seafood recipes and coastal cuisine. Like in St. Lucia, Jamaica had folks cooking out of their home and bringing their food to the roadside to sell to passersby. The complexity of flavor in dishes like escovitch (an evolution of skibaj, the African Arab dish by the Moors, who colonized Spain, where it became escabeche; Jamaica was a colony of Spain before the British took over) and their approach to pickling and acidity throughout their cuisine taught me about balance. I observed a common thread of seasonality and the presence of home gardens in the food. I still draw on these lessons of cooking with the seasons and eating what's in proximity.

The recipes in this chapter reflect my time in the many small restaurants and home kitchens I ate and studied in during my years in Jamaica. Stewed Oxtail and Spinner Dumplings (page 142) was a lesson for me in big flavor. Escovitch-Style Snapper (page 150) is a classic dish that is deceptively simple but every ingredient is doing work. And the Grilled Lobster with Cilantro Lime Butter (page 129) will take you right to the beachside, even if you're not grilling on a wheel spoke.

ACKEE FRITTERS

SERVES 4

Jamaica is the only island in the Caribbean that uses ackee to its fullest potential, despite the tree being found throughout the region. Ackee trees produce so much fruit. The texture of ackee is like uni (sea urchin) when you cook it; it feels silken and luxurious on the palate. I don't know why more islands don't cook with it, but every Jamaican spot I've been to serves it. These ackee fritters are a light appetizer or for lunch with a salad, a bite with a lot of flavor.

⅔ cup all-purpose flour

2 teaspoons baking powder

1½ teaspoons kosher salt

½ teaspoon freshly ground black pepper

½ cup chopped Spanish onion

1 red bell pepper, diced

1 tablespoon minced Scotch bonnet pepper

1 cup canned ackee, rinsed, drained, and crushed

1 tablespoon Baron West Indian Hot Sauce or Crystal hot sauce

1 large egg

¾ cup coconut milk

Canola oil, for frying

In a large bowl, sift together the flour, baking powder, ½ teaspoon of the salt, and the black pepper. Set aside.

In a medium saucepan on medium-high heat, add the onions, bell pepper, and Scotch bonnet pepper and sauté, stirring occasionally until tender, about 8 minutes. Season with the remaining 1 teaspoon of salt. Take off the heat and add the crushed ackee and hot sauce. Mix well.

In a small bowl, gently beat the egg and gradually add the coconut milk until smooth.

Transfer the vegetables to the bowl of seasoned flour. Stir gently to coat evenly. Add the coconut milk–egg mixture and fold in using a spatula. The mixture should look like a thick pancake batter.

In a large saucepan, add canola oil to a depth of 1 inch (about 2 cups) and heat on medium-high to 325°F; check using an instant-read thermometer. Line a plate with paper towels or fit a cooling rack in a sheet pan.

Use a tablespoon to scoop the batter and drop into the hot oil, repeating a few more times and taking care not to crowd the pan. Fry the fritters on both sides until evenly golden brown, about 3 minutes per side. Use a slotted spoon or tongs to remove them and set on the prepared plate to drain. Repeat with the remaining batter. Serve straight up, piping hot!

GINGER-COCONUT PLANTAIN PORRIDGE

SERVES 4

Living in Mo Bay, I'd find small, independent restaurants; to me, they were hidden gems. I remember one spot where the owner would make a different type of porridge each week. On weekends, he tended to serve a plantain porridge. I never caught his name, and this wasn't the kind of spot that had signage. In the Caribbean, restaurants can often be in the rear of someone's house, places where you just have to know what's up. I remember that he was Rastafarian, and he would always say, "Ital is vital," which is a formative and common saying in their culture. Ital refers to the plant-based diet honored by Rastafari, established in the early 1900s, that symbolizes a spiritual relationship with universal energy and life force. Off memory I've done my best to reconnect with his ginger-coconut plantain porridge, but I am differentiating here as I love what condensed milk does in this recipe—it adds a little fat and just enough sweetness. I love the texture of this dish (to me it's a big improvement on oatmeal), and the ginger with warming spices makes your tongue dance.

4 cups water

2 nearly ripe plantains (yellow with some black spots), peeled and sliced

1 ripe banana, peeled and sliced

1 (14-ounce) can sweetened condensed milk

1 cup rolled oats

1 cup coconut milk

2 teaspoons vanilla extract

1 teaspoon minced fresh ginger

1 teaspoon kosher salt

½ teaspoon grated nutmeg

1 cinnamon stick

SERVING

2 bananas, peeled and sliced

In a blender, combine the water, plantains and ripe banana, condensed milk, rolled oats, coconut milk, vanilla extract, ginger, salt, and nutmeg (depending on the size of your blender, you may want to divide the ingredients in half to blend in two batches). Puree until very smooth, for 1 to 2 minutes.

Transfer the mixture to a medium saucepan and place over low heat. Add the cinnamon stick and gently warm the mixture, stirring occasionally, until it thickens, 8 to 10 minutes.

To serve: Pour into individual bowls, garnish with the banana slices, and enjoy immediately.

CORNMEAL PORRIDGE

SERVES 4

In Jamaica, a favorite pastime of mine was stopping to patronize the roadside vendors. In Kingston, I loved this food stand, Juicy Blacks. He had a small setup, a single-room space. He only ever made one dish—cornmeal porridge, cooked in coconut milk. He'd come to the table to say what the day's garnishes would be, and he served the porridge in tin cans. It was rich and beautiful, and the simplicity of the dish always resonated with me. Enjoy it for breakfast or a snack. The molasses sets this one off.

3 cups coconut milk

2 cups water

½ cinnamon stick

½ teaspoon kosher salt

1 star anise pod

1 cup yellow cornmeal

½ cup sweetened condensed milk

1 teaspoon vanilla extract

½ teaspoon grated nutmeg

Light brown sugar or coconut sugar, to taste

SERVING

¼ cup molasses (optional)

1 teaspoon water (optional)

Fresh fruit medley (such as sliced banana, sliced mango, and blueberries)

In a large heavy-bottomed saucepan, add the coconut milk, water, cinnamon, salt, and star anise. Bring the mixture to a boil, then let simmer on low heat for 6 to 8 minutes to infuse the milk.

Gradually whisk in the cornmeal and keep whisking to prevent any lumps. Reduce the heat to low and cook, whisking occasionally, until the mixture thickens, about 10 minutes.

Add the condensed milk, vanilla extract, nutmeg, and sugar to your desired level of sweetness. Stir to combine and remove from the heat.

To serve: If you want to get fancy, brûlée the sliced mango and bananas before serving. To do so, in a medium heavy-bottomed saucepan, heat the brown sugar over medium heat, no stirring, until melted, about 10 minutes. Add the water and let it incorporate undisturbed for 1 minute. Add the sliced banana and mango, stir to evenly incorporate, then remove from the heat. The caramelization lends a nice depth to a simple and flavorful dish. (We don't brûlée the berries because they're too small and would overcook.)

Divide the porridge among serving bowls, top with the brûléed or fresh fruit, and enjoy immediately.

ACKEE, SALTFISH, AND FRIED DUMPLINGS

SERVES 6

My mother still lives in the house I grew up in, and we still have an ackee tree in front of our kitchen. As a child I never appreciated ackee; it's not a fruit that St. Lucians put into their dishes. When I moved to Jamaica, I quickly learned that ackee is king—ackee and saltfish is their national dish, and it was everywhere. I immediately loved and respected it. I called home and said, "Mum, there's *gold* in our backyard." She had only been sharing it with Jamaicans who lived on the island. Now when I go home, she has fresh ackee in the freezer ready and waiting.

Saltfish is often dismissed as poor people's food, owing to its history as sustenance for enslaved laborers (similar to how many African Americans reject pork, particularly entrails and offcuts). But saltfish is also the special something in many delicious, historical dishes. The blend of the cod with the nutty ackee is a perfect combo. If you don't have access to fresh ackee, canned is another option.

Most Caribbean islands have some form of fried bread for breakfast, often similar preparations with different names. Here, I am using my Bakes recipe (page 83), but we are honoring Jamaican vernacular by referring to them as fried dumplings.

1 pound saltfish fillet

Fried dumplings (see Bakes, page 83)

2 tablespoons canola oil

1 small Spanish onion, thinly sliced

2 medium tomatoes, cored and chopped

1 red bell pepper, thinly sliced

1 green bell pepper, thinly sliced

½ Scotch bonnet pepper, seeded and minced

4 garlic cloves, minced

1 (19-ounce) can ackee, rinsed and drained

2 scallions, thinly sliced

2 tablespoons thyme leaves

Kosher salt and freshly ground black pepper

In a medium bowl, submerge the saltfish in water and leave to soak overnight in the refrigerator. Change the water at least once during the soaking time. Drain.

Let's cook the excess salt out of the fish: In a medium saucepan, add the saltfish and cover with cold water by 2 inches. Bring to a boil and cook for 20 minutes. While the saltfish is boiling, make your fried dumplings.

Drain the fish, return it to the saucepan, and repeat the boiling and draining process twice more. Transfer the fillets to a medium bowl. If needed, clean the saltfish by removing all skin, scales, and pin bones. Use a fork to flake it into large chunks, then set aside.

In a medium skillet, heat the canola oil on medium. Add the onion, tomato, red and green bell peppers, Scotch bonnet, and garlic and reduce the heat to low. Sauté, stirring occasionally, until soft, about 8 minutes. Add the reserved cod and the ackee and scallions. Cook, stirring gently to keep the cod and ackee in large pieces, until warmed through, about 5 minutes. Add the thyme. Season with salt and pepper to taste, then set aside.

To serve: Cut an opening in the fried dumplings to form a little pocket and fill them with the ackee and saltfish. Serve immediately.

COCO BREAD

MAKES 8

Living in Mo Bay, I learned that everyone in the Caribbean has a bread that's unique to their culture. We have Creole Bread (page 105) in St. Lucia, but I quickly got down with this white loaf that's similar to a brioche. It's all about the fold. Coco bread has a double-folded triangle, sometimes seen as a half moon (when shaped as a half moon, it's traditionally sliced in half and served with a beef patty in between). It has to be folded over or it's not coco bread! This is more of a side dish and less so a breakfast item. It's got a density to it that makes it a perfect vessel to eat with jerk chicken.

1 cup coconut milk

6 tablespoons coconut oil, plus more for coating

2 tablespoons sugar

1 teaspoon kosher salt

¾ teaspoon active dry yeast

4 cups all-purpose flour, plus more for dusting

1 large egg, lightly beaten

1 teaspoon flaky sea salt

In a small saucepan, gently heat the coconut milk, coconut oil, and sugar over low heat for 1 minute, just to dissolve the sugar. Add the kosher salt and yeast and stir to incorporate. Transfer the liquid to a medium bowl.

Add the flour to the bowl and use your hands or a spatula to gently combine everything until a soft dough forms. Turn the dough onto a clean surface. Using your hands, knead the dough until smooth and elastic, for about 2 minutes. Shape it into a ball. Lightly grease a large bowl with coconut oil and place the dough in the greased bowl. Cover with plastic wrap and set it aside in a warm place to proof until it doubles in size, 1 to 1½ hours.

Heat the oven to 350°F. Line a baking tray with parchment paper.

On a floured surface, cut the dough into 8 equal portions, shaping each into a ball. Using a rolling pin, roll each ball into a 6-inch-wide round.

Brush each round with coconut oil on all sides, then fold into a half moon shape. Brush with more coconut oil and fold again to form a triangle.

Brush with the egg wash and sprinkle with sea salt.

Set each piece on the baking tray 2 inches apart. Bake until golden brown, about 15 minutes.

Serve immediately. Enjoy with pretty much anything!

CALLALOO

SERVES 2 TO 4

Leafy greens are part of countless West African cuisines and, consequently, Caribbean diaspora dishes. You'll find callaloo is a staple in people's gardens throughout Jamaica, where the name refers to amaranth leaves. In some places, like Trinidad and Tobago, callaloo refers to dasheen leaves. For this recipe, spinach is a fine substitute. Typically, the callaloo is simmered in broth or coconut milk with spices and aromatics. If you want a Jamaican breakfast of champions, get you a plate of Ackee and Saltfish (page 122), with callaloo and bammy, a cassava flatbread.

Heat a large saucepot over medium-high. Add the coconut oil, then the onion, tomato, scallion, thyme, garlic, salt, and cayenne pepper. Sauté the vegetables, stirring to combine, until the onion becomes translucent, 3 to 5 minutes.

Add the callaloo (or spinach). Sweat the leaves, stirring occasionally, for about 5 minutes so they begin to soften. Add the water. Reduce the heat to low and simmer, uncovered, until the leaves become tender, about 15 minutes. Serve hot.

1 tablespoon coconut oil

1 large yellow onion, sliced

1 beefsteak tomato, cut into ¼-inch dice

2 scallions, thinly sliced

2 sprigs of thyme, picked

2 garlic cloves, minced

1½ tablespoons kosher salt

¼ teaspoon cayenne pepper

4 cups tightly packed callaloo or spinach, chopped into 1-inch pieces

2 tablespoons water

SERVING SUGGESTION

Ackee and Saltfish (page 122), Whole Roasted Jerk Chicken (page 136), any steamed fish, or mixed with steamed rice.

GRILLED LOBSTER
WITH CILANTRO LIME BUTTER

SERVES 2

Working at the resort in Mo Bay, I was usually able to rely on two days off. On those days, I tried to explore different parts of Jamaica, particularly places only locals would go. I'd often take a boat off the mainland to Lime Cay, just outside of Kingston. The vibe was always quiet and relaxed, a drastic shift from the constant bustle of tourism in Mo Bay. There were only a handful of fishermen on the beach in Lime Cay, and one day I noticed a man with all these lobsters hanging on a long string. The fisherman would work with the folks who run the restaurants, basically beachside huts with grills and limited seating. I'd buy a lobster, he'd cut it in half and take it to the cook to grill for me. Then I would pay the cook for a drink and sides, like cabbage salad, boiled or roasted breadfruit, and of course, a square of Macaroni Pie (page 63). The cook would pour lime vinaigrette over the fresh grilled lobster. It is truly the best lobster I've had in my life. Here I'm adding fish sauce to ramp up the umami in the seafood.

1 cup (2 sticks) unsalted butter, softened

4 jalapeños, seeded and minced

3 tablespoons minced cilantro

3 tablespoons fish sauce

3 limes, zested and quartered

2 lobsters (about 2 pounds each; see Note)

¼ cup extra-virgin olive oil

Kosher salt and freshly ground black pepper

Build a medium-high fire in a charcoal grill or heat a gas grill to medium-high. Alternatively, heat a medium skillet over medium-high.

In a small bowl, mix the butter, jalapeños, cilantro, fish sauce, and lime zest and squeeze in the juice from half the lime quarters. Set aside.

If you have spiny lobster, defrost if necessary. Uncurl the tail and lay the lobster flat on a cutting board, belly side down. Use a heavy cleaver to split each lobster in half lengthwise from the head to the tail. Transfer the lobster halves, shell side down, to a sheet pan.

If you're using Maine lobster, uncurl its tail and place the live lobster on the cutting board, belly side down. Use a heavy cleaver to split the lobster in half lengthwise, from the head to the tail. Scoop out and discard the yellow-green innards and cut off the claws. Transfer the lobster halves, shell side down, to a sheet pan. Crack the claws and place them on the same sheet pan.

Drizzle the lobster halves with the oil and season with salt and pepper to taste.

Place the lobster halves (flesh side down) and claws (as applicable) on the grill or skillet and cook until the tail meat turns from translucent gray to white, 5 to 10 minutes. Turn over the lobster halves and claws and spread each with the butter mixture; continue cooking until the flesh is cooked through, up to 3 additional minutes. The halves will cook faster than the claws, so take those off the grill when they're ready. Serve immediately with the remaining lime wedges.

NOTE: In the islands we eat spiny lobster, which has a mildly sweet flavor and is less dense than Maine lobster. They don't have claws, so we just eat the tail meat. In the U.S., when spiny lobster is available, it's typically frozen. Most folks will likely have access to Maine lobster, which will be sold to you live. There is a subtle difference in overall taste, but the main thing is that prepping the lobster will be different depending on which type you get. If using a frozen spiny lobster, defrost it before proceeding with the recipe.

PICKLED GREEN MANGO
WITH CILANTRO DRESSING

SERVES 2

In secondary school in St. Lucia, we'd enjoy this as a snack during our breaks. Vendors would come with their baskets of beef patties (pastry hand pies with savory filling), tamarind balls, and mango– or golden apple-in-sauce, which is how we called this recipe. Mango-in-sauce was my favorite. They'd peel the fruit, slice it, then add it to a plastic sandwich bag with white vinegar, ginger, garlic, and chili flakes. In Jamaica, the Trinidadian influence of mango chow is popular, and I'd see folks eating this tangy side with things like jerk.

¾ cup extra-virgin olive oil

⅓ cup champagne vinegar

2 tablespoons Ginger-Chili Oil (page 269)

1 garlic clove, finely grated

4 green mangoes, peeled and diced into 2-inch cubes

1 small red onion, thinly sliced

1 bunch of cilantro, minced

2 teaspoons flaky sea salt

SERVING SUGGESTION

Whole Roasted Jerk Chicken (page 136) or Steamed Snapper with Pepper Ginger Sauce (page 48)

In a medium bowl, combine the olive oil, champagne vinegar, ginger-chili oil, and garlic. Whisk to fully incorporate. Add the mangoes, red onions, and cilantro to the bowl and mix again. Season with salt. Eat right away or refrigerate, covered, for up to 2 days.

JERK BUTTERED CORN

SERVES 4

Summer in Jamaica means grilling corn, sipping a Red Stripe, and big hearty laughs with friends. Throughout the Caribbean, when corn is in season, you find roadside grills set up with folks roasting local corn on the cob brushed with seasoned butter. It's a great snack on the go. I can't resist the sweet smell of sugars caramelizing on the grill. In Jamaica, the roast corn is served straight up, charred and plain; it's so good!

I took the spices you find in jerk seasoning and used them to make a compound butter that can go on just about anything—chicken, cauliflower, and definitely this corn. It will keep in the freezer for a month. The ranch-flavored breadcrumbs are my twist, too. It's got a fun crunch and the saltiness is a nice contrast with the jerk-inspired flavor. If you want a different flavor profile, skip the jerk butter prep, and use the Chili Butter (page 275) instead.

1 cup panko breadcrumbs

6 tablespoons ranch powder

1 cup (2 sticks) high-quality unsalted butter, such as Plugrà, softened

6 tablespoons light brown sugar

3 tablespoons cayenne pepper, plus ½ teaspoon for serving

3 tablespoons ground allspice

2 tablespoons ground ginger

1 tablespoon thyme leaves

1 tablespoon garlic powder

1 tablespoon onion powder

1 tablespoon ground cinnamon

½ teaspoon sweet paprika

4 ears of sweet yellow corn

Flaky sea salt

1 cup Aioli (page 269) or mayonnaise

1 lime, quartered

Heat the grill to 375°F and heat the oven to 325°F.

Place the breadcrumbs on a sheet pan and bake in the oven for 5 minutes. Stir to ensure even toasting and bake for another 5 minutes, until they're golden brown. Transfer to a bowl. Add the ranch powder, mix well, and set aside.

In a large bowl, add the butter, brown sugar, 3 tablespoons of cayenne pepper, and the allspice, ground ginger, thyme, garlic powder, onion powder, cinnamon, and paprika. Mix until well combined.

Take the corn ears and pull back the husks, but don't fully detach them. Generously rub the corn with the entire butter mixture and bring the husks back over the corn. You want them buttered and covered. Chill the corn in the refrigerator for 10 minutes.

Grill the covered ears for about 8 minutes, rotating to cook evenly on each side. Peel the husks back and continue to grill until the corn develops a brown-black char, another 10 minutes.

Season the grilled corn with sea salt to taste. Brush the corn with the aioli, then dust all over with the ranch breadcrumbs. Place the remaining ½ teaspoon of cayenne pepper on a small plate and dip the lime wedges in the pepper to cover. Serve the corn immediately with the seasoned lime wedges.

JERK FRIED CATFISH

SERVES 4

I didn't have catfish in Jamaica. I don't think we have catfish in the Caribbean at all. But after years in New Orleans, catfish has become my go-to, and this recipe is an example of cooking with what you have using recipes from where you've been. In Jamaica, you see jerked whole fish, like snapper, thrown on the grill, especially in spots like Negril where you're on the water. This dish combines island flavors with Gulf seafood. Catfish is slightly flaky, mildly sweet, and so moist. In this recipe you're going to make a dry jerk spice, soak the fish in spiced buttermilk, and dredge it in cornmeal, making a light but flavorful fish.

JERK SPICE

1 tablespoon cayenne pepper

2 tablespoons light brown sugar

1½ teaspoons sweet paprika

1 teaspoon garlic powder

1 teaspoon onion powder

½ teaspoon chili powder

3 tablespoons ground allspice

½ teaspoon ground cinnamon

½ teaspoon ground ginger

FISH BRINE

2 cups buttermilk

1 bunch of thyme

2 shallots, thinly sliced lengthwise

¼ cup Baron West Indian Hot Sauce, plus more for serving

3 tablespoons kosher salt

1 tablespoon red chili flakes

2 garlic cloves, smashed

4 (5-ounce) catfish fillets

COOKING THE FISH

1 cup all-purpose flour

½ cup rice flour or cornstarch

½ cup cornmeal

Canola oil, for frying

SERVING

Cabbage Salad with Tamarind Vinaigrette (page 252)

Make the jerk spice: In a small bowl, combine the cayenne pepper, brown sugar, paprika, garlic powder, onion powder, chili powder, allspice, cinnamon, and ginger. Set aside.

Make the fish brine: This is going to season the fish inside and out, but also the buttermilk here will tenderize the fish. In a large bowl, add the buttermilk, thyme, shallots, hot sauce, salt, chili flakes, garlic cloves, and 2 tablespoons of the jerk spice mix (reserve the remaining spice mix for the dredge; we'll get to that in a moment).

Add the catfish to the brine bowl and gently massage to fully coat the fish. Cover and place in the refrigerator for 1 to 4 hours before frying. When you're ready to cook, remove the bowl from the refrigerator but keep the fish in the brine.

Cook the fish: On a large plate, combine the remaining spice mix with the all-purpose flour, rice flour, and cornmeal.

In a large sauté pan, add canola oil to a depth of 1 inch (about 2 cups) and heat over medium-high to 350°F; check using an instant-read thermometer. Line a plate with paper towels.

Take one fillet out of the brine at a time, allowing excess to drip off. Place the fillet in the seasoned flour. Flip on both sides to ensure even coating. Place the fillet in the oil. Repeat with a second fillet. Do not crowd the pan; leave about 1 inch of space between fillets on all sides so they cook evenly.

Fry until the fillets are golden brown on both sides, about 3 minutes per side. To test the fish for doneness, use a cake tester or paring knife inserted into the thickest part of the fish. The flesh should easily flake when cut into. Use a spatula or slotted spoon to remove the fish, and allow to rest on the paper towel–lined plate. Repeat with the remaining fillets if necessary.

To serve: Eat immediately with extra hot sauce and cabbage salad.

WHOLE ROASTED JERK CHICKEN

SERVES 4

"Who jerkin the chicken!" The road stands in Jamaica have these jerk pits. The jerk method came from the Maroons as a way to cook and preserve food when they lived up in the mountains. Whether it's jerk chicken or pork, they're cooking the food on the allspice (pimento) branches. Traditionally jerk is cooked in the ground and covered up by the allspice—a practice influenced by Jamaica's Indigenous peoples but evolved as Africans cooked in the ground to not reveal their location as self-emancipated Maroons. This preparation is what gives jerk its iconic flavor, in addition to the spices used, which is why "jerk spice" can't really be separated from the way the meat is prepared.

Jerk is known all over the world (whether the flavor hits right is another conversation; I'll defer to the Jamaicans on that one!) because where Jamaicans go, their food follows.

I like to add roasted sweet potatoes and onions to the mix as a side dish. I slice some up and distribute them on the bottom of the roasting pan underneath the rack just before I put the chicken in the oven. The juices from the chicken will season the veggies as they cook together. If that's your thing, I'll cue you in the recipe. Note the optional overnight marinade.

JERK SAUCE
- ¼ cup extra-virgin olive oil
- 2 cups thinly sliced yellow onion
- 1 cup minced fresh ginger
- 1 cup Scotch bonnet peppers, halved
- 1 bunch of thyme
- 3 tablespoons light brown sugar
- ⅛ teaspoon kosher salt
- 3 tablespoons ground allspice
- 3 cinnamon sticks
- 4 cups water

BRINE
- 1 whole chicken (about 3 pounds), innards removed
- 4 cups water
- 2 cups kosher salt

ROASTING (OPTIONAL)
- 2 large sweet potatoes, sliced
- 2 medium red onions, sliced

SERVING SUGGESTION
- Coconut Rice and Peas (page 47) or Mirliton and Carrot Slaw (page 259)

Make the jerk sauce: In a large saucepot, add the olive oil and heat on medium-high. Sweat the onions, ginger, Scotch bonnet, thyme, and brown sugar, stirring occasionally, until the onions look dark golden brown, about 10 minutes. Add the salt. Add the allspice and cinnamon sticks and stir to incorporate. Reduce the heat to low and continue to cook, stirring occasionally, until the vegetables soften and look like a paste, about 10 minutes.

Add the water to the saucepot. Stir well and cover, then cook on low for another 2 hours; come back to the saucepot occasionally to give it a stir. As the sauce cooks, you're looking for it to reduce by about one-third in volume. Once the cinnamon stick is pliable, you're ready to puree the sauce.

Let's brine the chicken: First, spatchcock it. Place the chicken on a cutting board breast side down. Use kitchen shears to cut along one side of the backbone; don't remove it. Pull the legs away from one another. Flip the chicken over so the skin side is visible, then press down on the breastbone until it snaps so the chicken lies flat.

In a large bowl, add the water and salt. Stir to dissolve the salt. Submerge the chicken in the salted water. Cover and refrigerate for 1 hour. Remove the chicken from the brine.

Roast the chicken: Heat the oven to 400°F. Fit a rack in a roasting pan. If you're down to add the sweet potatoes and onions as mentioned earlier, now's the time to add them to the bottom of your roasting pan underneath the rack.

Transfer the jerk sauce (carefully!) to a blender. You can work in batches, and you can slightly crack the lid to allow the steam to escape. (Either use kitchen gloves or be sure to avoid direct contact with the sauce, as the raw peppers can be a skin irritant.) Puree until smooth; you'll have about 3 cups of jerk sauce.

Place the chicken on the rack. Use a spoon or wear gloves to distribute half of the jerk sauce all over the chicken, including inside the cavity, and loosen the skin at the breast so you can get the marinade in there, too. Get into all those little pockets to maximize the flavor. (You can cook right away, or leave to marinate uncovered in the refrigerator overnight to allow the skin to air dry. This makes for crispier skin once roasted.)

Place the chicken in the oven and cook for 45 minutes total to caramelize the seasoning and cook the chicken through. At the 25-minute mark, spoon the remaining jerk sauce all over the chicken—again just be careful about hand contact with the raw sauce. Continue roasting until the chicken is cooked: Use an instant-read thermometer inserted in the fleshy part of the thigh, which should read 165°F. Or use a skewer to puncture the thigh: The chicken is done cooking when the juices run clear. (Don't test the chicken breast, as white meat cooks the fastest.) Once the chicken is finished cooking, allow it to rest in the roasting pan for 5 minutes. Then you can carve it up and serve with your choice of sides.

BUSS UP SHUT ROTI

MAKES 6 ROTI

Buss up shut roti is Trinidadian in origin, and thanks to migration, the dish has traveled around the Caribbean. "Buss up shut" refers to the way we break up this bread, so it resembles a ripped-up shirt. It's one of my favorite foods. The technique for making roti can take practice because it's about getting the layering and flakiness just right. But once you get the rhythm, it's rewarding. I had buss up shut roti in St. Lucia, but it was more prevalent in Jamaica, where we use roti to swipe up curried goat or dal. I learned how to make roti while living in Jamaica but perfected my technique in New Orleans thanks to my Trini chef friend Lisa Nelson. She makes "island soul" Trinbagonian cuisine at her restaurant Queen Trini Lisa. Lisa is quite particular about the layers and how to expose them at the right time. She'd use two wooden paddles to contort and flip the dough on the tawa in such a precise way, it's masterful!

3 cups all-purpose flour, plus more for dusting

2 teaspoons baking powder

1½ teaspoons kosher salt

1 teaspoon sugar

1 tablespoon ghee or canola oil, plus ¼ cup for brushing

1¼ cups warm water, plus more as needed

Canola oil, for greasing

⅓ cup vegetable shortening or unsalted butter, softened

SERVING

Split Pea Dal (page 101)

EQUIPMENT

Tawa (you can also use a griddle, crepe pan, comal, or large sauté pan)

In a large bowl, mix the flour, baking powder, salt, and sugar until everything is incorporated.

Create a well in the dry mixture, then add 1 tablespoon of ghee, followed by the warm water. Knead the dough for 30 seconds to 1 minute to form a soft, sticky dough. Watch the consistency and add more warm water as needed. The dough should be pliable and soft.

Divide the dough into 6 equal pieces and cover with plastic wrap or a damp towel. Let the dough rest for 15 to 30 minutes at room temperature. Resting the dough helps relax the gluten, making it easier to work while producing a more tender roti. Oil a sheet pan and set it aside.

Heavily dust a cutting board or flat work surface with flour. Working with one dough segment at a time (leave the rest covered), use a rolling pin to roll out the dough into a circle, 3 to 4 inches wide and about ¼ inch thick. No need to make a perfect circle—just use these sizes to guide you.

With your fingers or a knife, smear about 1 tablespoon of the shortening on the surface of the dough circle, then lightly sprinkle it with flour. Use a paring knife to make one slit from the center of the circle to the edge. Lift one of the cut edges and roll the dough inward so you form a cone. On the wide end of the cone, you'll see you've made a coil. Pinch the outer edges of the cone together and fold the dough inward so the coils are no longer visible.

Place the dough on the oiled pan and cover with a damp cloth. Repeat this process for the other pieces, oiling each piece with a little canola to prevent the dough from drying out. Make sure the cones are not touching one another. Let the dough rest, covered, at room temperature, until the dough has increased in size by about a third, about 2 hours.

Heat the tawa on low heat. You're going to roll and cook one roti at a time. Dust a clean work surface with flour and gently flatten out each cone, then use a rolling pin to roll it out, working from the center outward. Working in a rhythm, rotate the dough outward each time you roll it; this helps to form a uniform circle. Each dough cone should roll out to be about 10 inches wide and ½ inch thick. Make sure each piece is thin at the edges.

Gently place one dough round on the griddle. Lightly brush the top with ghee and cook until tiny bubbles appear, about 30 seconds. Flip the dough, brush the surface with ghee, and wait 30 seconds. Repeat three more times. This process allows the layers to cook without drying out the roti. Wrap the roti in a clean cloth or towel, then give it a vigorous shake, or tap the enclosed cloth with a large spoon or spatula to shred the roti and expose the layers. Repeat with the remaining dough rounds. Keep any remaining roti covered.

To serve: Enjoy warm with dal.

STEWED OXTAIL AND SPINNER DUMPLINGS

SERVES 8

Jamaicans take their oxtails seriously. Growing up on St. Lucia, ours came from lean heifer cows, but in Jamaica their oxtails were on a whole other level. Marcia was a Jamaican cook I worked with at Sandals Ocho Rios. She invited me to her house one Sunday so I could experience traditional fare. She had beautiful, glazed oxtails in the pot. I took one look—they smelled so good—and I told her I had to learn how to make them. Graciously, she had me over the following weekend to school me, and you better believe I paid attention. You're benefiting here from those good notes I took on her technique. We both like to use red wine for added depth and richness, but that's not typical.

5 pounds oxtails, cut into 3-inch rounds

¼ cup freshly ground black pepper

2 tablespoons kosher salt

1 medium Spanish onion, roughly chopped

2 large carrots, peeled and roughly chopped

3 celery stalks, peeled and roughly chopped

2 cups tomato paste

1 cup browning

1 (750 ml) bottle red wine (such as merlot)

4 quarts Brown Stock (page 279) or beef stock

2 sprigs of rosemary

Spinner Dumpling dough (see page 88), rolled out but uncooked

Heat the oven to 375°F.

Heat a large Dutch oven on high heat. Generously season the oxtails with the black pepper and salt. Working in batches, sear the oxtails on all sides, 3 to 5 minutes on each side, so the surface is brown and the fat renders. Remove the oxtails from the pot and set aside.

Add the chopped onions, carrots, and celery (the mirepoix) and continue cooking over high heat for 10 minutes, stirring occasionally, until the mirepoix is caramelized. Reduce the heat to low and cook until it becomes a thick paste, about 5 minutes, then add the tomato paste and browning. Stir well and add the bottle of red wine. Keep cooking over low heat, stirring occasionally, until the wine reduces to demi sec ("half dry") and looks like a thick, burgundy-colored paste, about 10 minutes.

Add the oxtails back into the pot. Cover with the brown stock, bring to a simmer, and cook for 8 to 10 minutes to bring the stock together. Add the rosemary sprigs and place it in the oven. Leave it uncovered to allow the meat and braising liquid to caramelize. Braise for 30 minutes. After 30 minutes, cover the pot and reduce the oven temperature to 300°F. Cook for another 2 hours, or until the meat falls off the bone (check with a fork).

Remove the pot from the oven and set on the stovetop, uncovered. Place one ball of dough between your hands and as you move your hands in opposite directions to form a torpedo, flick the dough into the pot. Repeat with all the dough, then simmer on medium-high heat until the dumplings are cooked through, another 5 minutes. These are thick dumplings, so they won't float, but this is sufficient time for them to finish.

Serve immediately once your dumplings are done. In Jamaica, it's traditional to have the meat served on the bone, and we eat the bone-in meat using our hands.

BROWN STEW SNAPPER

SERVES 2

This is a Jamaican dish you'll find on pretty much any menu whether you're in-country or in the diaspora. The fish is fried, then finished in the oven or on the stovetop, then covered with the brown stew. Browning is a burnt sugar and water mix that we use in our cooking throughout the Caribbean to add color to dishes. You can replace the snapper with swordfish, salmon, or tuna steak.

SNAPPER

1 (1 to 1½ pound) whole red snapper, scaled and gutted

3 tablespoons Green Seasoning (page 274)

1½ tablespoons kosher salt

1 teaspoon minced garlic

½ teaspoon grated fresh ginger

½ teaspoon thyme leaves

½ teaspoon ground white pepper

1 lemon, zested and juiced

Canola oil, for frying

2 cups rice flour

BROWN STEW

1 medium Spanish onion, thinly sliced

1 red bell pepper, thinly sliced

1 teaspoon minced Scotch bonnet pepper

1 teaspoon thyme leaves

1 garlic clove, minced

½ teaspoon Green Seasoning (page 274)

1 fresh bay leaf

3 medium tomatoes, cut into ¼-inch dice

¼ cup sliced okra (¼-inch rounds)

¼ cup browning

2 cups Ginger Lemongrass Fumet (page 149) (or vegetable stock)

GARNISH

2 scallions, thinly sliced

SERVING

Coconut Rice and Peas (page 47)

NOTE: If you prefer, instead of frying the fish, simmer it in the brown stew sauce and bake in the oven for about 10 to 12 minutes at 350°F. Pour the stewed vegetables on top and then continue with the simmering instructions at the end.

Prepare the snapper: Rinse the fish. Drain and pat dry with paper towels or a clean towel. Using a paring knife, gently but firmly score the fish from the gill to the tail on both sides, along the belly's surface in crosshatches, about 2 inches apart. You want to go beneath the skin surface, but not so deep that you cut through the fish. When you're done, it should look like a stretched grid across the fish's surface.

Place the fish in a large bowl or on a sheet pan, then season with the green seasoning, salt, garlic, ginger, thyme, white pepper, and lemon juice and zest. Use your hands to gently and thoroughly coat the fish with the seasoning on the inside and out. Chill in the refrigerator for at least 30 minutes. Cover the fish if you marinate it overnight.

When you're ready to cook the fish, in a large skillet, add canola oil to a depth of 2 inches (about 1 cup) and heat over medium to 350°F; check using an instant-read thermometer.

Once the oil is ready, spread out the rice flour on a wide, flat plate. Remove the fish from the refrigerator and lightly shake off any excess marinade. Evenly dust the exterior with the rice flour.

Immediately add the coated fish to the skillet. Cook each side until golden brown, 3 to 4 minutes per side. Transfer the fish to a plate or cooling rack.

Make the brown stew: Drain most of the oil from the skillet, leaving about 3 tablespoons behind, or add the same amount of oil to a wide saucepan. Add the onion, bell pepper, Scotch bonnet, thyme, garlic, green seasoning, and bay leaf to the skillet or saucepan. Sauté over medium heat, stirring frequently to avoid any burns, until the onions are tender, about 2 minutes.

Add the tomatoes, okra, and browning. Continue to stir. Add the ginger lemongrass fumet and let the stew simmer until the vegetables soften and the sauce starts to thicken, about 5 minutes. Add the fish to the sauce and spoon it over the fish. Remove bay leaf and discard.

Top the stew and fish with scallions and enjoy immediately with Coconut Rice and Peas.

CURRIED RICE

SERVES 6

I saw this type of rice dish often in Jamaica, where they toast aromatics and allow them to infuse into the rice as it's cooking. I like the standout kick of the turmeric, garam masala, cardamom, ginger, and coriander. Curried rice is great with oxtails, fried fish, or chicken, but I like to eat it by itself or with a side salad.

2 tablespoons coconut oil

1 medium Spanish onion, diced

1 poblano pepper, diced

8 curry leaves

3 tablespoons kosher salt

3 tablespoons finely grated fresh turmeric

3 tablespoons garam masala

1 tablespoon minced fresh ginger

4 green cardamom pods, smashed

3 star anise pods

1 teaspoon coriander seeds

2 cups jasmine rice, rinsed 3 times until the water runs clear

1 Scotch bonnet pepper, torn

3 cups water

1 (14-ounce) can coconut milk

SERVING

Steamed Snapper with Pepper Ginger Sauce (page 48)

EQUIPMENT

Cheesecloth and twine

In a medium pot, add the coconut oil, then the onion, poblano pepper, and curry leaves. Cook over high heat and sweat out the vegetables, stirring occasionally until they soften, about 2 minutes. Season with the salt, then add the turmeric, garam masala, and ginger. Reduce the heat to low and cook until fragrant, about 2 more minutes.

Place the cardamom, star anise, and coriander in a piece of cheesecloth and tie with twine to form a sachet. Add the rice to the pot, then the sachet and Scotch bonnet. Cook on low heat, stirring occasionally to toast the rice grains, for about 5 minutes. Add the water and coconut milk and simmer on low heat, uncovered, until the water has evaporated and the rice is tender, about 20 minutes. Remove the sachet and pepper. Use a fork to fluff the rice, and serve hot.

POMPANO
WITH "PEPPERPOT" BROTH

SERVES 4

Pepperpot in Jamaica is a hearty stew, and traditional versions remind me of bouyon in St. Lucia. Pepperpot is often made with callaloo and ground provisions. Some folks add pig tails, shrimp, or fish. In Jamaica, the fish pepperpots feature pompano, dorado, or marlin. I'd have it in people's homes or at small restaurants on Hellshire Beach outside of Portmore, where folks go for seafood and family beach vibes. I'm riffing off traditional Jamaican pepperpot by making a smooth sauce as opposed to a rustic stew.

GINGER LEMONGRASS FUMET

2 pounds fish bones, cleaned

Ice water

¼ cup extra-virgin olive oil

½ cup roughly chopped lemongrass

½ cup roughly chopped fresh ginger

BROTH

¼ cup extra-virgin olive oil

1½ cups sliced okra (¼-inch rounds)

1 cup sliced Spanish onion

1 cup peeled and finely diced cassava

2 tablespoons kosher salt

1 tablespoon chopped Scotch bonnet pepper

1 (14-ounce) can coconut milk

1 cup sliced scallions

4 cups tightly packed callaloo, leaves separated and stems thinly sliced (or spinach)

FISH

2 (1 to 2 pounds each) whole pompanos, gutted and scaled (ask your fishmonger)

6 tablespoons extra-virgin olive oil

4 tablespoons kosher salt

3 tablespoons Chili Oil (page 271)

Make the Ginger Lemongrass Fumet: In a large pot, add the fish bones and cover with ice water. Cover the pot and set aside for 1 hour. This helps to remove fishy impurities from the stock and produces a richer flavor.

Heat the oven to 400°F. Line a sheet pan with foil.

Drain the bones and chop into 5-inch pieces. Put the bones on the prepared pan and lightly dress with 2 tablespoons of the olive oil. Spread the bones evenly on the tray and roast until they develop a golden brown color, about 20 minutes.

In a medium stockpot, add the remaining 2 tablespoons olive oil and heat for 1 minute over medium. Add

the lemongrass and ginger and sauté, stirring for 2 minutes, allowing the aromatics to release.

Add the bones and cover with cold water by a depth of 1 inch. Reduce the heat to medium-low and bring to a simmer. Cook for 45 minutes, during which time the bones will have softened and the broth will appear cloudy. Don't heat the broth longer than 45 minutes, as doing so can develop a bitter taste.

Strain the stock through a fine-mesh strainer. Bring down to room temperature and store in quart containers. Use right away, refrigerate for up to 3 days, or freeze for up to 1 month.

Make the broth: In a medium saucepan, add the olive oil and heat over medium. Add the okra, onions, cassava, salt, and Scotch bonnet. Sweat, stirring to incorporate, until the vegetables are lightly caramelized, about 8 minutes. Add the fumet, coconut milk, and scallions. Raise the heat and bring to a boil, then boil for 6 minutes. Reduce the heat to low and simmer for 12 more minutes; you'll see the broth thicken and the cassava should be soft. Remove from the heat, then add the callaloo stems and leaves. Transfer the broth to a blender in batches, then puree until smooth. Put the blended broth back into the pot and cover with a lid to keep warm. Set aside.

Make the fish: Heat the oven to 400°F. Line a sheet pan with foil.

Using a paring knife, gently but firmly score the fish from the gill to the tail on both sides, along the belly's surface in crosshatches, about 2 inches apart. You want to go just through the skin surface, but not so deep that you cut into the meat. It should look like a stretched grid across the fish's surface. Drizzle the olive oil onto the fish and gently rub it all over the flesh. Season one side of the fish with 1 tablespoon of the salt, holding your hand about 6 inches above the fish to ensure the salt evenly covers the whole fish. Flip the fish over and repeat, then season the other fish with the remaining salt.

Place the fish on the sheet pan and roast until a cake tester or toothpick inserted meets no resistance, 20 to 25 minutes.

Divide the broth between 2 shallow serving bowls to a 1-inch depth. Place a fish in each, drizzle with the chili oil, and serve immediately.

ESCOVITCH-STYLE SNAPPER

SERVES 4

Jamaica has had many settlers over the centuries, including the Spaniards, who brought escabeche, a method of preservation using vinegar that originated from the Moors in Africa. In Jamaica, tradition says the whole fish is fried, then drenched with the escovitch, a bright medley of dressed peppers, sautéed onions, and carrots that adds acid to the rich, crispy fish. I drew inspiration from a seafood stall on Hellshire Beach, outside of Portmore. It's often served with a fried bammy and rice and peas. We don't do escovitch in St. Lucia, but I saw how different techniques and flavors could emerge from using similar ingredients. With my version, I make a sauce with the carrots while still using the traditional escovitch to top it.

1 cup carrot juice (or 8 jumbo carrots, peeled and juiced)

1¼ cups (2½ sticks) unsalted butter

¼ cup all-purpose flour

3 lemons, zested and juiced

½ cup rice wine vinegar

1 jumbo carrot, peeled and thinly sliced into ribbons

1 small red onion, thinly sliced

Ice water

¼ cup canola oil

4 (5-ounce) skin-on red snapper or black bass fillets

4 tablespoons kosher salt

1 red bell pepper, thinly sliced

1 bunch of cilantro, leaves picked

3 limes, zested and juiced

GARNISH
Chili Oil (page 271)

EQUIPMENT
Juicer (optional)

Mandoline (great for the ribboned jumbo carrot)

Heat the oven to 375°F.

In a medium saucepan on high heat, bring the carrot juice to boil. Once it comes to boil, reduce the heat to medium and continue simmering until the volume reduces by half, 10 to 12 minutes. Set aside.

In a small saucepan on medium heat, brown the butter: Melt 1 cup (two sticks) of the butter and allow it to foam, undisturbed, until you smell a nutty aroma. Milk solids will start to brown and appear speckled (a good indicator that it's ready) in about 8 minutes. Don't burn your butter! Turn off the heat and immediately transfer the brown butter to a mug or small bowl.

Make the carrot beurre blanc: Using the same saucepan, melt the remaining ¼ cup of butter. Whisk in the flour and reduce the heat to low. Cook until the flour no longer smells raw and the roux is a thick paste, about 6 minutes. Whisk the roux into the reduced carrot juice. Set over high heat and bring to a boil, then allow it to boil for 2 minutes, continuing to stir. The roux will thicken the mixture. Remove from the heat and set aside. Add the lemon zest and the brown butter and whisk to emulsify the mixture. Return the pan to low heat to cook until it becomes a smooth sauce, about 5 minutes. Add the lemon juice and stir again. Remove from the heat.

In a small saucepan, bring the rice vinegar to a boil over high heat. Add the carrot ribbons to the saucepan, then immediately remove from the heat. In a small bowl, add the onions and cover with ice water. Allow to soak for 5 minutes, then drain and set aside (this reduces the harsh flavor from the raw onion).

Heat a large cast-iron or heavy-bottomed skillet on high heat and add the canola oil. Season the fillets evenly with the salt, then place the fish skin side down in the skillet. Allow them to crisp for 2 minutes or until the skin tightens and releases from the skillet surface. Place in the oven until the fish is cooked through, about 4 minutes. Use a toothpick or cake tester to check for doneness; there should be no resistance.

In a small bowl, add the red bell peppers, drained onions, pickled carrots with the cooked vinegar, and the cilantro. Dress with the lime zest and juice. Transfer the carrot beurre blanc to a serving plate, then place the fillets on top. Place a serving of the vegetables on top of each fish.

To garnish: Drizzle with chili oil for a subtle, spicy kick. Serve immediately.

TRINIDADIAN CORN AND PUMPKIN SOUP

SERVES 4 TO 6

This is a filling, humble dish that I especially love to make when hosting friends from Trinidad and Tobago. It's also *the* cure-all for hangovers during Carnival season when the drinking and dancing are at peak levels. I experienced my first Carnival in Trinidad, while I was living in Jamaica, which was quite an initiation.

J'ouvert—Kwéyòl for "opening day"—sets off Carnival each year. Following Lent, the occasion blends centuries-old traditions from African and French religious and spiritual practices. Carnival has its own flavor in the different countries where it's celebrated, but you can generally count on thousands of people ornately dressed and reveling in folktales brought to life. There's calypso dance, percussive music, stilt walking, stick fighting—a mixture of traditional rituals from Africa and the evolution of those expressions over time in the diaspora. Carnival is a big deal. It's a party, but it's not just about partying if you understand the subtext.

Trinidad is known for their extravagant costumes; it's the second biggest carnival after Brazil. (Brazil received the highest number of enslaved Africans, at eleven million, and they were the last country to abolish slavery, in 1888. Today Brazil has the largest number of African-descended people outside of the African continent.) During Carnival, your worries are thrown to the side; you let loose and release inhibitions. Frankly, not giving a damn is totally accepted. Each band has revelers hanging from the sides of huge trucks, and partiers wear bright colors with lots of feathers. Everyone's bare skin glistens after all the dancing.

If, like me, you're not in the parade, but you're dancing, sweating close to loud, imbibing, happy people. The music takes you, and you best allow it. It's not how you look anyway, it's how you feel. At least that's what I tell myself! Rum courage is a thing. And then, hours later when it's over, you've gotta eat.

2 tablespoons coconut oil

1 small Spanish onion, chopped

2 celery stalks, sliced

2 scallions, sliced

4 garlic cloves, minced

¾ cup split peas

1 red bell pepper, chopped

1 medium sweet potato, peeled and roughly chopped

1 bunch of thyme

¼ bunch of shado beni (culantro)

1 teaspoon freshly ground black pepper

Kosher salt

3 cups vegetable stock

3 cups warm water

5 ears of corn, sliced into 3-inch medallions

1 (14-ounce) can coconut milk

1 cup peeled and chopped pumpkin

1 medium carrot, chopped

1 Scotch bonnet pepper

DUMPLINGS

1 cup all-purpose flour

¼ teaspoon kosher salt

½ cup warm water

In a large stockpot or Dutch oven, heat the coconut oil on medium. Add the onion, celery, scallions, and garlic and sauté, stirring just to incorporate, until soft and translucent, about 5 minutes.

Add the split peas, bell pepper, and sweet potato, then stir and add the thyme, shado beni, black pepper, and kosher salt to taste. Cook, stirring to incorporate, until fragrant, 2 to 3 minutes. Pour in the vegetable stock along with the warm water. Bring the pot to a boil, then reduce the heat to medium-low. Cover and simmer, stirring occasionally, until the split peas are soft, about 30 minutes.

Using an immersion blender, puree the entire contents of the pot. Add the corn medallions, coconut milk, pumpkin, carrot, and Scotch bonnet. Stir and maintain at a simmer.

Make the dumplings: In a medium bowl, add the flour and salt. Gradually add water in intervals while kneading the flour mixture until it comes together into a cohesive ball of dough.

Pinch off a 2-inch piece of dough (about ½ ounce) and roll between your hands to create a long, tube-like dumpling.

Repeat with the remaining dough. Add all the dumplings to the pot at the same time, and gently stir. Continue to simmer the soup, no lid this time, for about another 20 minutes, until the dumplings rise to the top as they cook through. Remove the Scotch bonnet pepper, and taste—add additional salt to your preference. Serve hot.

TABLET KOKOYE

SERVES 4

You'll see these coconut drops throughout the Caribbean, particularly in Haiti; my Auntie Barbara, who lived in Kingston, used to make them. She called them "tablet kwéyòl," but they're pretty much the same all over. You'll see them individually wrapped in the markets; all the street vendors have them. Traditionally we use fresh coconut. The coconut is roughly chopped so the candy has big chunks of it, which makes for a fun texture.

When I lived in Ocho Rios, I would come down to Kingston on my days off and spend time with Auntie Barbara. She was actually my dad's aunt, so my great aunt. She was in her late sixties, and she was a trip. When I visited, we'd sit on the veranda that overlooked the city to watch the sun go down and the lights come on. This recipe is based on her version, where she used dried coconut chunks.

4 cups water

2 cups dried coconut chunks (or sweetened coconut flakes)

1½ cups raw coconut sugar

1 teaspoon ground cinnamon

1 star anise pod

2 teaspoons vanilla extract

Line a sheet pan with parchment paper and set aside.

In a large skillet, bring the water to a boil. Add the coconut chunks, coconut sugar, cinnamon, and star anise. Reduce the heat to low and cook, stirring occasionally, until the star anise and cinnamon become aromatic and the ingredients begin to meld and develop a slight caramel coloring, about 30 minutes. Remove the star anise and discard.

Add the vanilla extract to the pot and continue to cook on low for 3 minutes, stirring to incorporate.

Use two spoons to scoop the mixture from the pot and transfer to the sheet pan in 8 servings of about 2 tablespoons each. Allow the tablet kokoye to cool completely. Enjoy as a snack or dessert. They can hold in an airtight container at room temperature for up to 2 weeks.

PASSION FRUIT RUM PUNCH

MAKES 4

This is the kind of drink that instantly transports me to the Caribbean. I can immediately feel the sunset on my skin on Negril Beach. The cliffside has unobstructed views of the ocean, and it's the best place to watch the day slip away. I drink rum when I'm in the Caribbean; it gives me a sense of place.

You'll find various fruit rum punches throughout Jamaica, but this one draws a bit from home in St. Lucia. Passion fruit is one of my favorite fruits. It has a tart flavor that makes me happy and reminds me of my childhood. As a breakfast snack, my dad used to sprinkle granulated sugar on a ripe papaya and squeeze lime on top. It occurred to me that his morning treat might make a lovely cocktail, and with this combo, I was right.

Using a paring knife, slice the papaya in half. Use a spoon to seed the papaya. Cut one-third of the papaya into four 1-inch wedges for garnish and set aside.

Chop the rest of the papaya and place the pieces in a cocktail shaker. Use a muddler until the papaya is mashed into a pulp, 10 to 20 seconds.

Fill the cocktail shaker with ice. Add the white rum, dark rum, passion fruit puree, agave syrup, and lime juice. Shake well. Add several ice cubes to your rocks glasses. Strain the mix into the glasses.

Add the champagne as a float; each glass gets ½ ounce.

Prepare your garnish: Use a paring knife to make a small slit in the tip of the papaya wedges. Coat them evenly in the sugar and place them on the glass rims, then add a lime peel to each glass. Serve immediately.

1 small ripe papaya

Ice, for chilling and for serving

4 ounces white rum (such as Bounty)

4 ounces dark rum (such as Chairman's or Appleton)

4 ounces passion fruit puree

2 ounces agave syrup

2 ounces fresh lime juice (reserve the peel for garnish)

2 ounces champagne (or dry sparkling white wine)

GARNISH

4 tablespoons sugar

4 strips of lime peel

JAMAICAN BLUE DRAWS

MAKES 16

This is a traditional recipe for blue draws, a cornmeal pudding that's wrapped in banana leaves and boiled. During Christmastime in Jamaica, some people make these at home and share them as offerings to friends, similar to when you make a big pot of gumbo in Louisiana and share with friends or neighbors. I've seen versions of this dish all over the Caribbean during the holidays, reflecting the influence of Ghanaians. Blue draws are documented in Jamaica back to 1740. It originated with Ghana's Fante people who call it dokono, white corn pudding wrapped in banana leaf. In other parts of Ghana, it's referred to as comie, or kenkey—you can see this origin in the term that Bajans use for the dish, conkie. In St. Lucia we call it paime, and in Trinidad they call it pastelle. In Jamaican vernacular (and some Black vernacular in the States), "draws" means "underwear," and the twine you use to tie up the banana leaf parcels evokes the old-school drawstrings that would hold up your undies. It's said the "blue" comes from the color of the parcel after cooking.

2 cups yellow cornmeal

1½ cups cane sugar

1 cup cassava flour

½ teaspoon ground cinnamon

½ teaspoon ground nutmeg

½ teaspoon kosher salt

2 cups coconut milk

1 medium sweet potato, peeled and grated

1 cup sweetened coconut flakes

⅓ cup raisins

2 teaspoons vanilla extract

16 (8-inch square) banana leaves (about 2 pounds total)

EQUIPMENT

About 8 feet of butcher twine, cut into 6-inch lengths

In a large bowl, add the cornmeal, sugar, cassava flour, cinnamon, nutmeg, and salt. Whisk to combine. Add the coconut milk, whisking to make a thick, smooth batter. Add the grated sweet potato, coconut flakes, raisins, and vanilla. Stir to combine well.

Make the parcels: On a work surface, spread out a banana leaf. Spoon 3 tablespoons of the batter onto the center of the banana leaf, forming a small rectangle about 3 inches long (from top to bottom), and 1 inch wide (left to right). Cover the batter by folding the leaf over lengthwise, first by bringing one side over, then following with the second. The parcel should look like a standard-size envelope. Rotate the envelope laterally so the openings are on the left and right sides of the work surface. Now wrap, folding each side over to seal the batter inside. Use the butcher twine to tie the parcel closed, with one 6-inch strip in each direction so all sides of the parcel are enclosed. It looks like a present! Repeat with all the ingredients; you should have 16 parcels. (These can keep covered overnight in the refrigerator.)

Bring a large pot of water to boil over high heat.

Place all the parcels in the large pot to cook, uncovered, until the parcels are firm, 20 to 30 minutes. Check by carefully pressing the center of a parcel; it should be firm to the touch. Use a slotted spoon to remove and place the parcels on a plate. Cool for at least 10 minutes. You can enjoy right away or reserve for later. We enjoy these at room temperature. They will keep in the refrigerator for 2 days.

SORREL

SERVES 6

Throughout the Caribbean, we enjoy sorrel (also known as roselle, botanical name *Hibiscus sabdariffa*) as a daytime beverage during the Christmas season, and believe me, it's not Christmas if you don't have sorrel. While sorrel has its origins in West Africa and Asia (it's botanically related to okra), it's been documented in Jamaica as early as 1707, brought alongside the imported enslaved Africans, who were steeping the flowers with spices for beverages and medicinal purposes. Think bissap in Senegal, zobo in Nigeria, and in Mexico, agua de Jamaica—note the nod to the Caribbean! In the States, many southern Black cultures have red drink, where the absence of sorrel led to incorporating other reddish plants to make syrups, vinegars, and liqueurs. Red drink is also significant in the commemoration of Juneteenth, which originated with Black Texans.

Sorrel became popular during Christmas because that's the time of year when the flowering occurred in the Caribbean and West Africa, but now it's cultivated year-round. When the holidays come, everyone makes their batch. When I moved to Jamaica, I had little awareness about the food cultures of other Caribbean nations. During my first Christmas there, I started seeing sorrel at restaurants and shops, and it hit me like, "Oh! They do this here, too!" I was learning about the similarities and differences between regional cuisines.

In the evenings, you can add a little rum to the serving as an aperitif. We drink sorrel through the new year.

1 cinnamon stick, broken into pieces

2 star anise pods

3 cloves

2½ quarts water

1 cup sugar, plus more to taste

½ cup diced fresh ginger

2 cups dried sorrel

1 lime, sliced into rounds

1 pinch white rice (optional)

SERVING

Ice

1 orange, peeled and thinly sliced into rounds

St. Lucian dark rum, as desired

Heat a medium pot on medium-low for 2 minutes. Add the cinnamon, star anise, and cloves. Toast, stirring gently, until fragrant, 1 to 2 minutes. Add the water and sugar, stir to incorporate, then bring to a simmer over medium-low heat. Add the ginger and let simmer for 5 minutes to infuse the water. Add the dried sorrel and lime rounds. Remove from the heat. Let the sorrel and aromatics steep at room temperature for at least 45 minutes. For a more potent flavor, you can allow it to steep overnight or for a couple of days in the refrigerator. If you want effervescence in the sorrel, add the rice while it steeps overnight or in the refrigerator; the slow ferment is my mum's trick.

To serve: Strain the sorrel with a fine sieve and discard all the solids, then pour the drink into a pitcher. Serve over ice and garnish with orange slices. Drink as it is or add rum.

Liming

Liming is the act of doing nothing while hanging with your friends and family over food and drink and good vibes. If you're going on a lime in Jamaica, you can expect chill time on the beach with lots of laughter and equal parts rum. It might be what Black folks in the States call a kick back. There is no other purpose to the gathering than to just be with one another, and it often happens organically. Liming as a term originates in Trinidad and Tobago and is widely used throughout the region, though there are as many origin stories for the actual term as there are people who use it.

As in any place in the Americas that enslaved African people, the ability to rest after having your body worked to exhaustion was often branded as lazy and codified as illegal. Owing to the strong legacy of rebellion and revolt throughout all places and periods of slavery, gathering while Black, for any reason other than explicit labor, was seen as an opportunity for them to strategize and plan revolts (of which there were countless numbers) and thus treated with great suspicion by colonizers. So often today, our music and dances are banned or restricted. While lots of joy comes from liming, we know that our rest is political, too.

MIAMI
Florida

AN AFRO LATIN DIASPORA

Bienvenidos. Sak pasé.

Back in Ocho Rios, I'd decided that I wanted to leave the resort world of the Caribbean and try fine dining restaurants in the U.S. My chef told me that to work well there, I'd need culinary school. He told me I'd learn the foundational French recipes and techniques that are found in most fine dining environments in the States: the French mother sauces, which aren't in the Caribbean pantry; meat and fish butchery; knife cuts; wine knowledge; and patisserie. It was less about wanting to go to the States, and more about the available resources if I went.

As a chef, you never stop learning, and school was simply another place for me to get information. School in New York was my revelation that cooking could take me to places farther than I'd dreamed of, but after I finished school and worked a few months in a fine dining French restaurant, I didn't want to stay. I decided to head to Miami, where my sister Maya had been living. I told myself that after one year in Miami, I'd move back home to St. Lucia to open a restaurant. Around this time, I was always putting an end date on living in the U.S., extending my stays to get the knowledge I felt I needed.

I was naive; I thought all of Miami was like South Beach. My sister was married, had a child, and was living that suburban life outside the city—definitely not the routine I'd imagined. I hated it at first. I was in my early twenties, and I wanted to be on the scene, living The Life (whatever that was!)—not quiet residential streets. The drive to the beach was long, and the traffic in Miami is horrific. I wasn't making friends because I wasn't meeting people, and the city is spread out, so it can be hard to know where to go if you don't know where to go. Initially, I worked at a hotel where everyone was older than me. Ten months into my time, though, Miami Carnival popped up in October. Suddenly I was around my people! This was my first time seeing the many Caribbean folks in the city socializing together and creating an authentic Caribbean vibe. That flipped the switch. I stayed in Miami for eleven years.

Maya had told me how diverse Miami would be from a culinary perspective, and I wanted to learn about Afro Latin Caribbean food. I didn't realize it at the time, but I was essentially creating my own canon. I learned from kitchen colleagues and independent restaurants, and I soaked up the culture in a city that's home to Caribbean and Latin American diaspora cultures, with primary influence from Indigenous and African cultures. I was able to get a couple of jobs off the extension of my student visa, one of them working in Norman Van Aken's namesake fine dining Latin Caribbean restaurant.

I went for a stage (the French term for internship, essentially an audition, where the chefs observe you and you see how their kitchen works), and I was hired the same day. Norman was cooking with ingredients I knew from my background, like yuca (cassava to me) and conch, and he was doing intricate preparations with ingredients foreign to Caribbean repertoire. He had a cracked conch chowder where the conch was sliced thin and lightly breaded. The bright yellow broth was a base of clams and mussels, with orange juice, Scotch bonnet, saffron, star anise, and coconut milk. He made a puree with yuca, stuffed it into shrimp, then breaded and fried them. Deconstructing ingredients, using precise knife cuts, and using wine as a fortifying ingredient were all new ways of eating these foods I'd grown up with.

I started to ask myself why we as Caribbean people weren't presenting more of our food in this manner, out of curiosity, not as a criticism of what we did back home. We eat out a lot in St. Lucia, but restaurants for sitting down were for special occasions. Some had expressions that were in the arena of fine dining, but not like what I was seeing here. Growing up, many of us in the Caribbean are taught that the American way is the gold standard. Part of this is systemic, as our countries have been used as global assets by colonizing nations. Our countries were violently made to focus on cash crops with enslaved labor, then penalized for fighting for our independence (consider the example of Haiti), then restricted by dominating nations in where or how we could trade. It's an ongoing effort among many Caribbean nations to assert our political and economic value and cultural pride, and this happens in part by better understanding our history and finding a balance between influence and imitation. I wanted to be inspired by the American innovation I was witnessing, but I didn't want to lose the essence and respect I had for my Caribbean heritage.

I liked the possibility of being able to interpret my own food in a fine dining environment. At the time, I wanted to go back to St. Lucia and cook our food in a cheffed-up treatment. Often in the chef world, we use the word "elevated" to describe this kind of food, but writer Osayi Endolyn has challenged me that this echoes colonial ideas. Our food is already elevated, she told me as we worked on this book; that's why chefs like Norman were reaching for it! I am continually working to reframe my language to address these ongoing shifts that come from unlearning and decolonizing. At the time, I was excited about what could happen in my hands with this knowledge.

My student visa expired. I'd been at Norman's for just under one year. I had put in the paperwork early, but the waiting period was lengthy. I had to work undocumented for a time, so I found a catering side job to pay me in cash. I was nervous because I had no idea how long it would take for my paperwork to come through. During this period, I wasn't able to move freely. If something happened and I was pulled over and deported, I'd never be able to come back to the States. If I voluntarily left to go home for any reason, I wouldn't be able to return unless I applied and received a new visa. I knew people who'd been waiting for years; that option was basically a no-go. My experience with U.S. Immigration was horrible. They treated us so rudely. I would take unpaid time off to wait for hours in offices where they wouldn't let you eat or drink water, and sometimes they'd direct you to a line, and you'd realize hours later that they'd told you the wrong one. Then they'd tell you to come back the next day, as if I could afford another day off without pay. I watched officials yell at people who simply didn't have fluency in English, a lot of them Black or brown folks. Did they think yelling would suddenly make these folks speak better English? I could never understand that.

After nine stressful months, my paperwork came through. I got a job at the Versace Mansion.

Gianni Versace's private residence was known as the Versace Mansion, formally the Villa Casa Casuarina. After his death in 1997, it was sold as a residence, but the new owner transitioned it to a members-only club that accepted celebrity and high-roller clientele. At the time, the space felt like I was walking around Florence, Italy, instead of steps away from the beach in South Florida. Beautiful mosaics, fountains, gold-leaf details, and winding staircases. I was hired as a sous chef, then became the chef. The sky was the limit, given all the resources, but I was often catering to famous diners who wanted basic dishes that didn't allow for much creative exploration. My last year at the mansion, however, a restaurant consultant from Atlanta was hired to support the leadership team. Larry Miller showed romantic interest in me, but I was not about to date a colleague. Or so I thought. A year later, we had both moved on from the mansion, but we got married at the place!

When the recession hit in 2008, everyone was getting laid off; businesses were cutting back. I was able to find work at Scarpetta, a restaurant at the Fontainebleau hotel on Miami Beach. The job was a necessity because it's what I could get. I also thought it would be great to learn Italian and Mediterranean influences. By now, I'd determined I would not be moving back to St. Lucia on my original timeline. Larry and I were figuring out our lives together. I came on as executive sous chef and was promoted to executive chef. I learned about northern Italian cuisine, but thanks to the staff, I was getting schooled in the Latin diaspora. That and my time in the Caribbean and Central American restaurants around town would be influential takeaways.

I was cooking alongside folks from the Dominican Republic, Haiti, Cuba, Puerto Rico, Guatemala, Honduras, and Nicaragua, and a few Brazilians. The food they made for staff meal, which we ate as a team before dinner service, was always an expression of their home country's food. Yet again, I was excited to be exposed to interpretations of ingredients found on the menus across the Caribbean and Latin America. In St. Lucia, we like to fry our ripe plantains (also known as maduros), but we don't have a preparation like tostones, where underripe plantains are mashed and twice fried. It was a constant reminder that we come from similar but different places.

The recipes in this chapter center on my exposure to these Afro Latin culinary traditions. We've got Griot, Haiti's beloved fried pork mainstay (page 210). I fell in love with Shrimp Ceviche (page 187) because even in the seafood heaven of St. Lucia we don't have any! And the Coconut Flan (page 201) is going to set any day right.

HAM AND CHEESE CROQUETAS

SERVES 6

Croquetas in Miami are good any time of day; they were a definitive aspect of my eating there. Larry and I would go to a Cuban coffee shop called David's Café. We'd get a Cuban coffee, a pastelito, and a ham and cheese croqueta. Some mornings, we'd walk along the beach and have that quiet moment to start the day. Croquetas are also a lovely way to tee up the evening. We lived on a cute street called Española Way, neighbors with Tapas y Tintos, a spot owned by our friends Nicolas and Jordana. Nick's dad was the chef, the sweetest, hardest working man. We'd enjoy a lovely chilled red wine and croquetas before heading out for a night of dancing.

¼ cup (½ stick) unsalted butter

½ cup minced Spanish onion

2 tablespoons kosher salt, plus more as needed

2½ cups all-purpose flour

4 cups whole milk

1 teaspoon sweet paprika

⅛ teaspoon cayenne pepper

1 pinch freshly grated nutmeg

1 cup finely diced chicken (from a rotisserie chicken or poached chicken breast)

½ cup minced jamón serrano (Spanish cured ham)

1 cup grated Manchego cheese

Canola oil, for frying

2 large eggs, beaten

1 cup panko breadcrumbs

1 tablespoon water

Line a sheet pan with parchment paper.

In a medium saucepan, melt the butter over medium heat. Add the onions and cook, stirring occasionally, until they are translucent, about 5 minutes. Season with 1 tablespoon of the salt. Add 1½ cups of the flour and whisk until smooth. Cook, whisking continually, until the flour is cooked through and starts to take on a golden color, 5 to 8 minutes. Pour the milk into the flour mixture and cook, stirring continuously, until you have a thick sauce, about 2 minutes. Whisk in the paprika, cayenne pepper, and nutmeg. Add the chicken and ham, and sprinkle in the remaining 1 tablespoon of salt. Stir with a spatula and cook for another 2 minutes to incorporate. Remove from the heat. Use a spatula to fold in the cheese. The mixture should be thick and easy to mold in your hands. Carefully pick up a bit and try to form a ball with your hands; you want it firm to the touch but still a bit wet.

Spread the mixture on the lined sheet pan and let it cool to room temperature, or at least until cool enough to handle.

Meanwhile, in a small, deep saucepan, add canola oil to a depth of 2 inches (about 2 cups) and heat over medium-high to 350°F; check using an instant-read thermometer. Line a plate with paper towels.

When the mixture is cool, transfer to a piping bag. Cut about ¼ inch from the tip and pipe the filling onto a cutting board in 3-inch strips (you're aiming for about 24 croquetas).

Prepare your breading station: In 3 separate shallow plates, add the remaining 1 cup of flour, the beaten eggs, and the breadcrumbs. Add the water to the eggs and stir gently. Add a pinch of salt to each plate and gently mix.

Take one piece of filling and gently roll it in the flour, then dip it into the egg wash and let the excess drip off, then roll it in the breadcrumbs to coat, and transfer to a plate. Repeat with all the croquetas.

Add the croquetas to the hot oil in small batches, making sure that you don't crowd the pan and they are completely covered in the oil. Fry for 2 minutes, until they have a nice golden color, then use a spatula or tongs to flip the croquetas and fry for another minute. Transfer them to the paper towels to drain. Repeat with all the croquetas and serve hot.

GUAVA AND CHEESE PASTELITOS

MAKES 6

The Cuban cafés in Miami are always bustling. They are social havens for mixed generations to gather; you'll see folks catching up and sometimes playing dominoes. Any Cuban café or market you walk into, there will be these glossy pastries staring at you, but the heavy hitter spot in Miami is Versailles. While they're a full-service restaurant, they're chiefly known for their coffee, Cubano sandwiches, and pastries. I can't resist the pastelitos. The warm, jammy filling joins with cream cheese encased in the flakiest pastry dough. You can't go wrong starting your day with the rocket fuel of a cafecito (I could count on that triple espresso with sugar), or a café con leche, and this classic sweet bite.

Position a rack in the center and heat the oven to 375°F. Line a sheet pan with parchment paper.

In a small bowl, whisk the egg yolk with the milk until combined. Lightly flour a work surface. Unfold the puff pastry and cut it into six 4-inch squares.

Transfer the squares to the sheet pan. Place 1 slice of guava paste and 1 slice of cream cheese in the center of a square. Fold each square in half and press the ends with a fork to crimp the edges. Brush the pastry edges with some of the egg wash. Refrigerate until firm, about 15 minutes. Brush the pastries with the remaining egg wash and sprinkle with sugar.

Bake in the center of the oven, rotating the pan from front to back halfway through, until the pastries are golden, about 30 minutes. Let the pastelitos cool in the pan for at least 30 minutes before serving, to allow the molten guava to cool slightly.

1 large egg yolk

1 tablespoon whole milk

All-purpose flour, for dusting

1 (14-ounce) package all-butter puff pastry, thawed

6 ounces guava paste, cut into 6 slices (1 inch thick and 2 inches long)

6 ounces cream cheese, chilled and cut into 6 slices (1 inch thick and 2 inches long)

Turbinado sugar, for sprinkling

BEEF EMPANADAS

SERVES 6

You'll see empanadas in the Cuban coffee shops throughout Miami. When I'd get my morning coffee, I'd grab one on the run. Venezuelans put a boiled egg in their empanadas. Cubans may add olives and raisins. Mine lean closer to the Venezuelans' style.

Achiote seeds (also called annatto seeds) are bright orange, nestled inside red pods. We had an achiote tree in our backyard growing up. The seeds have a mild, sweet, nutty, and floral taste; they're less about flavor and more about color. In Mexican and Caribbean cooking, we use them to add color, but you can substitute turmeric. In the U.S., achiote seeds are typically found in the spice section.

DOUGH

2 cups all-purpose flour, plus more for dusting

1 tablespoon cane sugar

1 teaspoon kosher salt

¼ cup (½ stick) unsalted butter, cut into small pieces and chilled

2 large eggs, lightly beaten

¼ cup dry white wine

1 teaspoon white vinegar

FILLING

1 tablespoon extra-virgin olive oil

½ teaspoon ground achiote seeds

¼ pound lean ground beef

1 tablespoon kosher salt

1 teaspoon freshly ground black pepper

1 small Spanish onion, finely diced

¼ cup finely diced poblano pepper

1 garlic clove, minced

1 teaspoon sweet paprika

¼ teaspoon cayenne pepper

¼ cup tomato paste

¼ cup chicken stock

2 tablespoons chopped cilantro

1 cup grated Manchego cheese

Canola oil, for frying (optional)

SALSA VERDE

2 cups extra-virgin olive oil

3 bunches of flat-leaf parsley, minced

1 bunch of mint, leaves picked and minced

6 garlic cloves, grated

2 anchovies, minced (optional, but adds a lovely briny flavor)

1 tablespoon capers, drained and minced

1 teaspoon kosher salt

3 lemons, zested

Make the dough: In a food processor, pulse together the flour, sugar, and salt until combined, about 5 pulses. With the processor running, add the diced butter, slowly feeding in the pieces. Continue to pulse until the mixture resembles a coarse meal, about 2 minutes. Add the eggs, wine, and vinegar and keep pulsing until the dough just comes together, about 1 minute.

Transfer the dough to a lightly floured work surface. Using your hands, gently knead the dough until it's smooth, about 5 minutes. Wrap the dough in plastic wrap and refrigerate until firm, about 1 hour.

Make the filling: In a medium skillet, heat the olive oil on medium-low. Add the ground achiote and stir to incorporate. Raise the heat to high. Add the ground beef to the skillet and cook, using a wooden spoon to break up the meat so it cooks evenly. Cook the meat until it starts to brown, about 3 minutes. Add the salt and pepper and stir. Add the onion, poblano pepper, and garlic and cook, stirring occasionally, until the onion is softened, about 5 minutes. Stir in the paprika and cayenne. Add the tomato paste and stir again to fully incorporate. Add the chicken stock and bring to a simmer, then reduce to low heat. Cook, stirring occasionally, until the liquid has nearly evaporated, about 10 minutes. Stir in the cilantro and remove from the heat. Let the filling cool for about 10 minutes, just until it's easier to handle. Mix in the Manchego and set aside.

Shape the empanadas: Spread a generous amount of flour on a flat work surface. Coat the chilled dough with flour and roll it out to ⅛ inch thick. Use a 4½- to 5-inch round biscuit cutter to stamp out as many rounds as possible. Reroll the dough scraps and stamp out additional rounds if possible (you should have about 24). Don't waste a scrap! Brush any excess flour off the rounds and cover them with plastic wrap.

Assemble the empanadas: Work with 1 round at a time and keep the rest covered. Spoon 2 teaspoons of the filling onto one side of the dough round. Fold the dough over in half to enclose the filling and crimp the edges with a fork to seal in the filling.

Cover the empanada with plastic wrap while you form the remaining pastries.

(recipe continues)

At this point, the empanadas can be cooked or stored. Uncooked empanadas can be frozen for up to one month: Place them flat on a sheet pan (not touching) and when frozen solid, transfer to a freezer-safe bag.

Make the salsa verde: In a small bowl, use a fork to combine the olive oil, parsley, mint, garlic, anchovies (if using), capers, salt, and lemon zest. Mix well and reserve.

Cook the empanadas: To bake them, position a rack in the middle and heat the oven to 350°F. Line a sheet pan with parchment paper. Space the empanadas 2 inches apart on the sheet. Bake in the center of the oven until golden brown, 10 to 12 minutes.

To fry the empanadas, use a large deep skillet and add canola oil to a depth of 2 inches (about 3 cups) and heat on medium-high to 350°F; check using an instant-read thermometer. Heat the oven to 300°F to keep them warm. Line a plate with paper towels.

Fry about 4 empanadas at a time. After about 1 minute, turn them once and continue frying for another minute, until the empanadas are golden brown and crisp all over. Use a slotted spoon to remove them from the oil and drain on paper towels. You can transfer the empanadas to a sheet pan and keep them warm in the oven. Repeat with the remaining empanadas.

Serve the baked or fried empanadas immediately with the salsa verde.

SPICY BLACK BEANS

SERVES 6

Black beans are the unsung, hardworking star of many Latin meals. They're on every plate, but many of us take them for granted! Black beans take skill, man. Puerto Sagua on Miami Beach has the best black beans I've enjoyed, and I've consumed a lot. They'd plate them up as a side dish to vaca frita (check out my version on page 188). The fried crispy beef was a stunner, but I kept coming back for the beans. I always marveled that the beans were perfectly cooked, every one intact and not mushy. The zesty and spicy flavor is great, but the earthy cumin really sets it off. I'd always leave trying to pinpoint the precise spices I tasted. Puerto Sagua was never going to share their secret. But I think this take, featuring a piquant tomatillo salsa, comes pretty close! Note the advance preparation of soaking the beans overnight.

BEANS

4 cups dried black beans

1 tablespoon extra-virgin olive oil

3 small Spanish onions, finely diced

2 red bell peppers, finely diced

1 poblano pepper, finely diced

1 jalapeño, finely diced

1 tablespoon sliced garlic

1 tablespoon red chili flakes

½ teaspoon ground cumin

5 tablespoons kosher salt

2 tablespoons Tabasco ancho chili sauce

TOMATILLO SALSA

2 cups whole fresh tomatillos, husks removed

½ bunch of cilantro

½ jalapeño

1 lime, juiced

1 garlic clove

1 tablespoon kosher salt

SERVING SUGGESTION

This is a great companion with Griot (page 210), Tostones with Avocado (page 182), and steamed white rice.

Make the beans: In a large bowl, combine the beans and enough water to cover. Soak the beans at room temperature overnight (or for at least 4 hours). After soaking, drain the beans and set aside.

In a medium saucepot, add the olive oil. Sweat the onions, bell peppers, poblano, jalapeño, and garlic over medium heat, stirring occasionally, until they begin to color, about 3 minutes. Add the chili flakes and cumin and sweat until fragrant, about 1 more minute. (We're going to season the beans with salt at the end of cooking, not during. Adding salt too early can harden the outer layer and slow the cooking process. Some say it's a myth, but I believe it!)

Add the beans and enough fresh water to cover them by 4 inches. Simmer, uncovered, for 1 hour and then check for doneness. The beans are ready when they're tender enough to smush easily between your fingers. Transfer one-third of the beans to a blender or food processor and carefully puree (make sure to crack the lid to allow steam to escape), or use a handheld immersion blender to partially puree the beans in the pot. This helps make the beans super creamy. If removing to puree, return the pureed beans to the saucepot.

Now make the tomatillo salsa: In the blender (no need to clean it if you pureed beans; it's all going to the same place), add the tomatillos, cilantro, jalapeño, lime juice, garlic, and salt. Puree until smooth. Add the salsa to the beans.

Season the beans with the salt and Tabasco and serve. You'll want a nap soon after!

TOSTONES
WITH AVOCADO

SERVES 2

You'll find tostones in Haitian and Cuban restaurants around Miami. Plantain is unbelievably versatile, and tostones, made with green-skinned underripe plantains, are the perfect snack. In St. Lucia, we don't fry green plantains (except for chips; otherwise we boil or steam them), but I came to prefer this application after living in Miami. Since that time, it's become my personal breakfast meal, but typically you see this dish as a side with entrees like roasted or mojo chicken with rice and peas.

To make tostones, you need to know how to peel unripe plantain; unlike bananas, the peel doesn't easily fall away from the fruit. I remember when I was nine or ten, my dad asked me to peel some. Despite my effort, it was not going well. He kind of yelled at me like, "You don't know how to peel plantain? You're from the Caribbean!" I was so embarrassed! But it was also funny. He told me to score the plantain and submerge it in hot water so the peel can pull away from the flesh. This way you end up preserving most of the plantain, as without this step a lot of the flesh will come off with the peel. After that day I never forgot how to peel plantains, and that's how I'll teach you to do it here.

TOSTONES
2 underripe green plantains

Boiling water, as needed

Canola oil, for frying

1 teaspoon kosher salt

DIP
1 beefsteak tomato, diced

1 Florida avocado or 2 Hass avocados, large diced

2 tablespoons minced flat-leaf parsley

1 tablespoon Garlic Oil (page 271)

¼ teaspoon Ginger-Chili Oil (page 269)

1 teaspoon kosher salt

Prepare the tostones: Use a paring knife to cut the tips off each plantain. Following the plantain lengthwise on the outer curve, make an incision just deep enough to pierce the peel. Repeat the lengthwise incision on the inner curve. Place the whole plantains in a large bowl and cover with boiling water. Allow the plantains to rest submerged in the water for 15 minutes. Use tongs to remove the plantains from the bowl and set them on a flat work surface. Insert the paring knife at the end of one incision and flick the peel up to expose the flesh. Use your finger to run up the full length of the plantain to gently remove the peel. Repeat on the other side to gently remove the second peel, then repeat on the remaining plantain.

Slice the plantain into 2-inch-thick pieces.

In a medium saucepan, add canola oil to a depth of at least 2 inches (about 2 cups) and heat on medium to 350°F; check using an instant-read thermometer. Line a plate with paper towels.

Add a couple of the plantain chunks, ensuring that you have at least 1 inch of space in between them. Fry for 1 minute on each side, then flip and fry for another minute. You're not frying for color and doneness yet; this is to partially cook the plantain and get the starches going. Use tongs or a slotted spoon to transfer the fried chunks to the paper towels. Continue until all the plantain chunks have been fried once.

Move to a flat work surface. Place one plantain chunk on your cutting board at a time and use a small sauté pan or heavy-bottomed bowl to smash the chunk until it is ⅛ inch to ¼ inch thick. Repeat until all the plantain chunks are smashed into patties.

Return the oil in the saucepan to 350°F. Line another plate with paper towels.

Fry a couple of the patties at a time to prevent crowding. On this fry, you're looking for the tostones to develop a golden brown color, about 1 minute on each side. Remove from the oil and let cool on the paper towels. Season the tostones with the kosher salt.

Make the dip: In a small bowl, add the tomato, avocado, parsley, garlic oil, and ginger-chili oil. Season with the salt and stir to combine.

Serve the tostones immediately with the dip.

SHRIMP CEVICHE

SERVES 6

I'm lucky to have crossed paths with people who've generously shared their culture through food. Alejandro Choi was a Peruvian sous chef at the Versace Mansion; he did all the crudos—raw, lightly dressed fish dishes. (He'd also make papa rellena—mashed potatoes with beef and a boiled egg in the middle that was so good.) I'd always ask for extra cancha (roasted or deep-fried corn nuts) with my crudo because I love the texture combination. He treated the seafood with respect and care. With ceviche, some assume it's a random mix of seafood, salt, and citrus. But in Peru, there are intentional combinations of certain peppers with certain seafood, such as using yellow ají amarillo paste with shrimp. I've based this ceviche on Alejandro's version.

1 pound U10-size shrimp, peeled and deveined, cut horizontally

1 cup fresh lime juice

1 tablespoon kosher salt

2 grapefruits, peeled and supremed (divided into its natural segments; see Note)

1 avocado, diced

2 tablespoons extra-virgin olive oil

2 teaspoons flaky sea salt

1 teaspoon ají amarillo paste

1 teaspoon Ginger-Chili Oil (page 269)

1 small red onion, thinly sliced

1 bunch of cilantro, leaves picked

1 cup fried cancha or corn nuts

In a chilled medium bowl, combine the shrimp, lime juice, and kosher salt. Refrigerate for 20 minutes to cure—the acid from the lime juice essentially "cooks" the shrimp. The shrimp will turn from translucent to opaque white. Drain the excess juice and discard. Add the grapefruit segments, avocado, olive oil, flaky sea salt, ají amarillo paste, and ginger-chili oil. Stir gently.

Top with the red onion, cilantro leaves, and cancha. Serve immediately, while the shrimp is still very cold.

NOTE: To supreme, trim the top and bottom off the grapefruit. Place a flat side down and use the knife to trim off the remaining peel and pith, following the shape of the fruit. Turn the grapefruit on its side and slice along the membrane just into the center of the fruit, then repeat, slicing along the next membrane. The segment will release. Continue until the fruit is divided. (You can also separate the segments by hand.)

VACA FRITA
WITH YUCA FRIES

SERVES 4

Vaca frita, a Cuban staple, is a twice-cooked flank steak. First it's boiled, then it's fried. Similar to my introduction to griot, it was new for me to eat proteins treated this way. The membrane and fibers in flank can be chewy; it has been traditionally treated as a cheaper cut of beef. The dual cooking technique is an ingenious way to tenderize it and impart tons of flavor. When served, the meat resembles shredded hash browns, crisped up with sliced onions. Back at David's Café (home of the legendary pastelitos, page 176), vaca frita became *my* staple when I was off work. Larry and I would get this lunch with an ice-cold beer. The restaurant was always filled with music, laughter, and people talking shit to each other. It was such a feel-good time. At David's Café this was a big plate, with the vaca frita served with rice, black beans, and yuca fries with mojo sauce for dipping. This is a traditional take, based on my years of eating the dish.

1½ pounds flank steak, cut into 4 pieces

1 large Spanish onion, diced into 1-inch cubes

2 garlic cloves, smashed

2 thyme sprigs

2 bay leaves

4 tablespoons kosher salt, plus more to taste

1 large yuca, peeled and cut into 3-inch-long, 1-inch-thick strips

2 small red onions, thinly sliced

1 green bell pepper, quartered

¼ cup extra-virgin olive oil

¼ cups fresh lime juice

1 tablespoon red chili flakes

Canola oil, for frying

Freshly ground black pepper

1 lime, cut into wedges

SERVING

Mojo Vinaigrette (page 273)

Spicy Black Beans (page 181)

Cilantro Rice (page 197)

In a medium stockpot, add the flank steak, diced Spanish onions, garlic, thyme, bay leaves, and 2 tablespoons of the salt. Add enough water to cover and bring to a boil. Reduce the heat to medium-low and simmer for 20 minutes. The meat will be firm to the touch.

Remove the pot from the heat. Transfer the flank steak to a work surface and let cool. Strain the beef broth and reserve for another use (like cooking rice or braising short ribs). Use two forks to shred the steak and transfer it to a medium bowl. Set aside.

Line a sheet pan with paper towels. Place the yuca strips in a medium stockpot and cover with cold water. Bring to a boil and cook until fork tender, about 15 minutes. Use a slotted spoon or tongs to transfer the strips to the lined sheet pan and allow them to cool and dry for 10 minutes before frying.

In the bowl with the shredded beef, add the red onions, bell pepper, olive oil, lime juice, the remaining 2 tablespoons of salt, and the red chili flakes. Stir well and cover. Let the mixture marinate at room temperature for at least 30 minutes or up to 1 hour. (Don't marinate for more than an hour; the acidic lime juice will make the beef texture a bit mealy.)

While the beef is marinating, let's fry the yuca. In a large sauté pan, add canola oil to a depth of ¼ to ½ inch (about 1 cup) and heat on medium-high to 350°F; check using an instant-read thermometer. Line a plate with paper towels.

Add the yuca in small batches and fry until golden brown, about 2 minutes on each side. Use a slotted spoon to remove the fries and drain them on the paper towels. Season with salt to your taste preference.

To finish off the vaca frita, heat a large sauté pan on high until very hot. (We want this beef to be crispy, and heating the pan this way will heat the oil faster.) Add ¾ cup of canola oil (use more if needed) to the pan. Use tongs to spread the shredded beef mixture in a thin layer across the pan without crowding; you want as much of the beef to have contact with the pan as possible, so work in batches if necessary. Season with salt and pepper.

Cook over high heat, undisturbed, until crispy, about 3 minutes. If you move it around, the steak won't get crispy. Flip the beef and allow it to cook until crispy on the other side, about 3 minutes. Transfer to a platter. Continue until you've fried all the beef. Add the lime wedges to the platter.

To serve: Set out the vaca frita with the fried yuca, with a side of mojo vinaigrette for dipping, and enjoy immediately. This is a filling combo, but if you're doing it up, serve with Spicy Black Beans and Cilantro Rice.

ADOBO PORK
WITH SALSA VERDE

SERVES 4

Shout out to the Borinquen in Miami. They represent! There are many types of adobos: Mexican, Filipino, and this Puerto Rican–inspired one. The common thread is the marinade—that is, the acid—in this recipe by way of chimichurri. My friend Ricky Mungaray made a dish like this for me at his house. He's Nicaraguan, and he loved to cook with pork. I remember how the spice rub on the pork hit me, along with the earthy and acidic salsa verde. I added the plantain puree because I wanted a touch of sweetness, and it ties well with the chimichurri. It's a perfect balance with the heat of the pork. I add turmeric not just because the plantain puree brightens in color; good turmeric adds a subtle earthiness to the puree flavor that reminds me of the fresh turmeric we have in abundance in St. Lucia.

ADOBO SPICE
⅓ cup Guajillo chilies

2 tablespoons kosher salt

2 tablespoons sweet paprika

2 tablespoons garlic powder

4 teaspoons ground cumin

1 tablespoon onion powder

1½ teaspoons freshly ground black pepper

PLANTAIN PUREE
1 tablespoon extra-virgin olive oil

4 shallots, thinly sliced

½ cup thinly sliced Yukon Gold potatoes

1 cup 1-inch-thick slices of very ripe plantains (1 to 2, depending on size)

1 tablespoon diced fresh ginger

¼ teaspoon freshly grated turmeric

CHIMICHURRI
¼ cup red wine vinegar

2 tablespoons minced shallots

1 garlic clove, finely grated

1 cup extra-virgin olive oil

½ cup minced flat-leaf parsley

½ cup minced cilantro

2 tablespoons minced oregano

1 teaspoon kosher salt

PORK
2 (6 to 8-ounce) pork tenderloins, silver skin removed

2 tablespoons canola oil

Make the adobo spice: Heat a small dry skillet over high heat. Add the chilies and toast for 1 minute, until the skin starts to crackle and pop and they become aromatic. Turn them over and toast for another minute. Remove from the heat and allow them to cool. Add the toasted chilies and the salt, paprika, garlic powder, cumin, onion powder, and black pepper to a spice grinder and grind to a fine powder. Transfer to a small bowl or jar and set aside.

Make the plantain puree: In a large saucepot, add the olive oil and sweat the shallots and potatoes over medium heat, stirring occasionally, for about 3 minutes. You're not developing color, just providing enough heat so they become translucent. Add the sliced plantain, ginger, and turmeric. Add water to just barely cover (about 2 cups). Cook on low heat until the potatoes are tender, 15 to 20 minutes. Transfer the mixture to a blender. Carefully puree (with the center lid open to allow the steam to escape) until smooth, then pass the puree through a fine-mesh strainer. Set aside.

Make the chimichurri: In a small bowl, add the red wine vinegar, shallots, and garlic. Steep for 10 minutes. Add the olive oil, parsley, cilantro, oregano, and salt. Mix well and set aside.

Make the pork: Heat the oven to 375°F. Set a roasting rack in a sheet pan.

On a large plate, evenly spread the adobo spice. Roll the tenderloins in the spices until completely covered.

Heat a large sauté pan on high. Add the canola oil and sear the pork on all sides, for about 1 minute on each side, to char the spices. Transfer the tenderloins to the roasting rack. Roast in the oven until the pork is firm to the touch, an instant thermometer reads 145°F to 150°F, and the spices are completely caramelized, 10 to 12 minutes. Transfer to a cooling rack. Rest the pork for 3 minutes to allow the juices to evenly distribute before slicing into 1-inch-thick pieces.

To serve: Smear a plate with a generous serving of the plantain puree. Arrange the pork slices across the puree. Drizzle with the chimichurri on top and serve immediately.

FRIED PLANTAINS
WITH LIME VINAIGRETTE

SERVES 4

There's a Cuban restaurant on Miami Beach called Puerto Sagua. They've always had maduros in a lime dressing on offer, but you had to know to ask for it. My husband and I were regulars, and we loved the combination of the sweet and salty flavors with salsa verde. It felt simple but so flavorful and delicious, a way to make folks who came often feel special. This is my take on that dish. I love how the acid from the lime cuts into the sweet plantain.

VINAIGRETTE
½ cup packed arugula
½ cup packed mint leaves
½ cup canola oil
¼ cup extra-virgin olive oil
½ teaspoon finely grated lime zest
¼ cup fresh lime juice (from about 3 limes)
1 serrano chili or jalapeño, chopped (for less heat, remove the seeds)
½ teaspoon cane sugar
1 teaspoon kosher salt

FRIED PLANTAINS
Canola oil, for frying
3 very ripe black plantains
Kosher salt
½ cup cotija cheese, crumbled

Make the vinaigrette: In a blender, add the arugula, mint, canola oil, olive oil, lime zest and juice, chili, and sugar. Puree until the vinaigrette is combined but still looks chunky. Season with the salt and set aside.

Fry the plantains: In a large sauté pan, add canola oil to a depth of 2 inches (about 2 cups) and heat on medium to 350°F; check using an instant-read thermometer. Line a plate with paper towels.

Use a knife to cut the ends off the plantains and peel the skin. Slice the plantain into planks or strips about 3 inches long and 1 inch thick (depending on the size, you'll essentially slice the plantain in half in one direction, then cut each piece in half again in the other direction).

When the oil is ready, fry the plantains in batches, checking for them to become golden brown on all sides and turning as they finish, about 2 minutes per side. Use a slotted spoon to transfer the plantains to the lined plate. Season with salt to taste.

Transfer the plantains to a serving platter, add the crumbled salty cotija cheese, and dress with the vinaigrette. Enjoy immediately.

AREPAS

MAKES 4

When I was at Scarpetta, I worked with a Venezuelan cook named Danny Alas. When she made staff meal, she'd cook recipes from her homeland, including these arepas with queso fresco and various accompaniments. Linking up with Danny reminded me of the masa harina that my mum would bring back from her visits to Venezuela when I was a kid. She had good friends there and would visit a couple of times a year. We loved when Mum went to Venezuela, because it meant we'd be having arepas for breakfast at home in Moulin à Vent. My mum knew how to make arepas, but it was Danny who taught me the real-deal technique years later. You want a fluffy arepa so when you cut into it, it almost mimics a pudding consistency, with a crunchy exterior. I make these at home now, and they still feel like a treat.

1 cup masa harina (such as Masienda)
1 teaspoon kosher salt
1 cup hot water
Canola oil, for frying
Nonstick cooking spray (optional)

SERVING
1 Florida avocado, sliced
½ cup sliced queso fresco
1 jalapeño, thinly sliced
1 small red onion, thinly sliced
1 bunch of cilantro
4 fried eggs (optional)

In a medium bowl, stir together the masa harina and salt, then add the hot water while stirring with a fork until the mixture comes together to form a stiff dough. Cover with a damp cloth and let stand at room temperature for 20 minutes. The dough should appear firm, which indicates the flour is completely hydrated.

In a large Dutch oven, add the canola oil to a depth of 2 inches (about 4 cups) and heat on medium-high to 375°F; check using an instant-read thermometer. Line a plate with paper towels.

Transfer the dough to a work surface and use a dough cutter or knife to divide the dough into 4 equal pieces. Roll each piece into a ball. Place one dough ball between 2 sheets of wax paper and use a flat-bottomed skillet to gently press into a 4-inch-wide round (about ⅓ inch thick). Repeat with the remaining balls. (Note that you can use parchment paper, but you'll need to spray the paper with an oil spray to ensure the dough doesn't stick.)

Fry 1 to 2 arepas at a time in the hot oil until they're a light golden brown, about 3 minutes on each side. Use a spatula or slotted spoon to remove them and drain on the paper towels. Repeat with the remaining arepas.

To serve: Use a small knife to cut a 2-inch slit along one edge of each arepa. Serve family style with sliced avocado, queso fresco, jalapeños, red onion, and cilantro on the side so everyone can fill their arepa to their preference. If you want, add a fried egg. Enjoy hot.

SPICY PEEL-AND-EAT GARLIC SHRIMP

SERVES 4

Nicaraguan, Guatemalan, and Colombian communities live throughout the west side of Miami. Nicaraguan cuisine showcases Indigenous, Spanish, and Creole influences, and their interpretations of fish, shrimp, and other seafood dishes always grabbed my attention. In St. Lucia, we don't have shrimp; we eat crayfish. Seeing shrimp prepared in many variations in South Florida made me appreciate it.

I love how flavorful and simple this peel-and-eat garlic shrimp is. Typically camarones al ajillo are sautéed in garlic, butter, and lemon, which lets the freshest shrimp shine. I add chili to my version, in reference to the way we eat seafood back home, with a hefty dash of peppa sauce. We also serve these at Compère Lapin, as we have amazing shrimp in Louisiana.

To devein the shrimp, run the knife or shears down the spine of the shell and remove the vein. Repeat with all the shrimp and set aside.

In a large saucepan, heat the olive oil over medium-high. Place the shrimp in the pan in a single layer and season with the salt. Cook until they start to turn bright orange, flipping after 1½ minutes. Add the chili butter and use a spoon to baste (or coat) the shrimp with melted butter. When the shrimp are firm and opaque, after about 4 minutes, remove them from the skillet and set them on a plate. Add the garlic and rosemary sprigs to the pan. The butter will get foamy after 1 minute. Remove from the heat and pour over the shrimp.

To serve: Enjoy immediately with lemon wedges on the side. I love to eat the shrimp whole with the shells; that's where all the flavor is.

2 pounds U10-size shrimp, heads and shells on

3 tablespoons extra-virgin olive oil

1 tablespoon kosher salt

2 cups Chili Butter (page 275)

4 garlic cloves, thinly sliced

2 sprigs of rosemary

SERVING
1 lemon, cut into 4 wedges

CILANTRO RICE

SERVES 4

Felix Fernandez is a Dominican cook I used to work with in Miami. He was resourceful and creative, making delicious dishes out of basic ingredients. He'd make cilantro rice for staff meals using leftover cilantro stems. He added the stems to ginger, onions, water or vegetable stock, and jasmine rice, and at the very end, a ton of chopped cilantro leaves. This rice stood out to me; it takes on a gorgeous green color and has this mild, herbaceous flavor. It's great with grilled fish or chicken.

1 tablespoon canola oil

½ cup minced yellow onion

3 medium garlic cloves, thinly sliced

1 medium serrano chili, halved lengthwise and seeded

3 bunches of cilantro, leaves picked and stems reserved

1 tablespoon peeled, chopped fresh ginger

2 cups jasmine rice

1 tablespoon kosher salt

3⅓ cups chicken broth or water, plus more as needed

In a large Dutch oven or pot, add the canola oil on low heat. Sweat the onions, garlic, and chili, stirring occasionally, until translucent, about 3 minutes.

In a blender, puree the cilantro leaves and ginger with just enough water to make the puree smooth.

Finely chop the cilantro stems and add to the onions. Add the rice and stir to incorporate the ingredients. Season with the salt. Add the broth to cover the rice by 1 inch and steam, uncovered, for 15 minutes.

Stir in half of the cilantro puree and cover the pot. Cook until the rice is cooked through, 8 to 10 minutes.

Add the remaining cilantro puree. Fluff the rice and serve immediately.

COCONUT TRES LECHES CAKE

SERVES 6

Tres leches is standard fare for many people, but for me, when I first came to Miami, it was a new flavor and technique. Tres leches is a standout Latin American dessert that you'll find in the northern Caribbean, in Cuba, Puerto Rico, and the Dominican Republic. It's rich and moist from soaking in milk, and the coconut creaminess is decadent. It's the perfect dessert for a potluck or to keep in the refrigerator for up to a week. It's going to be on the menu in most Cuban spots along with flan, another influential dessert that would become my go-to (see page 201). For optional flair, bring out your cocoa stick (from Cocoa Tea, page 80) and grate it over your cake slice just prior to serving.

5 large eggs

¾ cup granulated sugar

1 cup all-purpose flour

2 (14-ounce) cans coconut milk

2 (14-ounce) cans condensed milk

2 (12-ounce) cans evaporated milk

1 cup heavy cream

¼ cup confectioners' sugar

GARNISH

2 cups toasted sweetened coconut flakes

Dulce de Leche (page 278)

Heat the oven to 325°F. Grease a 9 × 13-inch baking pan with a pat of butter.

For the cake: In a large bowl, whisk the eggs and granulated sugar until light and creamy, 6 to 8 minutes. Use a spatula to fold in the flour and mix to combine; a few lumps are okay, you just want to keep this light and airy.

Transfer the cake batter to the prepared pan. Bake for 15 to 20 minutes, until the cake is firm to the touch. Remove from the oven and allow it to cool to room temperature.

In a large bowl, add the coconut milk, condensed milk, and evaporated milk and gently stir. Reserve until the cake has cooled.

Slowly drizzle the cooled cake with the tres leches mixture, and soak for at least 1 hour and up to overnight in the fridge, allowing the cake to absorb the liquid.

Make the whipped cream: In a medium bowl (if whisking by hand or using an electric mixer) or the bowl of a stand mixer fitted with the whisk attachment, whip the heavy cream and confectioners' sugar. Whisk until the cream develops stiff peaks, 10 to 12 minutes by hand, or 6 to 8 minutes on medium speed if using a mixer. Spread the whipped cream over the cake.

To garnish: Top with the toasted coconut flakes, followed by a drizzle of dulce de leche. Enjoy immediately.

COCONUT FLAN

SERVES 2 TO 4

Being in Miami introduced me to flan. Roberto was one of my cooks at Scarpetta, and he treasured his mother's flan recipe. As a prep cook, he was often tasked with making staff meals, and he'd feature dishes like sancocho (a traditional Dominican stew), fried chicken, or braised pork with rice and beans. I couldn't wait to see what was hiding under that foil when I came in. When flan was on deck, the staff would be so happy. He never shared the recipe with me, and I don't blame him! But this version is inspired by what he made for us. Note the advance preparation of chilling the flan overnight.

1 cup sugar

1 tablespoon water

1 (14-ounce) can sweetened condensed milk

1 (14-ounce) can coconut milk

½ cup cream of coconut (I like Coco López)

5 large eggs

1 cup toasted sweetened coconut flakes

1 lime

Heat the oven to 300°F.

In a medium saucepan, add the sugar and water and cook over medium heat—no stirring. Let it start to caramelize (brown, not burn) around the edges, about 10 minutes, then reduce the heat to low. Pour the caramelized sugar into an 8-inch round baking dish and allow it to completely cool.

In a medium bowl, use a whisk to mix the condensed milk, coconut milk, cream of coconut, and eggs until just combined.

Once the sugar has cooled, pour the coconut custard on top of the caramel and place the dish in a larger ovenproof pan (such as a roasting pan). Fill the larger pan with enough room-temperature water to come 2 inches up the sides of the custard dish; you're creating a mini steam bath to allow for a slow bake. This way, the eggs won't curdle.

Bake until the custard is set, 30 to 45 minutes. When you jiggle the pan, the center should move just slightly.

Remove the custard dish from the steam bath and allow it to cool to room temperature for about 1 hour. Wrap in plastic wrap and transfer it to the refrigerator to chill overnight. When ready to serve, you can turn out the flan onto a plate, if you like. Garnish the flan with the toasted coconut flakes and zest the lime over the top.

MANGO CRÈME BRÛLÉE

SERVES 6

When it's mango season in Miami, it's like being back home in St. Lucia. Everyone who has a mango tree is giving them away because they have so many, and the range of colors on their skin catch the eye: red, orange, purple, and yellow. I was lucky to have friends who gave me the meatiest and juiciest ones. Of all the iterations of mango I'd seen around, it occurred to me that I hadn't had a mango crème brûlée yet. This custard is decadent, and when you shatter the sugar crust, you'll get the toasty coconut, the lime zest, and the brightness of the fruit.

2½ cups heavy cream

1 cup fresh mango puree (store-bought is okay)

7 large egg yolks

⅓ cup granulated sugar

1 teaspoon vanilla extract

Warm water, as needed

Turbinado sugar, for brûléeing

SERVING

1 ripe mango, diced

½ cup blackberries, halved

¼ cup toasted sweetened coconut flakes

1 lime

EQUIPMENT

6 (4-inch-wide) ramekins

Microplane

Heat the oven to 300°F.

In a medium bowl, combine the cream, mango puree, yolks, granulated sugar, and vanilla extract and whisk until fully incorporated. Distribute evenly among six 4-inch-wide ramekins and set them in a roasting pan. Add 1 inch of warm water to the roasting pan to make a water bath. This will keep the mixture from curdling or cooking the eggs in the mixture too fast (we don't want *scrambled* egg brûlée!).

Bake until the surface of the custard is set and firm to touch, about 30 minutes. Remove the ramekins from the roasting pan and chill them, uncovered, in the refrigerator for at least 1 hour or up to overnight.

When ready to serve, heat the broiler and position the rack in the center of the oven. (Of course, if you have a blowtorch on hand, skip this step and go for it!)

Place the ramekins on a sheet pan. Top each ramekin with a thin dusting of turbinado sugar and broil until the sugar is golden brown, 3 to 5 minutes. Watch closely! Rotate the individual ramekins for even browning, and remove them as they finish, to prevent burning.

To serve: Top each ramekin with diced mango, blackberries, and toasted coconut flakes, and use a microplane to zest the lime over to finish. Enjoy within 1 hour.

RUM CAKE

SERVES 6

Throughout the Caribbean (and therefore, its diaspora in Miami), you'll find different types of rum cake. It's traditional black cake in Trinidad and Tobago; in places like Cayman and Tortola, they make a white rum cake. In Miami, I saw the white version year-round, whereas the black cake (page 64) is usually made during Christmas, part of a practice of gifting the cake to loved ones. Many folks, like my mum, start soaking the fruits for black cake a year ahead. Black cakes are amazingly rich, sometimes a bit dense. For me, a little goes a long way. I love this cake because of its light flavor and spongy texture. Depending on the neighborhood, you might see these in a major grocery store, but I'd often find them in specialty shops. The rum gives the cake a caramelized sweetness, almost like honey. And everyone of all ages can enjoy this cake because the alcohol is all cooked off.

Position a rack in the center and heat the oven to 325°F. Spray an 8-inch cake tin with nonstick cooking spray and line it with parchment paper.

Use a stand mixer with paddle attachment to cream the butter and granulated sugar together on medium speed until it becomes light and fluffy, about 6 minutes. Reduce the speed to low and add the eggs, one by one, waiting until each is incorporated before adding the next. Add the oil, rum, milk, and vanilla. Mix on medium speed for 3 more minutes, until it forms a smooth batter.

Add the flour, baking powder, and salt and mix on low speed until the batter is smooth and all ingredients are incorporated, about 2 minutes.

Pour the mixture into the lined cake pan and place in the center of the oven. Bake for 20 to 30 minutes, rotating the pan halfway after 15 minutes. Check for doneness using a cake tester or toothpick; it should come out clean. Allow the cake to cool in the pan to room temperature, then dust with the confectioners' sugar right before serving. It can keep in an airtight container at room temperature for up to 1 week. Enjoy!

Nonstick cooking spray

2½ cups (5 sticks) unsalted butter, softened

1⅓ cups granulated sugar

4 large eggs

½ cup canola oil

⅓ cup Chairman's Reserve rum

⅓ cup whole milk

2 teaspoons vanilla extract

2 cups cake flour

1 tablespoon baking powder

1 teaspoon kosher salt

¼ cup confectioners' sugar

SERVING SUGGESTION

Pairs well with a snifter of aged rum, a side of ice cream, or a serving of fresh fruit.

CREOLE STEWED CONCH

SERVES 4

Creole stewed conch is a dish you find in St. Lucia (we call it lambi), but I found this in a lot of Miami Haitian restaurants, too. Miami is home to a huge Haitian diaspora. Little Haiti, just north of downtown, is where you'll find many shops and a vibrant arts and culture scene. This is where you hear Kreyòl, French, and English in the streets, and it's common to see the tap tap buses taking visitors on tours through the area. I'd been introduced to Haitian food in Jamaica, but being in Miami was a true immersion, given the size of its population.

A Creole sauce traditionally has tomatoes, pepper, onions, and thyme; it's a simple red sauce. In the States, you'll find conch in the freezer section (it's flash frozen as soon as it's caught), so all you need to do is defrost it. Stewed down, the shellfish is served with white rice.

1 pound conch

4 tablespoons kosher salt

½ teaspoon ground allspice

½ teaspoon freshly ground black pepper

¼ cup extra-virgin olive oil

2 shallots, thinly sliced

5 sprigs of thyme

3 garlic cloves, thinly sliced

1 cup white wine

¼ cup tomato paste

1 Scotch bonnet pepper, torn

2 cups water

1 cup vegetable stock or Ginger Lemongrass Fumet (page 149)

1 lemon, juiced

SERVING

Steamed white rice

Cut the conch into bite-size pieces, about 1-inch wide. Use a meat tenderizer to pound the flesh, but don't over-pound them: you want pieces that are about ⅛ inch thick.

In a small bowl, combine 2 tablespoons of the salt and the allspice and black pepper. Mix the conch and spice mix to evenly coat. Set aside.

In a medium pot, heat the olive oil on medium-high. Sauté the shallots, thyme sprigs, and garlic, stirring occasionally, just long enough to sweat and soften the vegetables, about 1 minute. Add the white wine and tomato paste, then stir to combine. Reduce the heat to medium and cook, stirring occasionally, to reduce the liquid by half, about 5 minutes.

Add the coated conch and torn pepper. Stir well. Add the water, vegetable stock, and the remaining 2 tablespoons of salt, and reduce the heat to low. Cover the pot and simmer, stirring from time to time, until the conch is tender, about 2 hours. You can insert a cake tester to check doneness; it should meet no resistance.

Finish with the lemon juice and stir well.

To serve: Enjoy hot with steamed white rice.

GRILLED SNAPPER COLLAR

SERVES 6

By now you know I have a thing for snapper, but what sets this preparation off is the pickled mango puree. Miami has a tropical climate, and many people have mango trees in their backyard. Just like in St. Lucia, when it's mango season, everyone is doing something with mangoes—jams, chutneys, you name it. Neighbors would sometimes leave a bag at my doorstep because they had so much. Mangoes can be enjoyed on the sour side or super ripe, so they lend themselves to many applications. We served a version of this dish at Compère Lapin in the summertime one year, and we couldn't keep up with the demand, it was so good.

PICKLED MANGO PUREE

2 cups white wine vinegar

1 cup cane sugar

2 large, ripe mangoes, peeled and roughly diced

FISH

2 cups honey

1 cup Baron West Indian Hot Sauce

1 tablespoon roughly chopped fresh ginger

6 red snapper collars

6 tablespoons extra-virgin olive oil

¼ cup kosher salt

GREEN MANGO AND RED ONION SLAW

1 large underripe mango, peeled and shaved with a mandoline (rotate the fruit around the pit)

1 medium red onion, shaved with a mandoline

½ cup cilantro leaves

¼ cup mint leaves

1 lemon, zested

1 lime, zested

3 to 4 tablespoons Mojo Vinaigrette (page 273), as needed

EQUIPMENT

Mandoline

Make the pickled mango puree: In a medium saucepan, add the white wine vinegar and sugar. Bring to a simmer over medium-low heat and cook to dissolve the sugar and reduce the volume by half, about 15 minutes. Remove from the heat.

Add the mango to a medium heat-safe bowl. Pour the melted sugar mixture over the mango and allow it to cool down to room temperature, 15 to 20 minutes.

Transfer the mango and liquid to a blender and puree until smooth. Set aside.

Make the fish: Heat the oven to 375°F. Fit a roasting rack in a sheet pan (see Note).

In a small pot, add the honey, hot sauce, and ginger, and stir to combine. Heat on low, stirring occasionally, just until it starts to bubble, 5 to 7 minutes. Strain out the ginger and transfer the hot honey to a small serving dish. Set aside.

Liberally coat the snapper collars with the olive oil and season with the salt. Arrange evenly on the roasting rack and roast until the skin becomes crispy, about 8 minutes.

Prepare the green mango and red onion slaw: While the fish is cooking, add the shaved slices of the green mango and red onion to a small bowl. Add the cilantro, mint, lemon zest, and lime zest. Add enough of the mojo vinaigrette to coat the fruit and veggies. Toss to combine and set aside.

Remove the fish from the oven and brush the collars with hot honey on the top and bottom. Flip the fish and continue to roast until cooked through and the honey caramelizes, about 5 minutes more, depending on the collar thickness.

Remove the fish from the oven. On a large serving plate, add all the pickled mango puree at the base, creating a small pool. Use tongs to arrange the roasted collars across the puree, then dress the fish with the mango-onion slaw. Serve immediately.

NOTE: Instead of roasting the fish, you may also grill it until cooked through and lightly charred on both sides.

GRIOT

SERVES 8

As a young cook, I was tracking so much information—from what I'd learned in culinary school, to what my chef expected of me, to watching my colleagues spin out dishes from their cultures in the back of the house. But an important part of any cook's development is eating out, and the Afro Latin restaurants in Miami are a wonderful education. Tap Tap was a Haitian restaurant on South Beach. They modeled the restaurant after the tap tap bus, the popular public transport in Haiti known for its bright red paint job with decorative leaves and parrots. The restaurant featured wooden benches and felt about the size of a school bus. When you walked into the space, you were instantly met with red and yellow hues; there was nothing mellow about this spot. The decor was from Haiti, and it felt vibrant and homey. Tap Tap was my first taste of Haitian food in a formal setting. Griot was their bestseller, a classic Haitian preparation of twice-cooked pork. It was juicy and tender and came with spicy pikliz, simple and so well done. Back in St. Lucia, we primarily braise or grill meats. I was intrigued by the marinade process with griot, and the texture of the pork after frying it. I would ask the chef about the technique and mess around in my own kitchen to replicate the flavors.

I was saddened to learn, on a trip to Miami after the pandemic, that Tap Tap had closed. But you'll get a hint of their hospitality, and the brightness of their classic dish, with this recipe. Note the advance preparation of marinating the griot overnight.

3 pounds boneless pork shoulder, cubed

1 large Spanish onion, chopped

1 red bell pepper, thinly sliced

½ bunch of flat-leaf parsley

10 sprigs of thyme

2 shallots, chopped

5 scallions, thinly sliced

2 oranges, juiced

2 limes, juiced

¼ cup kosher salt

1 Scotch bonnet pepper, sliced

6 garlic cloves, thinly sliced

1 tablespoon white wine vinegar

½ teaspoon freshly ground black pepper, plus more to taste

2 cups water

2 cups chicken stock

Canola oil, for frying

PIKLIZ

2 cups shredded white cabbage

1 cup grated carrot

1 red bell pepper, sliced

1 small red onion, thinly sliced

3 scallions, thinly sliced

1 Scotch bonnet pepper, torn

Kosher salt and freshly ground black pepper

2 cups white wine vinegar

¼ cup lime juice

SERVING

Steamed rice

Spicy Black Beans (page 181)

Fried Plantains with Lime Vinaigrette (page 191)

EQUIPMENT

2 pairs kitchen-safe gloves

2 (16-ounce) mason jars with lids

Marinate the pork: In a large bowl, add the cubed pork shoulder, chopped onion, bell pepper, parsley, thyme sprigs, shallots, scallions, orange and lime juices, salt, Scotch bonnet pepper, garlic, white wine vinegar, and black pepper. Wearing kitchen-safe gloves, use your hands to thoroughly mix the ingredients. Cover the bowl with plastic wrap and place it in the refrigerator to marinate overnight, 8 to 12 hours. This marinade will tenderize the shoulder, but don't go past 12 hours, as the acid in the marinade will break down the meat too much.

Meanwhile, make the pikliz: In a large bowl, combine the cabbage, carrots, bell pepper, onion, scallions, and Scotch bonnet. Add salt and black pepper to taste.

(recipe continues)

Wearing kitchen-safe gloves, use your hands to thoroughly mix. Divide the pikliz between two clean mason jars, packing down the contents. Divide the white wine vinegar and lime juice equally between the jars, covering the pikliz. Stir to incorporate. Screw the lids on and marinate in the refrigerator for at least 12 hours, then the pikliz will be ready to enjoy. (It can keep in the refrigerator for up to 1 month.)

Make the griot: Let the marinated pork shoulder start to come to room temperature for 10 minutes.

Heat the oven to 350°F.

Heat a large pot or Dutch oven on high. Add the water and chicken stock to the pot and bring to a boil. Add the pork to the pot. Leave uncovered and place it in the oven to braise until the pork is cooked through and tender, about 1½ hours. The pork will begin to caramelize, so halfway through the cooking time, turn the cubes over so the meat continues to brown evenly. Line a sheet pan with paper towels and set aside.

Remove the pot from the oven and use tongs or a slotted spoon to transfer the pork to the paper towel–lined tray to dry. Gently pat down the pork surface to ensure there is no moisture.

Use a clean large pot or Dutch oven to fry the griot. Add canola oil to a depth of 3 to 4 inches (about 5 to 6 cups) and heat on medium-high to 350°F; check using an instant-read thermometer. Line a plate with paper towels.

Add the pork to the oil in batches and fry, rotating as needed, until it develops a deep golden brown color, 5 to 7 minutes total. Use a slotted spoon to transfer the pork to the paper towel–lined plate to drain. Repeat with the remaining pork.

To serve: Enjoy the griot with steamed rice, spicy black beans, fried plantains, and the pikliz.

GUAVA-GLAZED RIBS

SERVES 4

Miami is home to plentiful guavas, which reminds me of guava season in St. Lucia. My husband, Larry, adapted this recipe in Miami after spending time with me and my family in St. Lucia. When it's guava season, it's time for guava juice, guava jam, guava mousse, guava everything! Beachside grilling is a fun pastime in Miami; it's almost always perfect weather for an outdoor meal. The sweet guava complements the smoked paprika and allspice here; it's a perfect combo. Note the advance preparation of marinating the ribs overnight.

1 cup Brown Stock (page 279)

1 cup honey

1 cup soy sauce

1 cup guava paste

½ cup apple cider vinegar

¼ cup sugar

¼ cup extra-virgin olive oil

1 Scotch bonnet pepper, torn

1 teaspoon smoked paprika

1 teaspoon rosemary leaves

1 teaspoon ground allspice

4 pounds baby back ribs, outer membrane removed

SERVING SUGGESTION

Creole Potato Salad (page 238) or Cabbage Salad with Tamarind Vinaigrette (page 252)

In a large microwave-safe bowl, mix the chicken broth, honey, soy sauce, guava paste, apple cider vinegar, sugar, olive oil, Scotch bonnet, paprika, rosemary, and allspice. Stir to combine, cover, and heat in the microwave for about 2 minutes; you're just gently warming the marinade to marry the ingredients. Or you can heat it on the stovetop in a small pot on low until the ingredients melt together. Allow the marinade to cool to room temperature.

Place the ribs in a large baking dish. Pour the marinade over the ribs, cover with plastic wrap or foil, and refrigerate overnight.

Heat the oven to 300°F.

Cover the baking dish with aluminum foil and bake for about 3 hours. The ribs are ready when they start to pull away from the bone. Remove the foil and switch the oven to broil. Broil for about 5 minutes on each side to caramelize the ribs, watching carefully.

Cut the ribs along the bone to portion according to your preference. Enjoy immediately.

NEW ORLEANS
Louisiana

COMING HOME TO CREOLE

Wazzam.

When the invitation to compete on *Top Chef* came through, I learned that we'd be filming in New Orleans. I would be gone for two months, and nobody could know why. How would I explain this to my Miami kitchen staff? I made up an excuse about going home to take care of a family member. I felt like such a liar! Chefs have to be on call for their restaurants because many things happen beyond our control. I believed in my team, but you do kind of worry. When I started filming, the producers took away my cell phone. I told Larry, "I need you to 'be' me; just text and email the staff." He'd text people about inventory and basic things to keep things moving along.

Suddenly I was roommates with a bunch of chefs I'd never met before in a beautiful house on Bourbon Street in the French Quarter. We'd be asked to report for filming and be greeted with something like: "Today you're going to be cooking in the swamp." The show was incredibly stressful, even while it was exciting, because you know that your every error is going to be highlighted. We had no TV, no books for entertainment, because they wanted to force us to interact with each other for the camera, even during downtime. But that could be challenging because there weren't many ways to decompress.

At first, I had my guard up during filming. I was thinking, *Hey I'm just little Nina from the islands trying to cook my Caribbean food.* I felt completely out of place. But after a few challenges I realized I was sticking around and I didn't have to perform crazy techniques to stand out. I remembered that my cooking was about local ingredients, seasonality. I remembered that in Jamaica, the best cooks were those roadside vendors who made one thing well, over and over. I wanted to create memorable flavors. In the end, I finished as runner-up, and it was a big thing—for me, but for others, too. I learned that viewers were pissed at the judges who docked me for my dessert, which to them wasn't a "true" dessert (a version of those banana pecan beignets is on page 266). Years later, people still message me or come to my restaurant and they're like, "You know you were robbed, right?" I'm like, *Guys! I'm good.*

Being on *Top Chef* changed my life. The show introduced me to New Orleans, and I found my culinary voice after all these years. I'd finally developed the confidence to cook *my* food. Returning to Miami after the show finished taping, I was clear that I needed my own place. This feeling got stronger after the show aired; it felt like others were also excited to see more expressions of Caribbean food. I looked for a restaurant space all over Miami, but nothing clicked. Offers that trickled in from other cities didn't seem like the right fit either. But then the call came to open in New Orleans' warehouse district. The space was already under construction, and Larry and I went to take a look. It was an instant yes.

New Orleans felt familiar to me when I first visited. I noticed the city's architecture first. The bright-colored cottages reminded me of the Caribbean. Creole or colonial style architecture painted in vibrant greens, reds, pinks, and yellows places me in St. Lucia. The vegetation in New Orleans forms a lush tropical landscape. But what I love the most about New Orleans comes down to the way people eat. They love to eat here. I've found that there's a deep appreciation for dining out and sharing food with big, extended family, friends, and neighbors. It's not just about being social and having good times. Folks cultivate community through food, and they strive to eat *well*. A stranger across the bar may try to share a spoonful of their crawfish bisque with you for no other reason than because that soup makes them so happy, they want someone else to experience it. In St. Lucia, I grew up in a culture where people shared their food. In our backyard, we had abundant fruit. Neighbors grew herbs, starchy veggies, spring onions, and mangoes, and we exchanged our respective harvests without hesitation. Someone always had extra seafood pepperpot, bouyon, or coco bread and would drop off a serving or loaf. New Orleans is the same. Nobody makes a crawfish boil or gumbo for a party of one. (I'm not sure it's possible, nor that it's a good idea to try!) I immediately felt comfortable here. In New Orleans, me and my St. Lucian food belonged.

When developing the concept for Compère Lapin, I didn't have a name yet. I searched online for Creole words in Louisiana. I was digging into the African history in the state and noted how similar it was to the history in the Caribbean, in terms of where enslaved people were taken from and the cultural traditions they carried with them. Africans imported into Louisiana came primarily from Senegambia, Bight of Benin, Bight of Biafra, and West-Central Africa, areas that denote modern-day Senegal, parts of Gambia, Benin, Nigeria, Angola, and the Republic of Congo. Africans were also taken from Liberia, Côte d'Ivoire, Ghana, Togo, and Cameroon. On a historical plantation tour in Louisiana, I saw the names of many of these women, men, and children commemorated, many of whom were Muslim. Enslaved people were also brought into the busy New Orleans port from Caribbean ports like Kingston, Jamaica. The Afro Creole foods, music, dances, and linguistic expressions so beloved in New Orleans today come from the incredible contributions of these Africans who went through horrors and still found ways to nurture, innovate, and thrive.

In my search, the folktale about Br'er Rabbit popped up in relationship to a plantation just outside the city, and I was struck that the same character and a similar story existed in this region as it did back home (although like many African cultural expressions in the U.S., the tale of Br'er Rabbit was co-opted and became a racialized way to mock Black folks; the character even led to the creation of the Bugs Bunny character). In our Caribbean traditional tale, Compère Lapin is a trickster who messes with other animals like the tiger and alligator. The lesson from brother rabbit is that you have to listen carefully because he isn't always giving you the real deal! I chose this name for the restaurant to signify my heritage and to (re)claim the related, but different, African diaspora history in the American South.

The opening menu reflected dishes I grew up eating and wanted to share in New Orleans. In Louisiana, people understand cooking out of necessity, folks have home gardens, and using all the parts of an animal is expected around here. I featured Caribbean recipes and drew from Louisiana influences, noticing the similarities to St. Lucia. We opened the restaurant with dishes like curried goat, drawing from home; conch croquettes inspired by Miami's Cuban croquetas; and buttermilk biscuits, the local dinner bread. We showcased Gulf seafood with shrimp in rundown sauce, a flex from Jamaica, and crudos that played off ceviche recipes I learned from my cooks in Miami, and we fried whole fish.

My mum and my sister Fiona gave me two banana plants to have in my New Orleans backyard. That plant is symbolic of St. Lucia, our prized crop for generations. My mum said you should always have ginger and turmeric in your garden. So a lot of ginger and turmeric is in my garden. I've got fresh herbs growing, like rosemary, parsley, and basil. We have citrus as well; satsuma is local here.

I live in the Bywater neighborhood in New Orleans. A woman down the street sells Snoballs and pralines. Another guy has a pickup truck setup, and he makes rotisserie chicken to sell. The aroma is so good. Being in New Orleans reminds me of being in Moulin à Vent. The people are friendly and kind, and the food bridges the Creole elements of New Orleans with my Caribbean Kwéyòl upbringing. There is truly a deep appreciation for cooking rituals and enjoying a meal with people you love that is unlike anything I've seen elsewhere.

BOUDIN BALLS

SERVES 12

Living in New Orleans as a contestant on *Top Chef*, I saw that many recipes are rooted in tradition. When I decided to move to the city and open a restaurant, I wanted to be sure I understood the framework of these important recipes: jambalaya, gumbo, crawfish bisque—dishes you'd see at family gatherings that take a while (and a few family members in the kitchen) to prepare. I leaned on folks like my friend Donald Link. A chef with multiple restaurants and a Cajun background (he's from Raine), he was generous to show me the ropes.

Boudin balls are a snack that comes from Cajun country, whose culture was developed in part by the Acadians en route from Nova Scotia and France. Boudin (pronounced "boo-dan") in Louisiana is as personal as gumbo, but essentially you've got a house-made sausage consisting of pork liver, pork shoulder, rice, our trinity (green bell pepper, onions, and celery), herbs, and seasonings. Boudin balls are often made from leftover boudin links. No one handles pork quite like the cooks of the South. Donald taught me about how during winter, the entirety of the pig is used, boudin being one expression. This recipe is inspired by Donald's own. Note the advance preparation of soaking the chicken livers overnight.

1 pound chicken livers

2 cups whole milk

5 pounds boneless pork shoulder

4 tablespoons kosher salt

4 cups diced Spanish onion

2 cups diced celery

2 cups diced green bell pepper

2 poblano peppers, diced

3 jalapeños, diced

4 garlic cloves, minced

1 tablespoon freshly ground black pepper

1 teaspoon cayenne pepper

1 cup Brown Stock (page 279), plus more if needed

6 cups cooked jasmine rice

2 cups sliced scallions, green and white parts

½ cup flat-leaf parsley, minced

FRYING

Canola oil

6 large eggs

2 cups water

4 cups all-purpose flour

4 tablespoons kosher salt, plus more as needed

4 cups panko breadcrumbs

SERVING

Creole mustard (such as Zatarain's)

Soak the chicken livers overnight: In a medium airtight container, add the livers and enough milk to just cover them. This process helps to extract any impurities and remove any metallic taste. Cover and refrigerate overnight. Drain and rinse with cool water, then pat dry with paper towels and set aside.

Prepare the mix: In a large pot, add the pork shoulder and cover with water. Bring to a boil, then reduce the heat to medium. Simmer, lid on, until fork tender, about 2 hours. Remove the pork and drain the liquid. Set aside.

Allow the meat to cool slightly and cut into chunks that will fit in a food processor. Pulse three times, until the meat reduces to chunky crumbles (you're not aiming for a fine or smooth mix).

Heat a large sauté pan on high. Add the drained chicken livers, but do not crowd the pan; you may need to work in batches. Season with 1 tablespoon of the salt on both sides. Sear the livers until they darken and shrink, flipping them over after 1 minute. Let them cool slightly, then finely chop. Add the chopped liver to a large bowl, add the chopped pork shoulder, and combine. Set aside.

Return the sauté pan to medium heat. Add the onions, celery, bell pepper, poblanos, jalapeños, and garlic. Sweat, stirring to incorporate, until they soften, about 3 minutes. Season with the remaining 3 tablespoons of salt and the black pepper and cayenne pepper. Add the brown stock and cook, stirring occasionally, until the vegetables are soft, about 8 minutes. The stock will reduce and absorb into the vegetables. Remove from the heat.

(recipe continues)

Add the pan mixture to the chopped meat. Use a spatula to fold in the rice, scallions, and parsley until the mixture comes together. You want the mixture to be neither crumbly nor soupy, but tight and cohesive; you should be able to form a ball with it. Add additional brown stock if you need more liquid.

Cover the bowl and let it chill for 1 hour in the refrigerator.

Use a tablespoon to scoop the mixture and roll in your hands to form round balls. Line a sheet pan with parchment paper and place the balls on the sheet pan. Chill the balls in the refrigerator for 30 minutes.

Fry the boudin balls: In a large Dutch oven, add canola oil to a depth of about 2 inches (about 4 cups) and heat over medium to 350°F; check with an instant-read thermometer. Line a sheet pan or plate with paper towels.

In a medium bowl, add the eggs and the water. Whisk until fully combined.

On one shallow plate, sprinkle 2 cups of flour and 2 tablespoons of the salt and mix. On another shallow plate, place 2 cups of the breadcrumbs and the remaining 2 tablespoons of salt and mix. (You're reserving some of the breading mix in case you need to refresh your plates, as during the process sometimes the flour and breadcrumbs can get clumpy and not cover the balls as well.)

Remove the chilled balls from the refrigerator. Roll one ball in the flour to fully cover. Dip the ball in the egg wash and use a slotted spoon or fork to remove, so the excess wash drips off. Roll the ball in the breadcrumbs, again making sure it's fully covered.

Fry the boudin balls in batches until golden brown on all sides, turning occasionally, 2 to 3 minutes per side. Use a slotted spoon to remove the balls and place them on the paper towels. Repeat with the remaining balls. Season with salt to taste.

To serve: Enjoy immediately with Creole mustard.

SHRIMP AND SCIALATIELLI PASTA
IN RUNDOWN SAUCE

SERVES 6 TO 8

This is one of my favorite noodles, made with milk, semolina, and 00 flour (no egg!). The texture is chewy and lends itself nicely to the shrimp in this dish. The scialatielli noodle is commonly found on the Amalfi coast in Italy, which is where I first had it.

I like to use every element of the shrimp, not just the flesh, which is what we're doing in this recipe—we're going to use the heads and the shells to make the sauce and impart flavor. Louisiana shrimp are the sweetest, and the heads contain prized, tasty fat that you want to make sure you extract into the process. Rundown sauce in Jamaican cooking is mostly used for stewing mackerel or cooking breadfruit or yams in the sauce, but I wanted to try it with a pasta. My best friend, Mike Pirolo, uses the word "luscious" when he tastes something that slaps with silky flavor, and this is one of those dishes. Eat this with bread to get every last drop of goodness.

SCIALATIELLI PASTA

6 cups 00 flour, plus more for dusting

⅓ cup semolina flour, plus more for dusting

1 bunch of basil, leaves picked

1 cup whole milk

1 cup kosher salt, for cooking the pasta

SHRIMP AND RUNDOWN SAUCE

1 pound head-on U10-size shrimp, peeled and deveined, shells reserved (see Note)

2 lemons, zested

2 limes, zested

2 oranges, zested

1½ cups extra-virgin olive oil

1 lemongrass stalk, roughly chopped

½ cup roughly chopped fresh ginger

2 cups tomato paste

3 (14-ounce) cans coconut milk

1 Scotch bonnet pepper, torn or cut in half

¼ cup minced scallions

¼ cup chopped basil

¼ cup chopped flat-leaf parsley

¼ cup chopped mint

¼ cup (½ stick) unsalted butter

EQUIPMENT

Stand mixer with pasta roller attachment and fettucine cutter attachment

NOTE: To clean the shrimp, completely remove the shells (heads and tails), but reserve all the shells and set aside. To devein the shrimp, run a paring knife down the flesh to remove the vein that runs along the back. Repeat with all the shrimp.

Prep the scialatielli pasta: In the bowl of a stand mixer fitted with the dough hook, add the 00 flour and semolina flour. Mix on low speed just to combine, about 1 minute. While the mixer is on, add the basil, then drizzle in the milk. Mix to fully incorporate, until the dough is firm and smooth, about 10 minutes. If you're in a drier area, you may need to add a splash of water; humidity can affect pasta just like any other dough. Continue to mix to further develop the gluten, another 10 minutes. Remove the dough and wrap completely in plastic wrap. Allow the dough to rest at room temperature for 30 minutes.

Use a dough cutter or knife to cut the dough into 3 slabs. On an unfloured surface, roll the dough slabs into 1-inch-thick rectangles. (The friction of an unfloured surface keeps the dough from sliding around.) Roll the rectangles, one at a time, through the stand mixer's pasta roller attachment. Set it at the widest opening for the first pass, then as you pass the rectangle through, reduce the setting each time until you get to the second-lowest setting. This builds the elasticity of the dough. You'll end up with dough rolled out to 3 to 4 inches wide and ¼- to ⅛-inch thickness. Add the fettucine cutter attachment to the stand mixer and pass each rectangle through, then transfer the pasta to a sheet pan. Dust the pasta with a mixture of a bit of semolina and 00 flour, just enough to lightly coat, and chill in the freezer for 15 minutes.

Make the shrimp and rundown sauce: Cut the shrimp in half horizontally (it's harder to overcook the shrimp this way). In a medium bowl, add the halved shrimp, the zest of the lemons, limes, and oranges, and ¼ cup of the olive oil. Use a spoon to coat the shrimp, then chill in the refrigerator, uncovered, for 10 to 15 minutes.

(recipe continues)

In a large stockpot, add 1 cup of the olive oil and heat on medium. Add the lemongrass and ginger and sauté, stirring occasionally, until aromatic, about 3 minutes. Add the shrimp shells and raise the heat to medium-high. Continue to sauté, stirring occasionally, until they turn bright pink, about 10 minutes.

Reduce the heat to low and add the tomato paste, stirring to incorporate. Cook until a thick paste forms, 4 to 5 minutes. Add the coconut milk and Scotch bonnet and just enough water to cover the shells, 3 to 4 cups. Stir to combine and allow the mixture to simmer, uncovered, until the stock forms a thick reddish-pink sauce, about 45 minutes. It will have the consistency of heavy cream.

Strain the sauce through a mesh strainer into a large bowl and discard the shells and aromatics. Set the sauce aside.

Cook the pasta: Rinse out your large stockpot and add about 8 cups of water and the salt (we want a salty ocean vibe!). Bring to a rolling boil and add all the pasta. Use tongs to gently stir and loosen the noodles. Continue to cook until the noodles float to the top, 3 to 4 minutes. Reserve 1 cup of the pasta water to adjust consistency of sauce if needed. Use a colander to strain the noodles and hold them in the colander.

Combine the pasta and rundown sauce: In a large sauté pan, add the remaining ¼ cup of the olive oil and heat on medium heat for 2 minutes. Add the scallions and cook, stirring occasionally, until they soften, about 1 minute. Transfer the rundown sauce to the sauté pan and continue cooking on medium heat until the sauce reduces by half, 5 to 6 minutes. The sauce will thicken and deepen in color. Add the cooked pasta and the shrimp. Reduce the heat to low and stir to evenly coat the noodles, cooking until the shrimp turns bright pink and firm, about 3 minutes. Remove from the heat and add the basil, parsley, and mint. Add the butter and stir to combine and melt the butter. Serve immediately.

CRAWFISH HUSHPUPPIES

SERVES 8 TO 10 (MAKES ABOUT 3 DOZEN)

In Jamaica, they have festivals, a fried bread made of cornmeal. I'd see these in the seafood stalls as a side with my fish and rice and peas. In New Orleans, I was introduced to hushpuppies, and after the first bite I was like, ah this is familiar. Savory with a subtle, almost hidden sweetness, this hushpuppy recipe adds our treasured Louisiana crawfish tails. At the peak of crawfish season, nothing is better than shucking the head and pinching the tail. For this use, you'll want to buy the tails cooked and cleaned (save the live ones for your crawfish boil!). Fold these succulent babies into the cornmeal batter and fry until golden brown—I can guarantee you'll eat a dozen in one sitting!

CILANTRO AIOLI

1 cup cilantro, leaves and stems

2 jalapeños, seeded and minced

2 tablespoons drained capers, plus ¼ cup of the brine

1 tablespoon smoked pimentón

1 tablespoon green Tabasco hot sauce

2 cups Aioli (page 269) or mayonnaise

1 tablespoon kosher salt

HUSHPUPPIES

Canola oil, for frying

2½ cups cornmeal

2¼ cups all-purpose flour

2 tablespoons sugar

1 tablespoon sweet paprika

5 teaspoons baking powder

4 teaspoons kosher salt

1 teaspoon garlic powder

1 teaspoon onion powder

6 tablespoons (¾ stick) unsalted butter, cubed

1 cup minced scallions

3 jalapeños, minced

3 cups buttermilk

3 large eggs

1 cup crawfish tails, cooked and cleaned

Make the cilantro aioli: In a blender, combine the cilantro, jalapeños, capers and brine, pimentón, and hot sauce with about one-third of the aioli. Blend on low speed until a coarse paste forms, about 30 seconds, then transfer to a medium bowl. Mix in the remaining aioli and season with the salt. Set aside.

Make the hushpuppies: In a large Dutch oven, add oil to a depth of 3 inches (5 to 6 cups) and heat on medium-high heat to 325°F; check using an instant-read thermometer. Line a plate with paper towels.

In a medium bowl, whisk together the cornmeal, all-purpose flour, sugar, paprika, baking powder, salt, garlic powder, and onion powder until combined. In a small saucepan, melt the butter on low heat (or if you prefer, microwave for 1 minute, just to melt). Add the scallions and jalapeños to the melted butter and stir to combine.

In a separate medium bowl, whisk the buttermilk and eggs together, then use a spatula to fold the buttermilk mixture into the dry mixture. Don't overwork the mixture. Now add the melted butter mixture and the crawfish. Stir to combine. The batter should be smooth and firm—a spoon should stand up straight in the center.

Use a 1-ounce scoop (approximately 2 tablespoons) to transfer the batter to the hot oil. Work in batches, cooking 6 to 8 pieces in the oil at a time. Cook until golden brown, about 2 minutes, then flip and cook until evenly browned, another 2 minutes. Use a slotted spoon to transfer to the paper towels. Repeat with the remaining batter.

Serve immediately with the cilantro aioli for dipping.

CHILLED CRAWFISH AND CORN SOUP

SERVES 6

This recipe celebrates late spring and crawfish season in the Gulf. We get beautiful sweet corn. And with crawfish, whenever you can get it, you celebrate it. The season begins to dwindle by late June. When you get into late spring, it's the perfect weather—crisp, not too humid, and not too cold.

This won't surprise you by now, but I love cooking with coconut. It adds a fatty creaminess. Our guests at BABs-Nola responded well to this dish. The sweet, plump crawfish add a bit of umami. The ginger and turmeric add a brightness and a subtle spiciness. Herbs bring in a pop of freshness. This soul-satisfying soup can be served chilled as directed here; it's perfect for hot days. For cooler days, skip the ice bath and serve hot.

12 ears of corn

4 tablespoons extra-virgin olive oil

1 cup thinly sliced Spanish onion

3 tablespoons kosher salt, plus more as needed

¼ cup minced fresh ginger

1 tablespoon minced lemongrass

1 teaspoon fresh grated turmeric

1 teaspoon red chili flakes

4 cups coconut milk

1 lemon, zested

3 mirlitons, cored and finely diced

2 cups crawfish tails, cooked and cleaned

GARNISH

1 radish, thinly sliced

½ bunch of basil, leaves picked

¼ bunch of mint, leaves picked

Shuck the corn: Remove the husks and use a knife to shave off the kernels. An easy method is to place a kitchen towel in the center of a mixing bowl. Hold an ear upright in the center of the towel, then use a chef's knife to shave off the kernels into the bowl. This way is steady and you avoid the kernels going everywhere. Set aside the kernels and reserve the cobs.

Snap the cobs in half and place them in a medium stockpot. Cover with water by 4 inches. Simmer on low heat, uncovered, for about 30 minutes. You're infusing the water with corn flavor. Remove and discard the cobs and set aside the corn stock; you'll have about 4 quarts.

In a large saucepot on medium heat, add 2 tablespoons of the oil and the onions. Sauté, stirring occasionally, until translucent, about 8 minutes. Season with the salt, then add the ginger, lemongrass, turmeric, red chili flakes, and three-quarters of the corn kernels. Reduce the heat to low and continue to sauté, stirring occasionally, for about 10 minutes. The corn will brighten in color as it caramelizes, and the onions will develop a golden brown color.

Add the coconut milk to the pot and pour in enough corn stock to cover by 2 to 3 inches. Cover and simmer on low heat for 30 to 40 minutes, adding more stock if the liquid reduces to expose the vegetables.

Fill a large bowl with ice water. Transfer the soup in batches to a blender and puree until smooth, about 1 minute (open the center lid to allow steam to escape). Put the soup in a medium bowl, add the lemon zest, and place the bowl in the ice bath. Chill for 10 minutes.

In a medium sauté pan, add the remaining 2 tablespoons of oil, and sauté the mirlitons and remaining corn kernels on high heat, stirring occasionally, until tender, about 1 minute. Season with a pinch of salt. Allow to cool.

When ready to serve, add a spoonful of the sautéed mirlitons and corn to each serving bowl. Add a spoonful of crawfish tails. Pour the soup around the sautéed vegetables and seafood.

To garnish: Top each serving with some of the radish, mint, and basil. Serve immediately.

FRIED OKRA
WITH PICKLED GREEN BEAN REMOULADE

SERVES 4

It's hard to overstate the symbolism of okra, which is all over New Orleans. "Gombo," a precursor to "gumbo," is the word for okra in many West African languages. It's obvious in the etymology and the African ancestry here that our most treasured dish in this part of the diaspora comes from the continent. Fried okra is delicious; it's an easy snack to prepare, and a quick dip in hot oil won't activate the slippery mouthfeel in okra's texture (though a lot of African dishes, like okro stew in Nigeria, certainly indicate that's the best part!).

PICKLED GREEN BEAN REMOULADE

- ½ cup pickled green beans (store-bought is fine)
- ¼ cup pickled cherry peppers, drained
- 2 tablespoons drained capers, plus 1 tablespoon of the brine
- 2 large eggs
- 2 teaspoons Dijon mustard
- 2 lemons, zested
- 1 garlic clove, finely grated
- 2 cups canola oil

FRIED OKRA

- Canola oil, for frying
- 2 cups sliced okra, cut into ½-inch rounds
- 1 cup buttermilk
- 2 tablespoons all-purpose flour
- 2 tablespoons cornmeal
- ¼ teaspoon kosher salt, plus more to taste
- ⅛ teaspoon freshly ground black pepper, plus more to taste

Make the pickled green bean remoulade: In a food processor, add the pickled green beans, cherry peppers, and capers and their brine, and pulse to finely chop. Add the eggs, Dijon mustard, lemon zest, and garlic and puree. With the processor running, slowly add the oil and continue to process until the entire mixture becomes thick and creamy. Refrigerate, covered, while you fry the okra (it can keep for 3 to 5 days).

Make the fried okra: In a deep-fat fryer or large sauté pan, add canola oil to a depth of 1½ inches (about 2½ cups) and heat on medium to 375°F; check using an instant-read thermometer. Line a plate with paper towels.

Pat the sliced okra dry with paper towels. In a shallow bowl, add the buttermilk. In another shallow bowl, combine the flour, cornmeal, salt, and pepper. Dip a piece of the okra in the buttermilk, then roll it around in the cornmeal mixture to coat. Add it to the oil and repeat with a few more pieces. Fry the okra, working in batches, until golden brown, 1 to 3 minutes on each side. Keep an eye on them. Use a slotted spoon to drain the fried okra and transfer to the paper towels. Repeat with the remaining slices.

Season with additional salt and pepper to your liking. Serve hot with the pickled green bean remoulade.

PHEASANT GUMBO

SERVES 6 TO 8

Gumbo in New Orleans typically features chicken, andouille sausage, shrimp, and crab (some folks have stronger opinions about separating the seafood, but the old Creole recipes tend to keep everything together). The lines between Creole and Cajun continue to blur; people think andouille is of New Orleans, but it's actually from Cajun country. Traditionally it's a Sunday dinner or festive dish. Gumbo, of course, centers okra, referencing the traditional okra stews from West Africa, mixed with the French influence of a flour roux that adds flavor and color. We also have okra stew in St. Lucia. But the first time I had *pheasant* gumbo, I was at JazzFest, a major late-spring music and culinary event that takes place over two weeks. I have never been to a music festival where people plan who they're going to watch perform as carefully as they plan what they're going to eat, but both are of great importance at JazzFest. Prejean's is a Cajun restaurant in Lafayette that has been around for fifty years, and they are a food vendor at the festival. Believe me when I say it's the best gumbo I have ever had.

I was intimidated about making gumbo because it's deeply personal to folks in New Orleans. Its origins are not as a restaurant dish; it's practically a family heirloom. Everyone has an opinion, and people know what they're talking about. But their interpretation gave me an understanding of how gumbo is hearty, but so delicate, from the roux toastiness to the consistency of the broth. The pheasant brings out a deep flavor. This is my take on their recipe. If you have trouble sourcing pheasant, substitute chicken or turkey.

2 (3-pound) whole pheasants, butchered into 6 pieces each, skin removed and reserved

6 tablespoons kosher salt

2 tablespoons Crystal hot sauce

1 tablespoon cayenne pepper

2 teaspoons freshly ground black pepper

4 cups sliced andouille sausage

2 cups sliced smoked sausage

½ cup canola oil

1 cup all-purpose flour

4 cups finely diced Spanish onions

1 cup finely diced celery

½ cup diced green bell pepper

2 garlic cloves, chopped

3 bay leaves

4 cups thinly sliced okra, cut into ¼-inch rounds

4 quarts Brown Stock (page 279)

1 bunch of scallions, sliced, for garnish

SERVING
Steamed white rice

In a large bowl, season the pheasant with 2 tablespoons of the salt and the hot sauce, cayenne pepper, and black pepper. Marinate in the refrigerator, uncovered, for 1 hour.

In a large pot, cook the reserved pheasant skin on medium heat, stirring occasionally, until the fat renders and the skin develops a golden brown color, about 3 minutes. Strain the contents. Place the strained fat back in the pot and discard the skin. Working in batches, add the pheasant pieces to the pot and sear on high heat until brown on all sides, about 10 minutes total. Transfer the pheasant to a plate.

Add the andouille and smoked sausages to the same pot on medium heat and cook, stirring occasionally, until golden brown all over, about 5 minutes, then transfer to another plate. Add the canola oil to the rendered fat.

Whisk the flour into the fat and keep whisking continuously on low heat until the flour turns a dark chocolate color, roughly 45 minutes. This roux requires patience, so keep the heat on low, keep stirring, and don't rush it!

Add the onions and cook on low heat, stirring occasionally, until golden brown, 5 to 6 minutes. Add the celery, peppers, garlic, bay leaves, and okra, and cook, stirring occasionally, until the vegetables are tender, about 10 minutes. Add 2 tablespoons of salt, stir, then deglaze with 2 cups of stock, scraping browned bits from the bottom of the pan.

Add the remaining stock and the pheasant to the pot and bring to a simmer. Let simmer on low heat until the pheasant falls off the bone, about 1 hour. Use tongs to remove the pheasant and use a fork to pick the meat off the bone. Return the meat to the pot and discard the bones. Return the sausage to the pot and warm through. Adjust the seasoning with the remaining 2 tablespoons of salt. Remove bay leaves and discard. Garnish with the scallions.

To serve: Enjoy with steamed rice.

BARBECUE SHRIMP

SERVES 4

New Orleans barbecue shrimp refers not to the cooking process of grilling, but to the rich flavor and color of the shrimp. My first time having this dish was at Emeril's and it blew my mind, the depth of flavor. Pascal's Manale, a classic restaurant in New Orleans, introduced this dish in the 1950s and other spots followed. The dish reminded me of having mackerel or crayfish in rundown sauce in Jamaica—the sauce is cooked down with tomatoes, coconut milk, and spices, and its super luscious complexity with the briny seafood is memorable. If you have access to shrimp from the Gulf, get them. You already know that sweetness is irreplaceable!

2 pounds U10-size shrimp, heads and shells on

2 tablespoons freshly ground black pepper

2 tablespoons Jerk Spice (page 134)

2 tablespoons extra-virgin olive oil

¼ cup minced Spanish onion

2 tablespoons minced garlic

2 cups water

½ cup Worcestershire sauce

¼ cup dry white wine

3 lemons, peeled and juiced (reserve the peels)

3 bay leaves

¼ teaspoon kosher salt

2 cups heavy cream

2 tablespoons unsalted butter

1 tablespoon chopped chives

SERVING SUGGESTION

Compère Lapin Buttermilk Biscuits (page 248) or thick slices of crusty bread

Peel the shrimp and completely remove the shells, but reserve the shells and set aside. To devein the shrimp, run a paring knife down the flesh to remove the vein that runs along the back. Repeat with all of the shrimp and set aside.

Transfer the shrimp to a medium bowl. Sprinkle the shrimp with the black pepper and 1 tablespoon of the jerk seasoning. Use your hands to coat the shrimp with the seasonings. Refrigerate the shrimp while you make the sauce base.

Heat 1 tablespoon of the oil in a large pot over high heat. When the oil is hot, add the onions and garlic and sauté, stirring occasionally, until softened, about 1 minute. Add the reserved shrimp shells and the remaining 1 tablespoon jerk seasoning. Cook, stirring occasionally, until the shells turn pink, about 2 minutes. Add the water, Worcestershire, white wine, lemon peels, bay leaves, and salt. Stir well and bring to a boil. Reduce the heat to low and simmer, uncovered, until it thickens and develops a caramel color, about 30 minutes. Remove from the heat and allow to cool for about 15 minutes. Use a fine-mesh strainer to strain the sauce into a small saucepan. You should have about 1½ cups. Discard the solids.

Bring the sauce to a boil and reduce to a simmer, stirring occasionally, until it becomes syrupy and dark brown, simmering for about 10 minutes. This will yield about 2 tablespoons of the barbecue sauce base.

Heat the remaining 1 tablespoon of oil in a large skillet over high heat. When the oil is hot, add the seasoned shrimp and sauté them, occasionally shaking the skillet, until the shrimp turn pink, about 2 minutes. Whisk the cream and butter into the barbecue base. Add to the shrimp and stir to coat. Reduce to the heat to low. After 2 minutes, flip the shrimp and use a spoon to baste the shrimp with the barbecue sauce. Continue to cook for another 2 minutes until the sauce again coats the shrimp. Add the lemon juice and stir to incorporate. Sprinkle with the chives.

Serve right away with buttermilk biscuits or thick slices of crusty bread.

CREOLE POTATO SALAD

SERVES 4

In many places, potato salad cues the start of summer barbecues and picnics; in New Orleans, we also eat it the rest of the year because we serve it with gumbo. It's common to serve a heaping spoonful of potato salad in your bowl of gumbo along with steamed white rice. The combo surprised me at first, but I became a fan. The trinity (green bell peppers, onions, and celery) with the Creole mustard sets Creole potato salad apart from any other variety I've had.

2 pounds new potatoes, diced into 1-inch pieces

½ cup plus 3 tablespoons kosher salt

8 slices bacon, cut into ½-inch strips (or 2 tablespoons extra-virgin olive oil)

2 green bell peppers, finely diced

1 small red onion, diced

1 cup Aioli (page 269) or Duke's mayonnaise

½ cup minced dill pickles, plus 3 tablespoons pickle juice

3 tablespoons Creole mustard (such as Zatarain's)

2 tablespoons diced celery

1 tablespoon Creole seasoning (such as Tony Chachere's)

4 hard-boiled eggs, roughly chopped

1 cup thinly sliced scallions

SERVING SUGGESTION

Serve as a side with your summer grilling or with gumbo on cooler days.

In a medium pot, add the diced potatoes and cover with water by 3 inches. Add the ½ cup salt and bring to a boil. Reduce the heat to medium and simmer, uncovered, for about 15 minutes, until the potatoes are fork tender. Use a colander to drain the potatoes. Lay them on a sheet pan and allow to cool.

If using the bacon, in a medium sauté pan, cook the bacon over medium heat, stirring occasionally, until crispy, about 10 minutes. Remove the bacon and keep the fat in the pan. If not using the bacon, add the olive oil. Add the bell peppers and red onions and sauté, stirring briefly, just to warm them through, about 1 minute.

Transfer the vegetables to a large bowl. Add the potatoes, aioli, pickles and their juice, Creole mustard, celery, and Creole seasoning. Roughly chop the bacon and add to the bowl. Season with the remaining 3 tablespoons of salt and gently fold in the hard-boiled eggs. Garnish with scallions and enjoy.

GLAZED DUCK
WITH DIRTY RICE

SERVES 4

One thing I love in Cajun country cooking is that nothing goes to waste, just like in the Caribbean. I learned about dirty rice in Louisiana; it's a delicious dish that traditionally features the chicken or pork end cuts, diced up and seasoned, then mixed in with leftover white rice. They call Louisiana the sportsman's paradise because there's so much hunting and fishing culture, and ducks are indeed fair game. I've gone duck hunting with Larry and his friends. We cleaned the duck, plucked the feathers, blanched it and removed the innards, then broke down the carcass. We used pretty much every part. This recipe is inspired by that hunting trip, but don't worry! I've got you covered with a duck breast—no hunting gear required. The flavor of brown stock is key; don't sub it out. I prefer D'Artagnan duck breast because it cooks evenly and it's not too chewy (you can ask your butcher). Note the advance preparation of steeping the glaze overnight.

GLAZE
6 green cardamom pods
2 teaspoons coriander seeds
3 whole cloves
1 teaspoon whole black peppercorns
1 teaspoon red chili flakes
⅓ cup Steen's cane syrup

SOUR CHERRY JUS
2 cups red wine
4 quarts Brown Stock (page 279)
1 sprig of rosemary
1 cup frozen sour cherries

DIRTY RICE
4 tablespoons extra-virgin olive oil
1 cup roughly chopped spicy Italian sausage (you can remove any casing)
½ cup minced chicken livers
1 teaspoon kosher salt, plus more to taste
1 teaspoon red chili flakes
1 medium Spanish onion, finely diced
½ cup finely diced celery
2 Italian long hot peppers, seeded and minced
2 tablespoons minced flat-leaf parsley
2 teaspoons minced oregano
2 garlic cloves, grated
2 cups steamed jasmine rice (such as Two Brooks Farm)

DUCK BREAST
2 tablespoons fennel seeds
2 teaspoons coriander seeds
½ teaspoon cumin seeds
⅛ teaspoon red chili flakes
4 (8-ounce) Long Island duck breasts, fat scored into crosshatches
2 tablespoons kosher salt

Make the glaze: Use the flat end of a knife to crush the cardamom pods so that the shells break. In a small pot, add the crushed cardamom (including the seeds!), coriander seeds, cloves, peppercorns, and chili flakes, followed by the syrup. Cook, uncovered, over low heat, stirring occasionally, to infuse the spices in the syrup, about 30 minutes. Remove from the heat and let steep overnight (8 to 10 hours) at room temperature.

Make the sour cherry jus: In a medium pot, add the wine and cook over high heat, stirring occasionally, to reduce to about one-third of the initial volume, about 45 minutes. Add the brown stock and continue cooking on high heat, stirring once in a while, to reduce to half of the starting volume, about 1 hour. Add the rosemary sprig and frozen cherries and keep cooking on high heat to reduce until the jus coats the back of a spoon, about 20 minutes. Use a fine-mesh strainer to remove the cherries and rosemary, which you can discard. Set the jus aside and keep warm. (You can make this 1 day before and keep in the refrigerator, or freeze for up to 1 week.)

Make the dirty rice: In a medium stockpot, add 2 tablespoons of the olive oil and the sausage and sauté over high heat, stirring occasionally, until golden brown, about 10 minutes.

Add the livers and continue cooking, stirring to cook evenly, until it browns, 8 to 10 minutes. Add the remaining 2 tablespoons of olive oil. Season with the 1 teaspoon of salt and the chili flakes, then add the onion, celery, peppers, parsley, oregano, and garlic. Cook, stirring to combine, until the vegetables are tender, 5 to 6 minutes. Add the cooked rice and stir well. Heat until the rice is warmed through.

Add additional salt to your taste preference. Set aside and keep warm.

Make the duck breast: Heat the oven to 350°F. Line a plate with paper towels.

In a large, dry sauté pan, lightly toast the fennel, coriander, cumin, and chili flakes on low heat, stirring occasionally, until fragrant, about 5 minutes. In a spice grinder, coarsely grind the toasted spices and set aside.

Raise the heat to medium. Season the duck breasts with the salt and place them, fatty side down, in the same sauté pan. Cook for 15 minutes; don't flip the breasts, as you want the fat to become crispy, but use a spoon to baste the rendered fat over the breast every 30 seconds or so. The hot fat helps to cook the meaty side of the duck breast slowly and gently and to ensure the duck is juicy. Cook until the skin is rendered and crispy and the meat becomes firm and plump, about 5 more minutes.

Transfer the duck breasts to the paper towel–lined plate.

Return the glaze that has been infusing to low heat and reheat just long enough for it to become viscous, about 10 minutes. Use a fine-mesh strainer to remove the spices, and reserve the glaze.

Transfer the duck breasts to a sheet pan with the crispy side up. Use a spoon to coat the duck skin with glaze, then sprinkle the ground spices on top.

Roast until the glaze caramelizes (keep an eye on it—don't burn the sugars), about 5 minutes, then let rest for 3 to 5 minutes. Slice the duck breast in half lengthwise. Serve the duck on top of the dirty rice and pour the sour cherry jus around the rice and the duck. Enjoy immediately.

OYSTER DRESSING

SERVES 4

During my first holiday season in New Orleans, my opening staff at Compère Lapin hipped me to the requisite dishes that had to be on the holiday table. I wanted to hear about their favorites, and immediately my very first hire, a line cook named Shonda Cross, yelled, "Chef! The dressing, of course!" I said, "Dressing?" I was then schooled on what dressing is: a cornbread-based side dish that may feature crab or oysters and goes great with holiday ham and turkey. My whole staff chimed in with the different types and the overall process. I made this recipe and have never looked back. It's a delight.

½ cup (1 stick) unsalted butter, plus more for the pan

1 cup minced scallions

½ cup minced Spanish onion

3 large celery stalks, minced

½ green bell pepper, minced

¼ teaspoon thyme leaves

1 teaspoon cayenne pepper

2 tablespoons kosher salt

½ to 1 cup Brown Stock (page 279), as needed

3 cups diced cornbread (1-inch cubes)

1 cup roughly chopped day-old bread or biscuits

2 dozen Gulf oysters, shucked (see Note; reserve their liquor)

¼ cup fresh lemon juice

¼ cup chopped flat-leaf parsley

1 tablespoon minced sage (or 1 teaspoon dried sage)

½ teaspoon ground white pepper

EQUIPMENT

Oyster knife (optional)

Clean kitchen towel (optional)

NOTE: In New Orleans, it's easy to buy shucked oysters; you'll find them in a pint-sized container in their liquor. But elsewhere, you may need to get the hang of shucking your own. It's easy to do. Rinse the oysters well to release any sediment and grit. Fold a kitchen towel into a rectangle. Hold the rectangle in your nondominant hand and fit the oyster into the folded towel, so the opening of the oyster is facing out and the oyster shell is parallel to your work surface (try not to tilt it in your hand). Keep a snug hold on the base of the oyster in your palm, and with your other hand, insert the tip of an oyster knife into the crevice and wiggle it around gently, but firmly, until the opening pops. Move the knife around the entire circumference until you can pry open the oyster and remove the top shell.

Be careful to not lose the liquor in the shell, as that's important flavor. Take the oyster knife and run it underneath the bottom of the oyster meat so you sever it from the muscles, but if serving raw, keep the meat in the shell. This allows for easy slurping when you and your friends start taking them down, one by one!

Heat the oven to 350°F. Grease an 8 × 8-inch baking dish with a pat of butter.

In a large sauté pan, melt ¼ cup (½ stick) of the butter over medium heat. Add the scallions, onions, celery, bell pepper, thyme, and cayenne. Sauté, stirring occasionally, until the vegetables are almost translucent, 5 minutes. Add 1 tablespoon of the salt, then add ½ cup of the stock and cook, stirring occasionally, to combine the ingredients, about 5 minutes, then remove from heat. Add the cornbread and day-old bread to the pan and stir to combine.

In a medium bowl, stir together the oysters, lemon juice, parsley, sage, remaining 1 tablespoon of salt, and the white pepper. Add to the bread mixture and stir well to combine. If the dressing seems too dry, add a little oyster liquor and up to ½ cup more broth; the mixture should be very moist.

Spoon the dressing into the baking dish. Cut the remaining ¼ cup (½ stick) of butter into small pieces and scatter over the top of the dressing.

Bake until the top and sides are brown, 30 to 40 minutes. Serve hot.

OYSTER PAN STEW

SERVES 2 TO 4

I can relate to having access to beautiful seafood all the time in St. Lucia, and people around the Gulf are in the same position. Seafood from this region is some of the best, hands down. Beyond the proximity, we have such a diverse variety all year long.

This dish can feel decadent but doesn't require a lot of work. The smoky, peppery flavors stand out, and when it all comes together, it's a visual stunner. During crawfish season, I add crawfish tails; those plump babies are sweet and tender and set this dish on fire.

1 dried ancho chili

2 cups panko breadcrumbs

1 cup (2 sticks) unsalted butter or Chili Butter (page 275)

1 small Spanish onion, finely diced

2 celery stalks, finely diced

1 poblano pepper, finely diced

2 tablespoons kosher salt

4 sprigs of thyme

2 tablespoons all-purpose flour

3 cups heavy cream

4 cups shucked Gulf oysters (see page 244; about 48 oysters)

3 tablespoons chopped flat-leaf parsley

1 lemon, zested and juiced

In a small bowl, cover the ancho chili with hot water. Allow to rehydrate until softened, 10 to 15 minutes, then drain. Remove the seeds, chop the chili, and set aside.

Heat a dry medium skillet over medium heat. Add the panko breadcrumbs and toast, stirring occasionally, until golden brown, 3 to 5 minutes. Transfer to a small bowl and set aside.

In a medium saucepot, melt the butter on low heat. Add the onions, celery, and poblano. Sauté, stirring briefly, until the onion and celery are translucent, about 2 minutes. Season with 1 tablespoon of the salt and the thyme. Add the flour and cook over low heat, stirring to combine, for 1 more minute.

Stir in the ancho chili. Add the cream and simmer, stirring to combine, until the mixture thickens to coat the back of a spoon, about 8 minutes.

Add the oysters and cook to warm through, about 1 minute. Then add the parsley, lemon zest and juice, and remaining 1 tablespoon of salt. Transfer to a serving bowl. Sprinkle the toasted breadcrumbs on top and serve immediately.

COMPÈRE LAPIN
BUTTERMILK BISCUITS

MAKES 12

Biscuits are important in the South, as any bread is vital to the culture where it's made. We have bakes in St. Lucia and roti in Trinidad; in the South, you get a lot of biscuits, which people take seriously. You'll find biscuits served with pimento cheese or served as a sandwich with fried chicken. Some folks do a drop batter, a wetter mixture that results in a cakier biscuit. But I prefer laminated biscuits using butter, where you alternate layering the flour dough with fat. When it bakes, the biscuit is super flaky. For me, the flakier the better. We didn't realize how many biscuits we'd go through at Compère Lapin, but everyone orders the biscuits: We make about one thousand on average each week.

5¼ cups all-purpose flour, plus more for dusting

2 cups cake flour

2 tablespoons cane sugar

1 tablespoon baking powder

2 tablespoons kosher salt

½ teaspoon baking soda

2 cups (4 sticks) unsalted butter, cold and diced into ¼-inch cubes

1 cup thinly sliced chives

2 cups plus 6 tablespoons buttermilk

1 large egg yolk

3 tablespoons flaky sea salt

SERVING SUGGESTION
Bacon Butter (page 275) or Honey Butter (page 274)

Heat the oven to 325°F. Line a sheet pan with parchment paper.

In the bowl of a stand mixer fitted with the paddle attachment, add the all-purpose and cake flours, sugar, baking powder, kosher salt, and baking soda. Add the butter and mix on a low speed for 5 to 8 minutes, until the mix develops into pea-sized balls. Add the chives and continue mixing for 1 minute, just to combine. Slowly add the 2 cups of the buttermilk and keep mixing until a firm, smooth, cohesive dough forms, about 5 minutes. Do not overmix the dough!

On a floured surface, turn out the dough and roll with a rolling pin into a rectangle about 12 × 4 inches and 2 inches thick. Use a dough cutter to cut the biscuits into twelve 2-inch squares. Place the squares on the sheet pan.

In a small bowl, whisk together the remaining 6 tablespoons of buttermilk and the egg yolk until combined to make an egg wash. Gently brush the egg wash over the top of the biscuits and sprinkle the flaky sea salt on top.

Bake until golden brown, rotating the pan after 10 minutes to ensure even baking, 20 to 30 minutes total. Serve immediately.

TEMPURA SHRIMP SANDWICH

SERVES 2

We take our sandwich history seriously in New Orleans: the muffuletta, from Italian immigrants, featuring cured meats and cheese with olive salad on a sesame loaf; the po' boy, a literal "poor boy's" sandwich that gained popularity in the 1930s for striking streetcar workers, initially with potatoes, bits of roast beef, and gravy; and the bánh mì, courtesy of our Vietnamese community—a hybrid of the French baguette, pork pâté, jalapeño, carrot, and cucumber.

Frady's One Stop is my go-to for po' boys, and my favorite is shrimp (you can get meat or fried seafood po' boys). When you order a po' boy, you can ask for it to be dressed (with mayo, lettuce, and tomatoes) and with debris (braised bits of roast beef, owing to the sandwich's origins). For a bánh mì, I go to the West Bank, across the bridge, fifteen minutes out of New Orleans, to a stand in the Hong Kong Market. I make a day of it and shop for fresh fish, marinades, and so on, and I always get an avocado bubble tea.

I was introduced to Vietnamese culture in New Orleans while filming *Top Chef*. At the dock, we met local fishermen in shrimping boots, who showed us their catch and cooked for us. It felt like being back on Hellshire Beach or Gros Islet. This recipe is my twist on a po 'boy–meets–bánh mì. I like tempura batter to keep the shrimp juicy, but with a crispy coating, and we dress it in pickled pineapple tartar sauce for a sweet tang.

TEMPURA BATTER

4 cups rice flour

1½ cups cold sparkling water

1 tablespoon kosher salt

VINAIGRETTE

½ cup fish sauce (such as Red Boat)

¼ cup Garlic Oil (page 271)

2 limes, zested and juiced

2 tablespoons light brown sugar

2 tablespoons chopped pickled red onion (store-bought is fine)

2 tablespoons toasted sesame oil

SANDWICH COMPONENTS

1 cup seasoned rice vinegar

1 jumbo carrot, thinly sliced

Canola oil, for frying

20 U10-size shrimp, peeled and deveined

Kosher salt

1 English cucumber, thinly sliced

2 jalapeños, thinly sliced

1 cup Pickled Pineapple Tartar Sauce (page 273)

1 large baguette, halved lengthwise and toasted (or 2 toasted brioche buns)

1 bunch of mint, picked

1 bunch of cilantro, leaves picked

SERVING SUGGESTION

Mixed greens salad, served with Mojo Vinaigrette (page 273)

Make the tempura batter: In a medium bowl, whisk together the rice flour, sparkling water, and salt. Mix until the batter coats a spoon; it should be thick like honey. (Using sparkling water makes the tempura light and airy when it fries up.) Cover and refrigerate until you're ready to fry the shrimp.

Make the vinaigrette: In a medium bowl, whisk together the fish sauce, garlic oil, lime zest and juice, brown sugar, pickled red onion, and sesame oil.

Prepare the sandwich components: In a small pot, heat the rice vinegar over high heat until boiling, then add the carrots. Remove from the heat. Allow to cool slightly for 15 minutes and then use a spoon to remove the carrots and reserve.

In a large Dutch oven, add canola oil to a depth of 4 inches (about 4 cups) and heat on high to 350°F; check using an instant-read thermometer. Line a plate with paper towels.

Remove the tempura batter from the refrigerator and if needed, use a fork or whisk to give it a quick stir to blend it again. Drop the shrimp into the tempura batter and toss to coat, then gently shake off any excess batter. Using a slotted spoon, dip the shrimp, one at a time, one-third of the way into the oil to allow the batter to set, about 20 seconds. Release the shrimp into the oil completely, repeat with a few more shrimp, and fry in batches until golden brown, about 2 minutes on each side. Use the slotted spoon to remove the shrimp and place them on the paper towels. Season with a pinch of salt. Repeat with the remaining shrimp.

In a small bowl, combine the cucumber, jalapeño, and pickled carrots with the vinaigrette and let marinate at room temperature for 2 minutes. Smear the tartar sauce on each half of your bread.

Use a fine-mesh strainer to drain the slaw. Evenly distribute the shrimp and vegetables across the baguette (or between the buns) and top with mint and cilantro. Cut the assembled baguette into 2 portions. Serve immediately.

CABBAGE SALAD
WITH TAMARIND VINAIGRETTE

SERVES 4

The Vietnamese population is strong in New Orleans. While I'd had Vietnamese food before, this was a different experience. It was my first time in a city with a large Asian community, and it felt like an immersion: I could go to grocery stores that fully catered to Vietnamese cuisine and be surrounded by foods I grew up with, thanks to the similar tropical environment (soursop, breadfruit, mangoes). I also encountered countless ingredients that were new to me, staples like dried fish, rice cakes, glass noodles, all kinds of dried chilies, and fermented vegetables. A common but iconic dish in Vietnamese cuisine is the green papaya salad, mixed with dried shrimp, chilies, peanuts, and fresh herbs, served in a sweet and sour nước chấm dressing (it has just the right amount of fish sauce).

My version features white cabbage, a callback to the side salads on a typical island plate, along with jerk-spiced peanuts and a tamarind lime vinaigrette. Don't use napa cabbage or red cabbage for this recipe; the white cabbage gives the perfect bite and texture.

Heat the oven to 300°F. Line a sheet pan with parchment paper.

In a medium bowl, toss the peanuts, jerk spice, and olive oil until the nuts are well coated. Transfer the seasoned peanuts to the prepared sheet pan. Roast until the nuts smell toasty and the spices have slightly darkened, stirring occasionally to ensure even roasting, about 10 minutes.

Allow to cool and then roughly chop the peanuts.

Make the dressing in a blender: Combine the fish sauce, sugar, lime zest and juice, chili, and tamarind concentrate. Blend until smooth.

In a large bowl, add the cabbage. Dress it in the tamarind vinaigrette and use tongs to gently toss so the dressing is fully distributed. Top the salad with the chopped jerk peanuts and torn cilantro, basil, and mint. Serve immediately.

1 cup roasted salted peanuts

2 tablespoons Jerk Spice (page 134)

1 tablespoon extra-virgin olive oil

½ cup fish sauce (such as Red Boat)

⅓ cup light brown sugar

4 limes, zested and juiced

1 fresh red Thai chili, minced

1 teaspoon tamarind concentrate

4 cups shredded white cabbage (about half of a large cabbage)

½ bunch of cilantro

½ cup basil leaves

½ cup mint leaves

COCONUT-BRAISED COLLARD GREENS

SERVES 4

In the South, collards are a must. I created this side dish for an event at Dooky Chase's, the iconic Creole restaurant shaped by chef Leah Chase, the true queen of twentieth-century Creole cooking. She transformed the 1940s autonomous sandwich shop owned by her husband's family into a fine dining restaurant that celebrated elegance in Black Southern cooking, and she did it from the height of Jim Crow until she passed at the age of ninety-six in 2019. The restaurant was not only a beacon for beautiful food and service; Mrs. Chase challenged the law by serving a racially mixed dining room. Under her leadership, Dooky Chase's became a destination for civil rights leaders like Martin Luther King, Jr., who went there for rest, restoration, and to strategize the movement. Mrs. Chase's leadership echoed that of many Black women throughout the South who used food to cultivate, and literally feed, the resistance.

Of course, I found cooking greens at Dooky Chase's to be nerve-racking! I love going to the restaurant, whose legacy in the Tremé neighborhood and far beyond continues under the leadership of Mrs. Chase's family. She always wanted folks to feel welcome in her dining room, and you feel the epitome of family there. Her grandchildren exude warmth and pride in their grandmother's legacy that beams throughout the space. Mrs. Chase was renowned for her art collection, which heralds great American masters, a living gallery. To be greeted by her family when I walked in for the event, I felt a little pressure! When Dook IV, Mrs. Chase's grandson and now the restaurant's chef, tasted my greens, he closed his eyes, smiled, and laughed, saying, "I would have never thought of cooking them with coconut milk." He winked and told me, "I may have to borrow this recipe." Using coconut milk to braise leafy greens is common for many African diaspora and Latin American cultures, but I felt blessed that my version came out right that day.

2 tablespoons coconut oil
1 large Spanish onion, thinly sliced
1 teaspoon cayenne pepper
1 teaspoon smoked paprika
3 bunches of collard greens, tough stem ends trimmed, stems and leaves sliced ½ inch wide
2 tablespoons kosher salt
2 (14-ounce) cans coconut milk

In a large saucepan on medium heat, add the coconut oil and sweat the onions, stirring occasionally, until translucent, about 3 minutes.

Add the cayenne pepper and paprika. Stir to evenly distribute, and cook until the spices are well incorporated, about 3 more minutes.

Add the collard greens and salt, then cook and stir occasionally until the greens soften, 5 to 10 minutes. Add the coconut milk, cover, and reduce the heat to low. Simmer until the greens are tender and the sauce is creamy, about 45 minutes. Serve immediately.

COPPER BUNNY COCKTAIL

MAKES 1

In New Orleans people know their food, but they know their drinks just as well. At Compère Lapin, we wanted a signature drink that pulled in Caribbean influences (the pineapple and ginger) and felt festive. The Copper Bunny has been on the menu since opening. It's best enjoyed on a sunny day with friends. We feature Dulce Vida tequila because we like the floral perfume of pineapple and its punchy jalapeño bite. Of course, we serve it in a Copper Bunny vessel, in reference to our namesake.

¾ ounce vodka (such as Absolut Elyx)

¾ ounce pineapple jalapeño tequila (such as Dulce Vida)

¾ ounce pineapple liqueur

¾ ounce ginger liqueur

1 ounce fresh lime juice

Crushed ice plus 2 ice cubes

4 ounces champagne (or other dry white sparkling wine)

EQUIPMENT

Cocktail shaker

Collins glass

In a cocktail shaker, add the vodka, tequila, and both liqueurs, and then the lime juice. Add two cubes of ice and gently shake three times to incorporate. Add crushed ice to a Collins glass and strain the mix into the glass. Top with the champagne and enjoy.

HOT FIRE CHICKEN

SERVES 6

In St. Lucia, when we eat our peppa sauce, it doesn't blow your socks off; it has a slow, flavorful build that enhances the food. I wanted a spicy chicken recipe that layers heat and flavor so the heat could build without dulling the palate. Don't get me wrong, the fire is there, but you'll also be able to taste the other food on the table! I achieve this by layering the heat in the different stages of the recipe: there's chili in the buttermilk brine and in the sauce. This subtle addition allows for a well-rounded, in-depth flavor and spice, instead of just blasting it at the end.

In various forms this dish has appeared at Compère Lapin, BABs-Nola, and now Nina's Creole Cottage. Top this with the Mirliton and Carrot Slaw (page 259). Note the advance preparation of brining the chicken overnight.

BRINE

4 cups buttermilk

1 bunch of thyme

6 tablespoons kosher salt

¼ cup Calabrian chili paste

3 tablespoons Jerk Spice (page 134)

2 shallots, thinly sliced

2 garlic cloves, smashed

1 tablespoon red chili flakes

6 boneless, skin-on chicken thighs (see Note)

FRYING

Canola oil

2 cups all-purpose flour

HOT FIRE SAUCE

⅔ cup light brown sugar

½ cup sweet paprika

½ cup cayenne pepper

1 tablespoon ground ginger

1 tablespoon onion powder

1 tablespoon garlic powder

1 teaspoon ground cinnamon

1 teaspoon ground nutmeg

4 cups Frank's RedHot Original Hot Sauce

1 cup water

1 tablespoon plus 1 teaspoon red wine vinegar

SERVING SUGGESTION

Top the chicken with Mirliton and Carrot Slaw (page 259).

NOTE: I've called for boneless chicken here to help with the uniformity of cooking, but if you prefer bone-in chicken for that added flavor, just use a probe thermometer and make sure it reads 165°F closest to the bone.

Brine the chicken: In a large lidded container, mix the buttermilk, thyme, salt, chili paste, jerk spice, shallot, garlic, and chili flakes. Add the chicken, cover, and let brine overnight in the refrigerator. Use tongs to remove the chicken from the brine, shaking off any excess. Set aside.

Prep the fryer: In a large Dutch oven, add canola oil to a depth of 3 to 4 inches (about 2 cups) and heat on medium heat to 350°F; check using an instant-read thermometer. Line a plate with paper towels.

Make the hot fire sauce: In a medium bowl, combine the brown sugar, paprika, cayenne pepper, ginger, onion powder, garlic powder, cinnamon, and nutmeg. Add the hot sauce, water, and red wine vinegar. Whisk to combine. Set aside.

Fry the chicken: Add the flour to a shallow plate. Dredge the chicken thighs in flour so both sides are evenly coated. The flour on the chicken will become a shaggy mess; that's fine.

Add a few thighs to the oil at a time, taking care not to crowd the pan, and fry, flipping at 6 to 8 minutes, at which point it will be golden brown. Cook until golden brown all over and cooked through, another 6 to 8 minutes. Transfer to the lined plate to drain, and repeat with the remaining thighs.

In batches, add the fried chicken to the bowl of hot fire sauce, and toss to evenly coat the chicken. Serve hot.

MIRLITON AND CARROT SLAW

SERVES 6

Raw mirliton tastes like a cross between apple and squash, with a crispy texture. It's used in countless applications in Louisiana: raw in salad; stuffed with crabmeat and shrimp, then roasted; or added to soups. Back home, we make a gratin with it (page 56) or boil it as a side. I'd never seen it in salads or stuffed before coming to New Orleans. At Compère Lapin, we serve this slaw as an accompaniment to Hot Fire Chicken (page 258). The vibe is not so much a creamy coleslaw but a cool, refreshing salad that offsets the heat from the sauce's spice and richness.

2 cups Mojo Vinaigrette (page 273)

Kosher salt

EQUIPMENT
Mandoline

3 jumbo carrots (8 inches, about ½ pound total)

3 mirliton (½ pound), cored

1 bunch of scallions, thinly sliced

Use a mandoline to thinly shave the carrots and mirliton. Place the vegetables in a large bowl and add the scallions.

Lightly dress the sliced vegetables with the mojo dressing and season with salt to taste. You can eat immediately or chill in the refrigerator, then serve.

SHRIMP RAGU AND CREAMY GRITS

SERVES 4 TO 6

Shrimp and grits are on almost every New Orleans breakfast menu. The stars are beautiful local shrimp and freshly milled stone-ground grits. I added some of my favorite ingredients from Asian cuisines to explore different flavors. The soy sauce and sambal add umami and layered spice, and the rice vinegar balances the richness of the dish. Note the advance preparation of soaking the grits overnight.

GRITS

1 cup stone-ground grits (not instant), such as Anson Mills (see Note)

2¼ cups whole milk

1 cup heavy cream

1 teaspoon kosher salt

1 cup freshly grated Parmesan cheese

¼ cup (½ stick) unsalted butter

SHRIMP RAGU

1 cup minced andouille sausage

½ cup extra-virgin olive oil

2 pounds U10/12-size shrimp, peeled and deveined

1 teaspoon kosher salt

2 cups thinly sliced scallions

3 garlic cloves, thinly sliced

¼ cup water

2 tablespoons rice wine vinegar

2 tablespoons sugar

2 tablespoons sambal oelek

2 tablespoons soy sauce

1 tablespoon minced fresh ginger

1 tablespoon minced celery

2 tablespoons unsalted butter, softened

1 lemon, zested

NOTE: Stone-ground grits are delicious, but they take longer to cook. Soaking in advance of cooking helps hydrate the kernels and reduces the cook time, and while the grinding process takes off the majority of the hull, some of it still needs to be removed for a smoother consistency.

Prep the grits: In a large container, cover the grits with water. Allow the grits to sit in the water for at least 2 hours or up to overnight. If you are soaking for a shorter period, stir occasionally to speed the release of the hulls from the kernels.

Once the grits are floating, skim the top and discard the hulls. Reserve ¾ cup of strained soaking water for cooking the grits later—the grits have imparted their flavor to the water, and we want to use it to enhance the dish. Drain the grits.

Make the grits: In a small pot, bring the milk, cream, and salt to a boil. Slowly stir the grits into the boiling liquid. Stir continuously and thoroughly until the grits are well mixed. Let the pot return to a boil, cover, and reduce the heat to low. Cook, stirring occasionally, for approximately 30 minutes. Add half of the reserved water from soaking the grits. Cook for another 30 minutes, then start to check the consistency. You're aiming for smooth, not coarse. Add more of the soaking water if necessary. The grits are done when they have a smooth and creamy texture, thick enough to coat the back of a spoon. Stir in the cheese and butter and keep warm.

Make the ragu: In a medium sauté pan, add the sausage and sauté over medium-high heat, stirring occasionally, until crispy, about 5 minutes. Add the olive oil, then the shrimp, and season with the salt. Add 1½ cups of the scallions (save the rest for garnish) and the garlic and cook, stirring constantly, until the vegetables soften, about 30 seconds. Add the water, rice wine vinegar, sugar, sambal, soy sauce, ginger, and celery. Stir well to combine and continue to cook, allowing the liquid to reduce by half, another 5 to 6 minutes. Add the butter and lemon zest (these make it extra luscious) and stir to combine. Remove from the heat.

To serve: Spoon the grits into shallow serving bowls. Top each with a serving of the shrimp ragu. Garnish with the reserved scallions. Enjoy immediately.

SWEET POTATO GNOCCHI

SERVES 6 TO 8

I came to this dish through wanting to connect a dish that I grew up with and the local culture of New Orleans. Sweet potatoes are all over the American South, and their sweet, subtle flavor makes them easy to incorporate in many different preparations. Pasta became my therapy when I was working in Miami, and I loved the act of forming gnocchi by hand—it can be meditative. In St. Lucia, we typically eat curried goat with steamed rice or roti, but I wondered how it might pair with a light sweet potato gnocchi. I love the way the sweet potato pasta soaks up the brothy stew. I serve this style of gnocchi with Curried Goat (page 96) at Compère Lapin, and it's become a definitive dish for the restaurant.

3 pounds sweet potatoes (such as Garnet)

¼ cup kosher salt

4 large egg yolks

4 cups all-purpose flour, plus more for dusting

½ cup semolina flour, for dusting

COOKING THE GNOCCHI

1 cup kosher salt

Sauce of your choice, such as Curried Goat (page 96) or the Rundown Sauce in the Shrimp and Scialatielli Pasta (page 225)

Heat the oven to 375°F. Fit a sheet pan with a roasting rack.

Place the sweet potatoes on the roasting rack and bake them until fork tender, about 1 hour. Set aside to cool.

When the potatoes are cool enough to handle, peel off the skins, then transfer the flesh to the bowl of a stand mixer fitted with the paddle attachment. On medium speed, blend until smooth, 10 to 12 minutes. Add the salt to the mixture.

Add the yolks to the blended sweet potatoes and mix on low speed until smooth, about 3 minutes. Gradually add 3 cups of all-purpose flour, 1 cup at a time, until the dough comes together, about 1 minute. It should be smooth, cohesive, and not tacky to the touch. Water content in sweet potatoes can vary, so add the flour slowly and watch the consistency; you may not need all the flour. Don't overwork the dough.

Scoop the dough into a piping bag and cut off ½ inch at the tip. (If you don't have a piping bag, use a large zip top bag and trim about ½ inch off one corner to create a small opening to pipe the dough through.) Sprinkle a clean work surface with the remaining 1 cup of all-purpose flour, using your fingers to spread it around.

Pipe the dough mixture onto the floured work surface, forming logs about 6 inches long. Pinching flour from your work surface, dust the top of the gnocchi logs, then use your flattened palm to gently pull the gnocchi toward yourself, ensuring that the log is fully formed and covered in flour. This prevents the pasta from sticking together when you cut it.

Using a dough cutter or knife, divide the logs into 1-inch pieces. Dust a sheet pan with the semolina and a bit more all-purpose flour. Arrange the gnocchi on the floured sheet pan, then place it in the freezer for 1 hour. (If you want to hold off on cooking the gnocchi until later, you can freeze the cut pieces overnight on the sheet pan, then transfer them to zip top bags or an airtight container for up to 30 days.)

Cook the gnocchi: In a large stockpot, bring 4 quarts of water to a boil. Add the salt. Yes, the whole cup! You want the water to taste a little less salty than the ocean.

Meanwhile, in large saucepan, bring the sauce to a simmer.

Working in batches so as not to overcrowd the pot, add the gnocchi to the boiling salted water. Maintaining high heat, cook the pasta until the gnocchi floats for about 1 minute, about 4 minutes total. Remove the gnocchi with a slotted spoon and add to the sauce. Repeat with the remaining gnocchi.

Simmer the pasta and sauce together for about 1 minute to bring it all together. Serve immediately.

PLANTAIN CREPES
WITH HONEY BUTTER

MAKES 8 CREPES

Plantains are one of my favorite things to eat. When they're very green or underripe, they can be treated like a starchy potato, and when very ripe, like a banana. Ripe plantains develop a deep, caramelized sweetness that make this crepe so, so good.

In New Orleans, breakfast and brunch are big celebrations with friends, especially on the weekends. These crepes are a fun way to start the day.

2 very ripe plantains (the skins should be black or nearly black), peeled, 1 left whole, 1 finely diced

¾ cup water

⅔ cup whole milk

5 large eggs

¼ cup (½ stick) unsalted butter, melted

¼ cup cane sugar

½ teaspoon grated nutmeg

1½ cups all-purpose flour

Canola oil, clarified butter, or cooking spray, for greasing

SERVING

½ cup cane syrup, warmed

Honey Butter (page 274), softened

Confectioners' sugar, for dusting

Dulce de Leche (page 278; optional)

In a food processor, add the whole plantain and puree until smooth. Add the water, milk, eggs, butter, cane sugar, and nutmeg and blend until it becomes a smooth paste. Add the flour and pulse several times, until the ingredients are thoroughly combined, about 1 minute. Transfer the batter to a bowl and cover. Rest it for at least 30 minutes in the refrigerator or up to overnight.

When ready to cook, use a rubber spatula to fold the diced plantain into the batter.

Heat a small skillet or saucepan on medium heat, then lightly coat the hot pan with canola oil. Pour in ½ cup of batter. Tilt the pan so the batter spreads across evenly. Cook the crepe for about 1 minute. When bubbles start to form, flip with a spatula and cook the other side, until the bottom is light brown, 1 to 2 minutes. Transfer to a serving plate and fold in half. Keep warm by covering with a clean kitchen towel. Repeat with the remaining batter.

To serve: Top with warm cane syrup and honey butter and generously dust with the confectioners' sugar, or drizzle with dulce de leche.

BANANA PECAN BEIGNETS

MAKES ABOUT 18

In preparation for filming in New Orleans, I assumed we'd have cooking challenges that reflected the city's culinary history. I tried to get acquainted with obvious choices before leaving Miami: gumbo, crawfish, and beignets, all dishes I hadn't had much experience with but knew were important to the culture. But my first real beignet was during filming at Café du Monde in the French Quarter. For the finale, I made banana pecan beignets as my dessert. The judges bashed me for it—"this isn't really a dessert," yadda yadda yadda. For a time, we featured them on Compère Lapin's menu—for *dessert*—and that fryer was always filled with beignets, let me tell you.

You'll make the beignet mixture, then fill it with banana cream and top it with rum caramel sauce, which has a touch of curry spice that brings forward a beautiful floral note.

BEIGNETS

¾ cup lukewarm water

½ cup granulated sugar

1¼ teaspoons active dry yeast

½ cup whole milk

1 large egg

1 teaspoon kosher salt

3¾ cups bread flour, plus more for dusting

5 tablespoons unsalted butter, softened

Canola oil, for frying

Confectioners' sugar, for dusting

PECAN RUM CARAMEL

2 cups heavy cream

2 tablespoons dark rum

1 teaspoon curry powder

2½ cups granulated sugar

1 teaspoon kosher salt

1 cup (2 sticks) unsalted butter

1 cup toasted and chopped pecans

BANANA CREAM FILLING

1 cup whole milk

½ cup granulated sugar

3 tablespoons all-purpose flour

⅛ teaspoon kosher salt

2 large egg yolks, slightly beaten

1 large very ripe banana

2 tablespoons fresh lemon juice

1 teaspoon vanilla extract

Prep the beignet dough: In a medium bowl, mix the lukewarm water, granulated sugar, and yeast. Cover and let stand for 10 minutes to allow the yeast to bloom.

In the bowl of a stand mixer fitted with the dough hook, add the milk, egg, and salt. Mix on low speed to combine until it's incorporated and foamy, about 2 minutes.

Add the bread flour to the yeast mixture and use a rubber spatula to gently combine. Add the flour mixture to the stand mixer bowl. Mix on low speed until the dough comes together and develops a sticky, stretchy texture, 6 to 8 minutes.

Add the butter and continue to mix on medium speed until the dough is smooth, 6 to 8 minutes. Remove the stand mixer bowl and cover with plastic wrap. Allow the dough to proof at room temperature until doubled in size, about 2 hours.

Make the pecan rum caramel: In a medium saucepan, heat the cream, rum, and curry powder over medium heat until just warmed through, 3 to 5 minutes. Set aside.

In a medium heavy-bottomed pot, melt the sugar and salt over medium heat, no stirring. Cook to develop an even, dark amber color, until it caramelizes, about 8 minutes. Remove from the heat and slowly whisk in the cream mixture. The sugar is hot, so temper the liquid gradually, whisking constantly as you pour. Don't rush this part, and do ensure the cream is warmed through. Keep mixing until everything is fully incorporated. Add the butter and whisk gently until combined. Strain the caramel through a fine-mesh strainer into the medium saucepan; this removes any crystallization. Add the pecans and stir to combine. Set aside.

Make the banana cream filling: In a medium heavy-bottomed saucepan, heat the milk on medium heat until it's very hot, but not boiling, 3 to 5 minutes.

In a medium bowl, mix the sugar, flour, and salt. Stir in the hot milk and beat with a whisk until well blended. Slowly add the beaten egg yolks to the bowl, taking care to temper them in so they adjust to the temperature without curdling (we don't want scrambled eggs!). Pour the mixture back into the saucepan and continue to stir vigorously over low heat until it thickens and becomes smooth, 2 to 3 minutes. Set aside to cool, but stir about every 30 seconds to ensure the mixture isn't sticking.

Mash or small dice the banana in a small bowl, then beat until smooth. Mix in the lemon juice and vanilla. Add the banana mixture to the cream filling in the saucepan and stir to fully combine.

Fry the beignets: In a medium pot, add canola oil to a depth of 2 inches (about 4 cups) and heat on medium to 325°F; check with an instant-read thermometer. Fit a cooling rack over a sheet pan.

Flour a work surface and use a rolling pin to roll out the dough to a rectangle ⅓ inch thick. With a dough cutter or knife, cut 2-ounce portions for the beignets (about a 3-inch square; the rough sizing is more for uniformity of cooking than appearance). You'll have about 18 beignets.

Drop the dough squares into the oil, cooking in batches to not crowd the pan, and fry until golden brown, 2 to 3 minutes on each side. Use a slotted spoon to transfer them to the cooling rack to drain. Repeat with the remaining dough.

Assemble the beignets: Scoop the filling into a piping bag with ¼-inch attachment, or a zip top bag with ¼ inch of the corner trimmed off. Make a small incision in the center of one side of a beignet and fill with some of the banana cream. Repeat until all are filled. Drizzle with the pecan rum caramel, then dust with a shitload of confectioners' sugar. Go crazy! Enjoy warm.

PANTRY

AIOLI

We use a blended oil in this recipe for the best flavor combination. Straight-up olive oil is a bit too intense. Canola oil is neutral, but used alone in this application, it can taste a bit flat. The blended oil strikes a happy medium.

2 large egg yolks

1 lemon, zested and juiced

1½ teaspoons Dijon mustard

½ garlic clove, grated

2 cups blended oil, chilled (see Note)

½ teaspoon kosher salt

EQUIPMENT
Food processor

NOTE: You can purchase blended oil or make it yourself: Whisk together 3 parts canola oil to 1 part extra-virgin olive oil and store in an airtight container.

In a food processor, add the egg yolks, lemon zest and juice, mustard, and garlic. Put the lid on and begin to blend while you slowly drizzle the chilled blended oil into the mix. Blend until it's emulsified, about 4 minutes. As you add the oil, the color will turn from yellow to white. It should look creamy, not quite a puree or paste.

If you don't have a food processor, you can do this manually with a bit of elbow grease. In this scenario, we want to keep the bowl steady so you can whisk and emulsify the ingredients without the bowl moving around on the counter. Take a large pot and line it with a clean dish towel. Set your bowl in the lined pot; the bowl should be snug. Whisk the egg yolks, lemon zest and juice, mustard, and garlic together as you very slowly drizzle in the chilled blended oil, and whisk constantly for 8 to 10 minutes until you get a creamy, cohesive mixture.

For both methods, add the salt and mix to combine. Store the aioli in an airtight container; it will keep, refrigerated, for up to 1 week.

USE IN
Crawfish Hushpuppies (page 229)
Pickled Pineapple Tartar Sauce (page 273)
Fried Okra with Pickled Green Bean Remoulade (page 233)

GINGER-CHILI OIL

The potency of ginger is often underestimated! It's a wonderful spice element to include in many recipes, and combining it with the chili oil makes for a well-rounded, spicy addition.

1 cup canola oil

2 tablespoons minced fresh ginger

2 teaspoons red chili flakes

In a medium pot, add the oil and ginger. Bring to a simmer over low heat, then cook for 10 minutes to extract all the ginger flavor.

Remove the pot from the heat and add the chili flakes. Let cool to room temperature. Strain through a fine-mesh strainer and discard the ginger and chili flakes. Keep the oil in an airtight container in the refrigerator for up to 2 months.

USE IN
Pickled Green Mango with Cilantro Dressing (page 130)
Tostones with Avocado (page 182)

CHILI OIL

Chili oil is a staple in my pantry because it offers a bit of spice and a lot of control over how much heat you put in at once (versus throwing in a pepper). It's great to finish off a dish or keep at the table.

¼ cup red chili flakes
1 cup extra-virgin olive oil

In a small pot, add the chili flakes, cover with the oil, and bring to a simmer over low heat, then remove from the heat. Allow to cool for 20 minutes. For milder spice, you can use a fine-mesh strainer to remove the flakes from the oil. Or you can opt to not strain (that's my vibe), and the chili flakes continue to lend spice and heat over time—the gift that keeps on giving. Store in an airtight container; it will keep at room temperature for up to 3 months.

USE IN
Cow Heel Soup (page 95)
Escovitch-Style Snapper (page 150)
Pompano with "Pepperpot" Broth (page 149)

GARLIC OIL

MAKES 1 CUP

This infused oil has a distinctive garlicky flavor but with a subtle sweetness, and when you add it to a dish, the garlic doesn't overpower other flavors.

1 head garlic
1 cup extra-virgin olive oil

Cut the garlic head in half crosswise (leave the skin on; there's flavor and nutrients in there). Add to a small pot and add the oil. Simmer over low heat until the garlic is tender and caramelized, about 20 minutes. Use a slotted spoon to remove the garlic head. Squeeze the pulp into the oil for a robust, intense flavor (or use the pulp in a marinade for any seafood or meat). Store the oil in an airtight container and keep in the refrigerator for up to 1 week.

NOTE: Do not keep garlic oil at room temperature except when using, and don't keep this oil beyond a week, as it can harbor harmful bacteria.

USE IN
Whole Roasted Snapper (page 79)
Tostones with Avocado (page 182)
Tempura Shrimp Sandwich (page 251)

PICKLED PINEAPPLE TARTAR SAUCE

MAKES 2 CUPS

You might be surprised by the addition of pickled pineapple in a tartar sauce, but stay with me. You can put this on so many dishes! I love the creaminess of the aioli, the saltiness of the capers, and the sweet and acidic pickled pineapple. It just might become your new favorite.

PICKLED PINEAPPLE
¼ cup rice wine vinegar

1 tablespoon finely diced pineapple (fresh is best)

TARTAR SAUCE
2 cups Aioli (page 269)

¼ cup cilantro

1½ tablespoons seeded, minced jalapeño

1½ tablespoons chopped capers

½ teaspoon smoked paprika (such as La Dalia)

½ teaspoon Crystal hot sauce

1 teaspoon kosher salt

Pickle the pineapple: In a small saucepan, bring the rice wine vinegar to a simmer over low heat. Place the pineapple in a small bowl and pour the vinegar over it. Set aside to cool.

Make the tartar sauce: In a food processor, combine 1 cup of the aioli and the cilantro, jalapeño, capers, paprika, and hot sauce. Strain the pickled pineapple, reserving the pickling liquid, and add all the fruit to the processor plus a splash of the liquid. Pulse until you have a coarse, chunky, but well-mixed texture. Transfer the tartar sauce to a medium bowl and add the remaining 1 cup of aioli. Use a large spoon or spatula to mix well, then season with salt; add more pickling liquid to taste. The tartar sauce will keep in an airtight container in the refrigerator for up to 5 days.

USE IN
Accra Fritters (page 84)
Ackee Fritters (page 119)
Tempura Shrimp Sandwich (page 251)

MOJO VINAIGRETTE

MAKES 2 CUPS

Living in Miami introduced me to mojo, a citrusy condiment that warms up with cumin spice. I add Dijon mustard to an otherwise traditional recipe, which makes for a creamier vinaigrette. It can be used as a marinade and dressing and is always balanced and bright.

1 orange

1 lemon

1 lime

2 cups fresh orange juice

2 tablespoons fresh lemon juice

2 tablespoons fresh lime juice

1 cup canola oil

½ cup extra-virgin olive oil

2 garlic cloves, finely grated

1 teaspoon chopped Scotch bonnet pepper

1 tablespoon Dijon mustard

3 tablespoons sherry vinegar, or to taste

1 teaspoon chopped oregano

⅛ teaspoon ground cumin

2 tablespoons kosher salt, or to taste

Start by grating the zest from the orange, lemon, and lime, and reserve the zest.

In a small saucepan, add the orange, lemon, and lime juices. Cook over medium heat, stirring occasionally, until the juices reduce to half the volume, about 15 minutes. Set aside.

In a separate small pot, add the canola oil, olive oil, garlic, and Scotch bonnet. Cook on low and simmer until the garlic becomes a bit foamy about 5 minutes. Remove from the heat and set aside to cool.

In a blender, combine the reduced juice and the mustard. As you blend, slowly drizzle in the infused oil until the liquid emulsifies, about 2 minutes.

Transfer the dressing to a small bowl, then add the citrus zests, sherry vinegar to taste, oregano, and cumin. Add salt to your taste preference. Whisk to combine.

Use immediately. Any leftovers will keep in an airtight container in the refrigerator for up to 5 days.

USE IN
Mirliton and Carrot Slaw (page 259)
Coconut Rice and Peas with Chicken (page 47)

GREEN SEASONING

MAKES 2 CUPS

In every St. Lucian home, we have a bottle of green seasoning. It goes on everything; use it to marinate fish or meat, or add to rice. People make their own blend based on what they have in their home gardens.

1½ cups extra-virgin olive oil

1 bunch of scallions, roots trimmed, sliced into 1-inch pieces

½ cup roughly chopped cilantro

½ cup roughly chopped flat-leaf parsley

1 small green bell pepper, chopped

2 tablespoons roughly chopped fresh ginger

½ teaspoon chopped Scotch bonnet pepper

1½ teaspoons kosher salt

In a blender, add the olive oil, scallions, cilantro, parsley, bell pepper, ginger, Scotch bonnet, and salt. Puree until smooth, about 2 minutes. Transfer to an airtight container; it will keep, refrigerated, for up to 2 weeks.

USE IN
Brown Stew Snapper (page 145)
Stuffed Crab Backs (page 50)

HONEY BUTTER

MAKES 1¾ CUPS

This is versatile, sweet compound butter, and the honey adds a creamy texture.

1 cup (2 sticks) salted butter, softened (use a high-quality butter like Plugrà)

¾ cup organic honey

In a small bowl, add the butter and honey. Use a rubber spatula to mix until fully incorporated. Transfer to an airtight container and refrigerate for 1 week or freeze for up to 1 month (divide into deli cup containers for easy portioning). You can also leave this butter at room temperature for up to 3 days for easy spreading on toast or buttermilk biscuits.

USE IN
Cassava Sweet Bread (page 106)
Creole Bread (page 105)
Buttermilk Biscuits (page 248)
Plantain Crepes (page 264)

BACON BUTTER

MAKES 2 CUPS

This is versatile, savory compound butter. Infusing a butter with flavors adds new depth—in this case, a smoky enhancement.

¼ pound bacon (I like Benton's bacon; it's nice and smoky)

1 cup (2 sticks) salted butter, softened (use a high-quality butter such as Plugrà)

Roughly chop the bacon and place in a medium sauté pan. Cook on low heat, stirring to ensure even cooking, until the bacon firm ups and start to curl, 8 to 10 minutes. It will develop a chestnut color, but you're cooking the bacon not to crisp, but to use its fattiness in the butter.

Strain and reserve the rendered fat and let cool. Transfer the cooked bacon to a work surface and use a knife to mince it. Add the minced bacon, reserved fat, and softened butter to a small bowl. Use a rubber spatula to evenly combine. Transfer to an airtight container. Freeze for up to 30 days or refrigerate for up to 1 week (divide into deli cup containers for easy portioning). You can also leave the butter at room temperature for up to 3 days for easy spreading on biscuits or toast.

USE IN
Cassava Sweet Bread (page 106)
Creole Bread (page 105)
Buttermilk Biscuits (page 248)

CHILI BUTTER

MAKES 1 CUP

Calabrian chilies have a hint of sweetness—they're not too aggressive or overpowering. Don't be scared of a little sweet heat! They're perfect for an infused oil or, as in this case, a butter to add kick to your cooking.

1 cup (2 sticks) salted butter, softened (use a high-quality butter like Plugrà)

¼ cup Calabrian chili paste

½ lemon, zested

In a medium bowl, combine the butter, chili paste, and lemon zest. Use a rubber spatula to evenly combine and stir until the paste is well incorporated throughout the butter. Keep in an airtight container for up to 1 week in the refrigerator or 30 days in the freezer (divide into deli cup containers for easy portioning).

USE IN
Cassava Sweet Bread (page 106)
Jerk Buttered Corn (page 133)
Oyster Pan Stew (page 247)

AIOLI (PAGE 269)

CILANTRO AIOLI (PAGE 229)

MOJO (PAGE 273)

GREEN SEASONING (PAGE 274)

PICKLED PINEAPPLE TARTAR
SAUCE (PAGE 273)

DULCE DE LECHE

MAKES 1 CUP

Add dulce de leche to toast, pie, ice cream, or anything where you want a sweet hit. I especially love it sandwiched in the traditional South American sugar cookie alfajores.

1 (14-ounce) can sweetened condensed milk

This is the easiest thing! Take the label off the can and place the can in a medium pot. Cover the can with water *all* the way to the top of the pot and turn the heat to high. Once the water begins to boil, reduce the heat to medium-high and cook, covered, for 4 to 6 hours. Make sure you keep topping off the pot with water, just enough to cover the can.

Test the can at the 4-hour mark: Remove it and allow to cool slightly, for about 10 minutes. Give the can a shake. If there is a viscous sound, if it sounds like liquid is sloshing around, then keep cooking the canned milk and check back hourly until done. When you shake the can and you don't feel or hear anything jiggling, the dulce de leche is ready. And it's worth the wait!

Use tongs to remove the can from the water and allow it to cool for about 10 minutes. Pop open the can and transfer the dulce de leche into an airtight container. It will keep in the refrigerator for up to 2 weeks.

USE IN
Coconut Tres Leches Cake (page 198)
Plantain Crepes (page 264)

BROWN STOCK

MAKES ABOUT 6 QUARTS

I use brown stock in everything. In every region I've lived in, brown stock has been a fixture for stews and sauces. It's an easy way to layer deep flavors throughout a dish; there's just no substitute! You can save chicken bones from deboning or roasting chicken and keep them in the freezer until you've got enough to make stock.

5 pounds chicken carcasses

¼ cup canola oil

2 large Spanish onions, roughly chopped

1 jumbo carrot, roughly chopped

3 celery stalks, roughly chopped

3 cups white wine

1 (14-ounce) can tomato paste

1 bunch of thyme

Heat the oven to 400°F. Line two sheet pans with foil.

Place the chicken bones on the prepared sheet pans and roast until they become golden brown, about 30 minutes. (You can strain and reserve the fat that comes from this step; I use it to cook vegetables for any chicken dish or add it to my jerk chicken sauce.)

Heat a large stockpot over medium-high heat. Add the oil, then wait 1 minute to allow it to fully heat. Add the onions, carrot, and celery. Sauté, stirring occasionally, until the onions are translucent, 10 minutes or so. Add the wine and cook, stirring occasionally, until the wine reduces to about ½ cup, about 5 more minutes.

Add the tomato paste and thyme and reduce the heat to low. Add the roasted chicken bones and follow with enough cool water to cover the bones by 4 inches.

Raise the heat to high, bring to a boil, and boil for 10 minutes. Reduce the heat to low and cook, uncovered, at a low simmer until the stock has a reddish-brown color and reduces by about one-third, about 4 hours. Use a ladle to occasionally skim and discard the impurities that float to the top.

Use tongs to remove the bones from the pot, then use a fine-mesh strainer to strain the stock.

Allow the stock to cool completely before storing in airtight containers. If not using right away, freeze for up to 1 month.

USE IN

Adobo Pork with Salsa Verde (page 190)
Beef Pepperpot (page 87)
Boudin Balls (page 223)
Bouyon (page 88)
Coconut Rice and Peas with Chicken (page 47)
Curried Goat (page 96)
Glazed Duck with Dirty Rice (page 240)
Guava-Glazed Ribs (page 213)
Pheasant Gumbo (page 234)
Stewed Oxtail and Spinner Dumplings (page 142)

Acknowledgments

I am thankful to have created this book with Osayi Endolyn, without whom my prideful Caribbean journey would not be told. Thank you for your patience and guidance; I am forever grateful.

To my family: My granny for being tough as nails and keeping me in the kitchen at a very young age. My mum and dad for believing in me, giving me the confidence to do what I love, understanding and appreciating farming, and for the access to amazing produce in our garden.

To my siblings, Sean, Jeannine, Maya, and Fiona, for tasting some of the mishaps that I made as a young cook and still cheering me on.

To Brittany Conerly, for making my food look vibrant on these pages. To Kasimu Harris, for documenting the beautiful spaces I lived in on my journey. Zoe Maya Jones Abudu, thank you for your care and attention to detail during recipe testing.

To my amazing staff at Compère Lapin, BABs-Nola, and Nina's Creole Cottage—without you none of this is possible. Shonda Cross, Hector Suarez, Chad Kuczek, Ray Ingerham, and Jayda Drury, thank you for your tireless work. The staff at Sandals La Toc, Mo Bay, and Ochi for your teaching a small-island girl all the things while having a blast in Jamdown!

My professional journey would not be possible without the following chefs—Thank you Chef Daniel Boulud, Chef Alex Lee, and Chef Bradford Thompson for teaching me the meaning of excellence when I was fresh out of culinary school. Chef Norman Van Aken, for encouraging me to hone my Caribbean flavors. Chef Scott Conant for showing me the beauty of simplicity when cooking. Chef Marcus Samuelsson, for your mentorship; the knowledge you have given me is priceless. Chef David Kinch and Chef Donald Link, for breaking bread with me.

To the Chase family for your kindness and for welcoming me to the Crescent City; you all are culinary royalty in my eyes. I often look to the sky to see if Mrs. Leah is smiling.

My friendships over the years have kept me grounded while having all kinds of fun: Thank you Mike and Jenn Pirolo, Kate and Aberra Larcher, and Kingsley John.

To the loves of my life, Larry, Hank, and Buster, for your unconditional love, hugs, and kisses. I will love you always.

Index